Cocos2d-x Intermediate Level: Elevating Your Game Development Skills

Cocos2d-x Series

Kameron Hussain and Frahaan Hussain

Published by Sonar Publishing, 2023.

COCOS2D-X INTERMEDIATE LEVEL: ELEVATING YOUR GAME DEVELOPMENT SKILLS

First edition. November 30, 2023.

ISBN: 979-8223589334

Written by Kameron Hussain and Frahaan Hussain.

Table of Contents

Step 2: Prepare Text for Translation

Step 3: Translate Text

Step 4: Implement Localization

Step 5: Handle Text Expansion and Contraction

Step 6: Cultural Considerations

Step 7: Testing and Quality Assurance

Step 8: Ongoing Maintenance

17.4 Internationalization Best Practices

1. Use Unicode for Text Handling

2. Externalize Text and Assets

3. Use String IDs

4. Support Dynamic Text Layout

5. Consider Right-to-Left (RTL) Languages

6. Maintain a Language Selection Mechanism

7. Collaborate with Native Speakers

8. Test Thoroughly

17.5 Legal Considerations in Global Markets

1. Age Ratings and Content Restrictions

2. Compliance with Privacy Laws

3. Intellectual Property Rights

19.1 Narrative and Storytelling Techniques

1. World Building

2. Character Development

3. Branching Narratives

4. Non-linear Storytelling

5. Environmental Storytelling

6. Subtext and Themes

7. Foreshadowing

8. Player-Driven Stories

9. Audio and Sound Design

10. Dynamic Events

11. Pacing and Rhythm

12. Ethical Considerations

13. Playtesting and Iteration

14. Storytelling Tools

19.2 Creating Immersive Game Worlds

1. Detailed Environments

2. Consistent Art Style

3. Dynamic Lighting and Shadows

4. Soundscapes

5. Interactive Elements

6. Lore and Backstory

7. Day-Night Cycle and Weather

8. Environmental Storytelling

9. World Map and Navigation

10. Player Agency

11. Cultural Diversity

12. Hidden Secrets and Easter Eggs

13. Environmental Challenges

14. Playtesting and Iteration

19.3 Player Psychology and Engagement

1. Reward Systems

2. Progression Mechanics

3. Flow State

4. Social Interaction

5. FOMO (Fear of Missing Out)

6. Autonomy and Choice

7. Immersion and Escapism

8. Challenge and Mastery

9. Surprise and Delight

10. Feedback and Progress Tracking

11. Emotion and Storytelling

12. Player Empowerment

13. Anticipation and Teasers

14. Playtesting and Feedback

19.4 Ethical Game Design

1. Player Well-Being

2. Fair Monetization

3. Inclusivity and Representation

4. Age-Appropriate Content

5. Privacy and Data Security

6. Accessibility

7. Social Responsibility

8. Transparency

9. Ethical Testing

10. Community Moderation

11. Accountability

12. Ethical Leadership

19.5 Innovations in Game Mechanics

1. Procedural Generation

4. Immersive Storytelling

5. Spatial Audio

6. Gesture and Voice Controls

7. Training and Simulation

8. Performance Optimization

9. User Experience and Comfort

20.4 The Role of AI in Future Game Development

1. AI-Driven Gameplay

2. Personalized Player Experiences

3. Dynamic Content Generation

4. Natural Language Processing (NLP)

5. Emotional AI

6. AI for Content Moderation

7. AI-Enhanced Graphics and Animation

8. Data-Driven Game Design

9. AI-Powered Quality Assurance

10. Ethical Considerations

20.5 Preparing for the Next Generation of Gaming

1. Advanced Hardware Capabilities

2. Ray Tracing and Realistic Lighting

3. 5G and Low Latency Networking

4. Immersive Audio Experiences

5. Cross-Platform and Cross-Reality Gaming

6. Sustainability and Green Game Development

7. Player Data Privacy and Security

8. Accessibility and Inclusivity

9. Ethical Game Design

10. Community Building and Engagement

Chapter 1: Understanding the Core of Cocos2d-x

Section 1.1: Introduction to Advanced Cocos2d-x

Cocos2d-x is a powerful open-source game development framework that allows developers to create cross-platform games with ease. In this section, we will introduce you to the fundamentals of Cocos2d-x and its key features.

Cocos2d-x is written in C++, which makes it a popular choice for developers looking for high performance and efficiency in their game development projects. It provides a robust set of tools and libraries for game creation, including support for 2D graphics, audio, physics, and user input.

History of Cocos2d-x

Cocos2d-x has a rich history dating back to its initial release in 2010. It was originally a port of the popular Cocos2d framework, which was primarily used for iOS game development. Cocos2d-x was created to extend this functionality to multiple platforms, including Android, Windows, macOS, and Linux.

Over the years, Cocos2d-x has evolved and gained a strong community of developers who contribute to its development and create a wide range of games and applications using the framework. It has become a versatile and reliable choice for both indie developers and large game studios.

Key Features of Cocos2d-x

Cocos2d-x offers a range of features that make it a preferred choice for game development:

1. **Cross-Platform Compatibility**: Cocos2d-x allows you to write your game code once and deploy it on multiple platforms, reducing development time and effort.
2. **High Performance**: Being built in C++, Cocos2d-x provides excellent performance, making it suitable for graphics-intensive games.
3. **2D Graphics Rendering**: The framework includes a powerful 2D rendering engine that supports sprites, animations, and particle systems.
4. **Audio Support**: Cocos2d-x provides tools for handling audio effects and music within your games.
5. **Physics Engine Integration**: It offers integration with popular physics engines like Box2D and Chipmunk, enabling realistic physics simulations in your games.
6. **User Input Handling**: Cocos2d-x simplifies user input handling, making it easy to manage touch events, gestures, and keyboard input.
7. **Rich Community and Resources**: With a vibrant community and extensive documentation, Cocos2d-x offers valuable resources for developers to learn and troubleshoot issues.

Getting Started with Cocos2d-x

To get started with Cocos2d-x, you'll need to set up your development environment and install the necessary tools and dependencies. Here's a basic outline of the steps:

1. **Installation**: Download and install Cocos2d-x from the

official website or repository.

2. **Creating a New Project**: Use the Cocos2d-x command-line tools to create a new project.
3. **Coding Your Game**: Start writing your game code using C++, making use of the Cocos2d-x libraries and APIs.
4. **Testing and Debugging**: Use the built-in debugging tools and emulators to test your game.
5. **Deployment**: Once your game is ready, you can deploy it to various platforms, including iOS, Android, and desktop.

In the upcoming sections of this book, we will dive deeper into the architecture and advanced features of Cocos2d-x, helping you become proficient in game development with this versatile framework. Whether you're a beginner or an experienced developer, Cocos2d-x has something to offer for your game development journey.

Section 1.2: Deep Dive into Cocos2d-x Architecture

In this section, we will take a comprehensive look at the architecture of Cocos2d-x, which forms the foundation for developing games and applications using this framework.

Core Components of Cocos2d-x

Cocos2d-x is built around several core components that interact to create a game:

1. **Director**: The Director is responsible for managing the game loop and scene transitions. It controls the flow of the game, updating and rendering scenes in the correct order.
2. **Scene**: A Scene represents a single screen or game level. It

can contain multiple layers and game objects. Scenes are switched by the Director as the game progresses.

3. **Layer**: Layers are used to organize game elements within a scene. They can contain sprites, labels, and other visual and interactive elements.
4. **Node**: Nodes are the fundamental building blocks of a Cocos2d-x game. Everything in a scene is a node, including sprites, labels, and custom game objects. Nodes can be positioned, scaled, and rotated, and they form a hierarchical structure.
5. **Sprite**: Sprites are 2D images or animated characters. They are often used to represent game characters, items, or background elements. Cocos2d-x provides efficient sprite rendering.
6. **Action**: Actions are used to animate nodes in Cocos2d-x. You can move, rotate, scale, and perform other transformations on nodes using actions. Actions can be sequenced and combined to create complex animations.

Game Loop in Cocos2d-x

Cocos2d-x follows a typical game loop structure. Here's a simplified overview of how the game loop works:

1. **Initialization**: The game initializes its components, such as the Director, Scenes, and Layers.
2. **Input Handling**: User input, including touch events and keyboard input, is processed in this phase.
3. **Update**: The game updates the state of game objects and performs logic calculations. This includes character movement, collision detection, and game events.
4. **Rendering**: The game renders the current frame, displaying all visible game elements.

5. **Repeat**: The loop repeats, continuously updating and rendering frames, creating the illusion of animation and interactivity.

Cocos2d-x Rendering Pipeline

Cocos2d-x utilizes a rendering pipeline to display graphics on the screen. It includes the following stages:

1. **Scene Graph**: All visible nodes are organized in a hierarchical scene graph. This structure allows efficient traversal and rendering of nodes.
2. **Culling and Batching**: Cocos2d-x performs culling to determine which nodes are within the camera's view frustum. Batching is used to reduce draw calls by combining similar nodes into a single batch.
3. **Shader Programs**: Shader programs control how nodes are rendered. Cocos2d-x supports custom shaders for advanced rendering effects.
4. **OpenGL Rendering**: The final step involves rendering the nodes using OpenGL, taking into account transformations, textures, and shaders.

Event Handling and Callbacks

Cocos2d-x provides event handling mechanisms to respond to user input and other events. Events can be handled through callbacks and listeners. For example, you can register a touch event listener to detect when a user taps the screen or interacts with a specific node.

Here's a simple example of registering a touch event listener in Cocos2d-x:

```
// Create a touch listener
```

```
auto touchListener = EventListenerTouchOneByOne::create();

touchListener->onTouchBegan = [](Touch* touch, Event* event) {

// Handle touch began event here

return true; // Return true to consume the touch event

};

// Add the listener to the event dispatcher

Director::getInstance()->getEventDispatcher()->addEventListenerWithSc
yourNode);
```

In this code, we create a touch listener and define a callback function for the "touch began" event. When a touch event occurs on *yourNode*, the callback is executed.

Conclusion

Understanding the architecture of Cocos2d-x is crucial for developing games efficiently and effectively. In this section, we've explored the core components, the game loop, the rendering pipeline, and event handling mechanisms that form the backbone of Cocos2d-x game development. With this knowledge, you'll be well-prepared to dive deeper into advanced topics and create compelling games using this framework.

Section 1.3: Optimizing Game Performance in Cocos2d-x

Optimizing game performance is a critical aspect of game development, as it ensures that your game runs smoothly on a variety of devices and provides an enjoyable gaming experience. In this section, we will explore various techniques and best practices for optimizing the performance of your Cocos2d-x games.

Profiling Your Game

Before diving into optimization, it's essential to understand where your game's performance bottlenecks are. Profiling tools can help you identify areas that need improvement. Cocos2d-x provides built-in profiling tools that allow you to measure frame rates, memory usage, and more.

One of the most commonly used profiling tools is the **Director's Display Stats**. By enabling this feature, you can display real-time performance metrics on the screen, including frames per second (FPS), draw calls, and memory usage. Here's how to enable it:

```
// Enable display stats

Director::getInstance()->setDisplayStats(true);
```

Additionally, you can use external profiling tools like **Instrument** on iOS or **Android Profiler** on Android to get a deeper understanding of your game's performance characteristics.

Texture and Sprite Optimization

Textures and sprites are central to most 2D games. Optimizing how you use and manage them can significantly impact performance:

1. **Texture Atlas**: Use texture atlases to combine multiple textures into a single image. This reduces draw calls and improves rendering performance. Cocos2d-x provides tools for creating texture atlases.
2. **Sprite Sheets**: Combine multiple sprites into a single sprite sheet. This reduces the number of draw calls and

minimizes texture switching.

3. **Texture Compression**: Use texture compression formats (e.g., PVR, ETC, ASTC) to reduce texture memory usage and improve loading times.
4. **Texture Size**: Be mindful of texture sizes. Large textures consume more memory and may not fit on some devices. Use appropriate texture sizes for different screen resolutions.

Batch Rendering

Batch rendering is a technique that groups multiple sprites or objects into a single draw call, reducing the overhead of rendering individual objects. Cocos2d-x provides tools to enable batch rendering for sprite nodes. For example:

```
// Enable batch rendering for a sprite

yourSprite->setBatchNode(batchNode);
```

By using batch rendering, you can significantly improve rendering performance, especially when dealing with many sprites on the screen simultaneously.

Memory Management

Effective memory management is crucial for maintaining good game performance:

1. **Object Pooling**: Implement object pooling to reuse game objects (e.g., bullets, enemies) instead of creating and destroying them frequently.
2. **Texture Memory**: Be aware of texture memory usage. Unload textures that are not currently in use to free up memory.

3. **Resource Loading**: Load game assets efficiently and only when needed. Preload essential assets to reduce loading times during gameplay.
4. **Avoid Memory Leaks**: Carefully manage object references to prevent memory leaks. Use smart pointers and Cocos2d-x's memory management features.

CPU and GPU Optimization

Optimizing CPU and GPU usage is vital for maintaining smooth gameplay:

1. **CPU**: Minimize CPU usage by optimizing game logic, avoiding unnecessary calculations, and using efficient data structures.
2. **GPU**: Optimize rendering by reducing the number of draw calls, using appropriate shaders, and avoiding expensive graphical effects that may strain the GPU.

Multithreading

Cocos2d-x supports multithreading, allowing you to offload non-rendering tasks to separate threads. This can improve overall performance by distributing the workload across multiple CPU cores. Be cautious when using multithreading, as improper implementation can lead to synchronization issues and bugs.

Testing on Target Devices

Finally, always test your game on a variety of target devices, including low-end and high-end hardware. Performance can vary significantly between devices, so it's essential to ensure your game runs smoothly on all supported platforms.

In conclusion, optimizing game performance in Cocos2d-x involves a combination of profiling, resource management, rendering optimization, and efficient coding practices. By following these guidelines and continuously monitoring and fine-tuning your game, you can create a high-performance and enjoyable gaming experience for players on various devices.

Section 1.4: Advanced Graphics and Animation Techniques

In this section, we'll explore advanced graphics and animation techniques in Cocos2d-x to enhance the visual appeal of your games. These techniques go beyond the basics and allow you to create stunning and dynamic visuals.

Particle Systems and Special Effects

Particle systems are a powerful tool for creating various visual effects in games, such as fire, smoke, explosions, and magical spells. Cocos2d-x provides a built-in particle system that you can easily integrate into your games. Here's a basic example of creating a particle system:

```
// Create a particle system

auto particleSystem = ParticleSystemQuad::create("particles/fire.plist");

// Add the particle system to a layer

yourLayer->addChild(particleSystem);
```

You can customize particle systems by creating your own particle plist files or by modifying existing ones to achieve the desired effect.

Advanced Animation Techniques

Cocos2d-x offers advanced animation capabilities to bring your game characters and objects to life:

1. **Sprite Animation**: You can create sprite animations by defining a series of frames and their timings. Cocos2d-x provides a sprite frame animation system that simplifies this process.

```
// Create a sprite frame animation
auto animation = Animation::createWithSpriteFrames(frames, delay);
auto animate = Animate::create(animation);
yourSprite->runAction(animate);
```

1. **Spine Animation**: Cocos2d-x supports the Spine 2D skeletal animation system, allowing you to create complex character animations with bone hierarchies and mesh deformations.

```
// Create a Spine skeleton animation
auto skeletonNode = SkeletonAnimation::createWithJsonFile("spine/character.json", "spine/character.atlas", 1.0f);
yourLayer->addChild(skeletonNode);
```

1. **Timeline Animations**: You can use timeline-based animations to create scripted sequences of actions. This is useful for cinematic sequences or scripted events in your

game.

```
// Create a timeline action
auto timeline = Timeline::create();
timeline->addFrame([=](){
// Action to perform at a specific time
}, 2.0f); // Time in seconds
yourNode->runAction(timeline);
```

Integrating 3D Elements in a 2D Engine

While Cocos2d-x is primarily a 2D game engine, you can still integrate 3D elements into your games for added depth and visual appeal. You can use 3D models, shaders, and effects to enhance your 2D scenes.

To incorporate 3D elements, you can use libraries like OpenGL or third-party plugins that provide 3D rendering capabilities. Cocos2d-x also has limited 3D support, allowing you to display 3D models, but it's not as robust as dedicated 3D engines.

Shader Programming in Cocos2d-x

Shader programming gives you fine-grained control over how objects are rendered in your game. Cocos2d-x supports custom shader development, allowing you to create stunning visual effects. You can write shaders in GLSL (OpenGL Shading Language) and integrate them into your game.

```
// Create a custom shader program
```

```
auto customShader = GLProgram::createWithFilenames("shaders/custom.vert", "shaders/custom.frag");

yourSprite->setGLProgram(customShader);
```

With custom shaders, you can achieve effects like water ripples, distortion, dynamic lighting, and more.

Real-time Rendering Optimization

Optimizing real-time rendering performance is crucial for smooth gameplay. Here are some optimization techniques:

1. **Batching**: As mentioned earlier, batch rendering combines multiple objects into a single draw call, reducing CPU overhead.
2. **Culling**: Implement frustum culling to skip rendering objects that are outside the camera's view, saving GPU processing.
3. **Level of Detail (LOD)**: For 3D elements, implement LOD techniques to reduce the complexity of models based on their distance from the camera.
4. **Texture Atlases**: Use texture atlases to minimize texture binding and improve rendering performance.
5. **Shader Optimization**: Write efficient shaders and avoid expensive computations in shaders.

Incorporating these advanced graphics and animation techniques into your Cocos2d-x game can elevate its visual quality and create a more immersive gaming experience for players. However, it's essential to balance visual effects with performance to ensure that your game runs smoothly on a wide range of devices.

Section 1.5: Cross-platform Development

Nuances

Cross-platform game development is the process of creating games that can run on multiple platforms, such as iOS, Android, Windows, macOS, and more. Cocos2d-x is known for its cross-platform capabilities, but there are nuances and considerations you need to be aware of when developing games for different target platforms.

Platform-Specific Code

While Cocos2d-x allows you to write most of your game code in C++, you may encounter situations where you need to write platform-specific code to access device features or implement platform-specific functionality. This is typically done using conditional compilation.

```
#if CC_TARGET_PLATFORM == CC_PLATFORM_IOS

// iOS-specific code

#elif CC_TARGET_PLATFORM == CC_PLATFORM_ANDROID

// Android-specific code

#elif CC_TARGET_PLATFORM == CC_PLATFORM_WIN32

// Windows-specific code

#endif
```

Common scenarios for platform-specific code include handling in-app purchases, integrating with platform-specific services (e.g., Game Center, Google Play Services), and managing device permissions.

Screen Size and Resolution

Different platforms have varying screen sizes and resolutions, so it's essential to design your game to be responsive. Cocos2d-x provides tools to help you adapt your game's user interface and content to different screen sizes.

1. **Viewports**: Use viewports to define the visible area of your game. This allows you to scale and position game elements dynamically based on the device's screen size.

```
// Set the design resolution and policy

Director::getInstance()->getOpenGLView()->setDesignResolutionSize(d
designHeight, ResolutionPolicy::SHOW_ALL);
```

1. **Asset Scaling**: Create multiple sets of assets (images, sprites) for different screen resolutions and load the appropriate set at runtime. Cocos2d-x's resource loading system can assist with this.
2. **Responsive UI**: Design user interfaces (UI) that can adapt to different screen sizes and aspect ratios. Use anchor points and relative positioning for UI elements.

Input Methods

Different platforms have varying input methods, such as touchscreens, mouse and keyboard, game controllers, and more. When developing cross-platform games, you need to consider how players will interact with your game on different devices.

Cocos2d-x provides input handling mechanisms that abstract the underlying input methods. You can use event listeners to handle touch events, keyboard input, and even game controller input in a consistent manner.

```
// Create a keyboard event listener

auto keyboardListener = EventListenerKeyboard::create();

keyboardListener->onKeyPressed = [](EventKeyboard::KeyCode keyCode, Event* event){

// Handle key press event

};

Director::getInstance()->getEventDispatcher()->addEventListenerWithSc
yourNode);
```

Performance Considerations

Each platform has its performance characteristics, and optimizing your game for each platform is essential. Low-end devices may have limited CPU and GPU power, so you should profile and test your game on a range of devices to ensure it runs smoothly.

Additionally, some platforms may have restrictions or limitations that impact performance. For example, iOS devices may have stricter memory limitations compared to Android devices.

Testing and Debugging

Testing your game thoroughly on each target platform is crucial. Emulators and simulators can help, but real-device testing is essential to identify platform-specific issues.

Cocos2d-x provides tools for remote debugging and testing on actual devices. You can connect your development environment to a physical device for debugging and testing purposes.

In conclusion, cross-platform game development with Cocos2d-x offers the advantage of reaching a broader audience, but it comes with its own set of challenges. Understanding and addressing platform-specific nuances, optimizing performance, and thorough testing are key to delivering a successful cross-platform game that provides a consistent and enjoyable experience across different devices and operating systems.

Chapter 2: Advanced Graphics and Animation

Section 2.1: Particle Systems and Special Effects

Particle systems are a valuable tool in game development for creating a wide range of visual effects, from dynamic fire and smoke to sparkling magic spells. Cocos2d-x provides a built-in particle system that allows developers to generate and control these effects efficiently.

Understanding Particle Systems

A particle system is a collection of small, individually controlled graphical elements called particles. These particles can represent various visual elements, such as sparks, smoke, raindrops, or even abstract effects. By emitting and manipulating particles over time, you can create complex and dynamic visual effects that enhance the overall look and feel of your game.

Cocos2d-x's particle system allows you to customize the appearance, behavior, and motion of particles. You can control factors like particle size, color, opacity, speed, direction, and lifespan, enabling you to achieve a wide range of visual effects.

Creating a Basic Particle System

Let's start by creating a basic particle system in Cocos2d-x. Below is an example of how to set up a simple particle system that creates a burst of particles:

```
// Create a particle system
```

```
auto particleSystem = ParticleSystemQuad::create("particles/fire.plist");

// Add the particle system to a layer

yourLayer->addChild(particleSystem);
```

In this code, we create a particle system by loading a predefined configuration file ("particles/fire.plist"). You can find various preconfigured particle effects within Cocos2d-x, or you can create your own custom particle effects using tools like Particle Designer.

Customizing Particle Effects

Cocos2d-x allows you to customize particle effects to match your game's style and requirements. You can modify various properties of the particle system, such as emission rate, particle size, speed, color, and more.

Here's an example of how to change the particle size and color of a particle system:

```
// Customize particle properties

particleSystem->setStartSize(10.0f);

particleSystem->setEndSize(20.0f);

particleSystem->setStartColor(Color4F(1.0f, 0.5f, 0.0f, 1.0f));

particleSystem->setEndColor(Color4F(0.0f, 0.0f, 0.0f, 0.0f));
```

In this code, we set the initial particle size to 10.0 units, the final size to 20.0 units, and the start and end colors to orange and transparent black, respectively.

Particle System Lifecycle

Particle systems in Cocos2d-x have a lifecycle that includes the following phases:

1. **Birth**: Particles are created at the emitter's position with initial properties.
2. **Update**: Particles move and change properties over time based on predefined rules and behaviors.
3. **Death**: Particles that have reached the end of their lifespan are removed from the system.
4. **Reuse**: Particles that have died can be reused for new births to maintain a constant number of particles in the system.

Advanced Particle Effects

Cocos2d-x's particle system is versatile and can be used to create a wide variety of effects beyond simple bursts. You can create effects like continuous fire, smoke trails, falling leaves, and even simulate complex natural phenomena.

To create more advanced effects, you can customize particle properties, apply gravity, adjust emission rates, and add forces like wind to influence particle motion. Experimenting with these parameters allows you to achieve the desired visual effect for your game.

In conclusion, particle systems are a powerful tool for enhancing the visual appeal of your games. Cocos2d-x's built-in particle system simplifies the creation of various effects, from basic bursts to complex and dynamic animations. By understanding particle system properties and customizing them to fit your game's style, you can create stunning and immersive visual experiences for your players.

Section 2.2: Advanced Animation Techniques

Animation is a fundamental aspect of game development that brings characters, objects, and the game world to life. Cocos2d-x provides a range of advanced animation techniques to create engaging and dynamic gameplay experiences.

Sprite Frame Animation

Sprite frame animation is a common technique used to animate 2D characters and objects in games. It involves displaying a sequence of images or frames at a specific rate to create the illusion of motion. Cocos2d-x simplifies the process of creating and playing sprite frame animations.

Creating Sprite Frame Animations

To create a sprite frame animation, you need a set of individual frames and a timing sequence. Here's a basic example of creating a sprite frame animation in Cocos2d-x:

```
// Create a vector to hold sprite frames

Vector<SpriteFrame*> frames;

// Load sprite frames from a sprite sheet or individual images

for (int i = 1; i <= numFrames; ++i) {

char frameName[100];

sprintf(frameName, "frame_%02d.png", i);

auto frame = SpriteFrameCache::getInstance()->getSpriteFrameByName(frameName);
```

```
frames.pushBack(frame);

}

// Create an animation from the frames

auto animation = Animation::createWithSpriteFrames(frames, frameDuration);

// Create an animate action to run the animation

auto animate = Animate::create(animation);

// Apply the animate action to a sprite

yourSprite->runAction(animate);
```

In this code, we load individual sprite frames from a sprite sheet or image files, create an animation from those frames, and then apply the animation to a sprite.

Sprite Sheet and Texture Packer

Using sprite sheets or texture atlases is a common practice in sprite frame animation. Sprite sheets combine multiple frames into a single image, reducing memory overhead and improving performance. Tools like Texture Packer can help you create optimized sprite sheets for your game.

Spine Animation

Spine is a 2D skeletal animation tool that allows you to create complex character animations with bones, joints, and mesh deformations. Cocos2d-x provides support for Spine animations, making it easier to integrate intricate character animations into your games.

Using Spine Animations

To use Spine animations in Cocos2d-x, you'll need to create or export your animations using the Spine tool and then import them into your project. Once imported, you can load and display Spine animations like this:

```
// Load a Spine skeleton animation
auto skeletonNode = SkeletonAnimation::createWithJsonFile("spine/character.json", "spine/character.atlas", 1.0f);
// Add the skeleton to a layer
yourLayer->addChild(skeletonNode);
```

This code demonstrates how to load a Spine skeleton animation and add it to a Cocos2d-x layer.

Timeline-Based Animations

Timeline-based animations allow you to create scripted sequences of actions that can be used for cinematic sequences, scripted events, or any situation where you need precise control over animation timing.

Creating Timeline Animations

In Cocos2d-x, you can create timeline animations by adding actions to a timeline sequence. Here's a simplified example:

```
// Create a timeline action
auto timeline = Timeline::create();
// Add actions to the timeline
```

```
timeline->addFrame([=]() {
// Action to perform at a specific time
}, 2.0f); // Time in seconds
// Run the timeline action
yourNode->runAction(timeline);
```

In this code, we create a timeline and add an action to it with a specified time delay. When the timeline runs, the action will be executed at the specified time.

Easing Functions

Easing functions (also known as easing curves or interpolation functions) control the rate of change of animation properties over time. Cocos2d-x provides a variety of easing functions that allow you to achieve different animation effects, such as smooth accelerations, decelerations, and bounces.

You can apply easing functions to actions in your animations to control how objects move, scale, or fade in and out over time.

Advanced Animation Techniques

Advanced animation techniques in Cocos2d-x go beyond basic frame-by-frame animations. These techniques include ragdoll physics for realistic character movement, inverse kinematics (IK) for precise control over character limbs, and dynamic mesh deformations for organic character animations.

To implement advanced animation techniques, you may need to use third-party libraries or create custom solutions tailored to your game's requirements.

In summary, advanced animation techniques in Cocos2d-x provide the tools you need to create dynamic and engaging gameplay experiences. Whether you're animating characters, objects, or special effects, mastering these techniques will help you bring your game to life and captivate your players.

Section 2.3: Integrating 3D Elements in a 2D Engine

Cocos2d-x is primarily known as a 2D game engine, but there are scenarios where you might want to integrate 3D elements into your 2D game. This can add depth and visual appeal to your game world. While Cocos2d-x is not a full-fledged 3D engine, it does offer limited support for incorporating 3D elements.

Use Cases for 3D Integration

Before diving into the technical details of integrating 3D elements, it's essential to understand why you might want to do it. Here are some common use cases:

1. **Parallax Effects**: You can create parallax backgrounds with 3D layers to add depth and realism to your 2D game.
2. **3D Models**: Integrate 3D models for characters or objects that need more complex animations or interactions.
3. **Terrain and Terrain Generation**: Use 3D terrain for platformers or games with height-based mechanics.
4. **Special Effects**: Some special effects, like water ripples or dynamic lighting, can benefit from 3D elements.

3D Integration Techniques

Cocos2d-x provides several techniques for integrating 3D elements into your 2D game. While these techniques won't turn Cocos2d-x into a full 3D engine, they allow for creative solutions.

1. **Layering**: You can create 3D layers and render them behind or in front of your 2D scenes to achieve parallax effects. For example, you can have a 3D layer with a scrolling starfield in the background.
2. **Using Third-Party Libraries**: Cocos2d-x allows you to integrate third-party 3D rendering libraries like OpenGL for more advanced 3D rendering. This approach requires significant knowledge of 3D programming.
3. **Limited 3D Support**: Cocos2d-x has limited built-in support for rendering basic 3D models using the *Sprite3D* class. You can load and display 3D models in your game.

Here's a basic example of how to load and display a 3D model using *Sprite3D*:

```
// Create a 3D model node

auto model = Sprite3D::create("models/character.c3b");

// Set the position and scale of the model

model->setPosition(Vec2(x, y));

model->setScale(0.1f);

// Add the model to your scene or layer

yourLayer->addChild(model);
```

In this code, we create a *Sprite3D* node and load a 3D model from a file. We then set its position and scale and add it to the game scene or layer.

Limitations and Considerations

While integrating 3D elements can add visual appeal, it comes with limitations and considerations:

1. **Performance**: 3D rendering can be computationally expensive. Ensure that your game can maintain a smooth frame rate when incorporating 3D elements, especially on lower-end devices.
2. **Art Assets**: 3D models require different art assets and may increase the overall size of your game.
3. **Complexity**: Integrating 3D elements adds complexity to your game development process, as it involves a different set of skills and tools.
4. **Compatibility**: Not all platforms or devices may support 3D rendering equally. Test your game on various target platforms to ensure compatibility.
5. **Balancing 2D and 3D**: Finding the right balance between 2D and 3D elements is crucial to maintaining a cohesive visual style in your game.

In conclusion, while Cocos2d-x is primarily a 2D game engine, it offers limited support for integrating 3D elements. Understanding the use cases, techniques, and limitations of 3D integration can help you make informed decisions when enhancing your 2D game with 3D elements.

Section 2.4: Shader Programming in Cocos2d-x

Shader programming is a powerful technique used to control how objects are rendered in your game. Cocos2d-x supports custom shader development, allowing you to create stunning visual effects and manipulate the appearance of game elements in real-time.

Understanding Shaders

In the context of game development, a shader is a program that runs on the GPU (Graphics Processing Unit) and is responsible for rendering objects. Shaders control various aspects of rendering, such as color, lighting, and texture mapping. There are two main types of shaders:

1. **Vertex Shader**: This shader operates on individual vertices of 3D models, transforming their positions and passing data to the fragment shader.
2. **Fragment Shader (Pixel Shader)**: The fragment shader determines the final color of each pixel on the screen. It can apply lighting, textures, and other visual effects.

GLSL (OpenGL Shading Language)

Cocos2d-x uses GLSL (OpenGL Shading Language) for writing shaders. GLSL is a C-like language designed for GPU programming. To create custom shaders in Cocos2d-x, you'll need to write GLSL code.

Creating Custom Shaders

To create a custom shader in Cocos2d-x, you can follow these general steps:

1. **Write the Shader Code**: Create a *.vert* file for the vertex shader and a *.frag* file for the fragment shader. Write your shader code in these files.
2. **Load the Shader**: Load the shader code from the *.vert* and *.frag* files into your Cocos2d-x project.
3. **Create a Shader Program**: Compile the shader code and create a shader program using Cocos2d-x's *GLProgram* class.

```
// Create a custom shader program

auto customShader = GLProgram::createWithFilenames("shaders/custom.vert", "shaders/custom.frag");
```

1. **Apply the Shader**: Apply the custom shader program to the sprite or object you want to render with the shader.

```
// Apply the custom shader to a sprite

yourSprite->setGLProgram(customShader);
```

Common Shader Effects

Custom shaders in Cocos2d-x can be used to achieve various visual effects, including:

- **Dynamic Lighting**: Simulate realistic lighting effects, such as shadows, highlights, and specular reflections, on game objects.

- **Distortion and Warping**: Create effects like water ripples, heat waves, or glass distortion by displacing vertices based on shader logic.

- **Post-Processing Effects**: Apply post-processing effects to the entire screen, such as blurs, color adjustments, and screen transitions.

- **Animations and Transitions**: Implement custom animations and transitions between game scenes or elements.

- **Outline and Glow**: Add outlines or glowing effects to game objects to make them stand out.

Shader Uniforms and Attributes

In GLSL shaders, you can use uniforms and attributes to pass data between the CPU and GPU. Uniforms are values that are constant during the rendering of an object, while attributes are values that vary per vertex.

In Cocos2d-x, you can set uniform values using the *setUniformLocationWith** methods, and you can pass custom attributes using the *setVertexAttribPointer* method.

Performance Considerations

While shaders can create visually stunning effects, they can also be computationally expensive. It's crucial to optimize your shaders to ensure good performance, especially on lower-end devices.

Some performance considerations for shader programming include minimizing the number of shader calculations, avoiding unnecessary branching in your code, and optimizing memory access.

Debugging and Testing

Debugging shaders can be challenging because they run on the GPU, making traditional debugging techniques less effective. Cocos2d-x provides some tools and techniques for shader debugging, such as uniform value inspection and shader validation.

Testing shaders on different devices and resolutions is essential to ensure that your effects work as intended across various platforms.

In summary, shader programming in Cocos2d-x allows you to create custom visual effects and control how objects are rendered in your game. By understanding GLSL, creating custom shaders, and considering performance and debugging, you can leverage the power of shaders to enhance the graphics and aesthetics of your game.

Section 2.5: Real-time Rendering Optimization

Optimizing real-time rendering is crucial for maintaining smooth and responsive gameplay in your Cocos2d-x games. Efficient rendering ensures that your game can run at a consistent frame rate, even on devices with limited hardware resources. In this section, we'll explore various techniques and best practices for optimizing the rendering performance of your Cocos2d-x games.

Batch Rendering

Batch rendering is a technique that involves grouping similar objects together and rendering them in a single draw call. This reduces the overhead of making multiple draw calls to the GPU, which can significantly improve rendering performance.

Cocos2d-x provides tools for batching sprites and other graphical elements. You can use *SpriteBatchNode* or *SpriteFrameCache* to group and render multiple sprites efficiently. Here's an example of how to use *SpriteBatchNode*:

```
// Create a sprite batch node

auto batchNode = SpriteBatchNode::create("sprite_sheet.png");

// Create sprites and add them to the batch node

auto sprite1 = Sprite::createWithSpriteFrameName("sprite1.png");

auto sprite2 = Sprite::createWithSpriteFrameName("sprite2.png");

batchNode->addChild(sprite1);

batchNode->addChild(sprite2);
```

Texture Atlas

Texture atlases are a way to store multiple textures in a single image, reducing the number of texture switches during rendering. Cocos2d-x supports the use of texture atlases to optimize rendering performance. Tools like Texture Packer can help you create optimized texture atlases for your game assets.

Culling

Culling is the process of determining which objects or portions of the game world are visible to the camera and should be rendered. Implementing culling in your game can significantly reduce the number of objects that need to be rendered, improving performance.

Cocos2d-x provides built-in camera and view management features that can help you implement culling effectively. By only rendering what is visible on the screen, you can save valuable GPU resources.

Level of Detail (LOD)

Level of Detail (LOD) is a technique used in 3D rendering to adjust the level of detail in an object based on its distance from the camera. In 2D games with perspective effects or zooming, you can apply a similar concept to optimize rendering.

For example, if you have background elements that become smaller as the camera zooms out, you can switch to lower-resolution textures or simpler representations of those elements to save rendering resources.

Particle System Optimization

Particle systems can be performance-intensive, especially when many particles are on-screen. To optimize particle systems in Cocos2d-x, consider the following:

- Limit the number of active particles if possible.
- Use simple particle shapes instead of complex textures.
- Opt for additive blending for certain effects.
- Group similar particle systems and use batching techniques.

GPU Profiling

Profiling your game's rendering performance is essential to identify bottlenecks and areas for improvement. Cocos2d-x provides tools for GPU profiling, allowing you to measure the GPU time spent on rendering each frame.

By using GPU profiling, you can pinpoint which rendering operations are consuming the most GPU resources and focus your optimization efforts accordingly.

Minimize Overdraw

Overdraw occurs when multiple objects are drawn on top of each other, and the GPU has to render each pixel multiple times. To minimize overdraw, use techniques like depth testing and sorting to ensure that only visible pixels are rendered.

Additionally, avoid using fully transparent pixels in textures whenever possible, as they can contribute to overdraw.

Dynamic Resolution

Cocos2d-x supports dynamic resolution scaling, which allows your game to adapt to different screen sizes and resolutions. By using the appropriate resolution policy, you can ensure that your game looks good on a variety of devices without sacrificing performance.

Multithreading

In some cases, multithreading can be used to optimize rendering performance, especially for CPU-bound tasks like physics calculations or AI. However, multithreading in game development can be complex and requires careful synchronization to avoid issues. Cocos2d-x provides support for multithreading, but it should be used judiciously and with a clear understanding of its implications.

In conclusion, optimizing real-time rendering in Cocos2d-x is essential for delivering a smooth and enjoyable gaming experience.

By implementing batch rendering, using texture atlases, applying culling and LOD techniques, optimizing particle systems, profiling GPU performance, minimizing overdraw, and considering dynamic resolution and multithreading, you can achieve excellent rendering performance for your Cocos2d-x games across a wide range of devices.

Chapter 3: Sophisticated Gameplay Mechanics

Section 3.1: Implementing AI and Pathfinding

Artificial Intelligence (AI) plays a crucial role in creating engaging and challenging gameplay experiences. Whether it's controlling non-player characters (NPCs), designing enemy behaviors, or optimizing character movement, implementing AI and pathfinding is a fundamental aspect of game development. In this section, we'll explore how to integrate AI and pathfinding techniques into your Cocos2d-x game.

The Importance of AI in Games

AI in games is responsible for making decisions, simulating behaviors, and reacting to player actions. It can provide lifelike character interactions, challenging opponents, and dynamic game environments. AI enhances gameplay by creating immersion, unpredictability, and a sense of challenge.

Pathfinding Algorithms

Pathfinding is a core AI technique used to find the shortest or most efficient path from one point to another within a game world. Cocos2d-x supports various pathfinding algorithms, including:

1. A Algorithm*

The A* (A-star) algorithm is one of the most popular pathfinding algorithms in game development. It finds the shortest path while efficiently exploring possible routes. Cocos2d-x provides support for A* pathfinding through libraries like Cocos2d-x A* and third-party plugins.

Here's a simplified example of using the A* algorithm in Cocos2d-x:

```
// Create a grid map representing the game world

GridMap gridMap = createGridMap();

// Find a path from start position to end position using A*

PathFinder pathFinder(gridMap);

Path path = pathFinder.findPath(startPosition, endPosition);
```

In this code, we create a grid map of the game world and use the A* algorithm to find a path from a start position to an end position.

2. Dijkstra's Algorithm

Dijkstra's algorithm finds the shortest path in a weighted graph. It is less efficient than A* for game pathfinding because it explores all possible routes without heuristic guidance. However, it can be useful in certain situations, such as when all edges have the same cost.

3. Navigation Mesh

Navigation meshes (navmeshes) are polygonal representations of the game world that simplify pathfinding. Cocos2d-x supports navigation meshes through tools like Recast Navigation. Navmeshes are often used in games with complex 3D environments where traditional grid-based pathfinding is impractical.

Implementing AI Behaviors

Integrating AI behaviors into your game involves defining decision-making processes for NPCs or entities. Cocos2d-x provides various approaches to implement AI behaviors:

Finite State Machines (FSM)

FSMs are a common method for modeling AI behaviors. In an FSM, an AI character can be in one of several states, each with its own set of rules and actions. Transitions between states occur based on specific conditions or events.

Here's a basic example of an FSM implementation in Cocos2d-x:

```
class AICharacter {
public:
enum class State { IDLE, PATROL, CHASE, ATTACK };
void update() {
switch (currentState) {
case State::IDLE:
// Implement IDLE behavior
break;
case State::PATROL:
// Implement PATROL behavior
break;
case State::CHASE:
```

```
// Implement CHASE behavior
break;
case State::ATTACK:
// Implement ATTACK behavior
break;
}
}
// Other AICharacter methods and properties
};
```

In this example, the *AICharacter* class uses an FSM to manage different behaviors based on its current state.

Behavior Trees

Behavior trees are hierarchical structures that represent AI decision-making. They consist of nodes that define specific behaviors, conditions, or composite tasks. Behavior trees are flexible and can model complex AI logic.

Cocos2d-x provides libraries and tools for implementing behavior trees, making it easier to create AI behaviors for your game characters.

Pathfinding Integration

To integrate pathfinding into your Cocos2d-x game, you'll typically follow these steps:

1. Create a map or grid representation of the game world where each cell represents an area that can be traversed.
2. Use a pathfinding algorithm like A* to find the shortest path from the character's current position to the target position.
3. Implement movement logic to follow the computed path, making sure the character navigates around obstacles.

Here's a high-level example of pathfinding integration:

```
// Find a path using pathfinding algorithm

Path path = findPath(character.getPosition(), target.getPosition());

// Follow the path by moving the character

for (auto& point : path) {

character.moveTo(point);

}
```

This code snippet demonstrates the basic process of using pathfinding to navigate a character to a target position.

AI Optimization and Performance

Efficient AI is essential for maintaining smooth gameplay. Here are some optimization techniques for AI in Cocos2d-x:

- **Avoid Excessive Computations**: Minimize unnecessary AI calculations, especially in update loops. Use caching and lazy evaluation where applicable.

- **Use Spatial Data Structures**: Organize game entities into spatial data structures like quadtrees or octrees to optimize collision detection and AI queries.

- **Multithreading**: Consider offloading AI calculations to separate threads to prevent blocking the main game loop.

- **Bounding Volume Checks**: Use bounding volumes (e.g., bounding boxes or spheres) for collision and visibility checks to reduce the number of precise calculations.

- **Level of Detail**: Apply LOD techniques to AI behaviors, simplifying calculations for objects that are far away from the player's view.

Debugging and Testing

Testing and debugging AI can be challenging due to the complexity of AI behaviors. Cocos2d-x provides debugging tools and features to help you visualize AI paths, states, and behaviors. Logging and visualization tools can aid in diagnosing issues and fine-tuning AI logic.

In conclusion, implementing AI and pathfinding in your Cocos2d-x game is essential for creating engaging and challenging gameplay experiences. Whether you're using pathfinding algorithms like A*, finite state machines, or behavior trees, understanding AI optimization techniques and debugging tools will help you create AI-driven characters and entities that enhance your game's immersion and fun factor.

Section 3.2: Physics Engine Integration and

Customization

Integrating a physics engine into your Cocos2d-x game is a fundamental step in creating realistic and interactive gameplay experiences. Physics engines simulate the physical behavior of game objects, allowing them to respond to forces, collisions, and interactions in a natural way. Cocos2d-x provides built-in support for physics through the Cocos2d-x Physics module, which is based on the popular open-source physics engine, Chipmunk.

Why Use a Physics Engine?

Physics engines offer several advantages in game development:

1. **Realism**: They provide realistic object movement, collision, and response to forces, enhancing the immersive quality of your game.
2. **Interactivity**: Physics engines enable dynamic interactions between game objects, making gameplay more engaging and enjoyable.
3. **Efficiency**: Physics engines are optimized for performance, ensuring smooth gameplay even with complex simulations.
4. **Simplification**: They simplify the process of implementing physics, reducing the need for manual calculations and coding.

Cocos2d-x Physics Module

The Cocos2d-x Physics module provides a convenient way to integrate physics into your game. It offers support for features like rigid bodies, collision detection, joints, and various shapes.

Here's a high-level overview of integrating and using the Cocos2d-x Physics module:

1. **Enabling Physics**: To use physics, you need to enable the Physics module in your Cocos2d-x project. This is typically done during project setup.
2. **Creating Physics Worlds**: You can create one or more physics worlds in your game, each representing a separate physics simulation. Worlds can have different properties like gravity and boundaries.
3. **Adding Physics Bodies**: Attach physics bodies to game objects like sprites or nodes. A physics body defines the physical properties of the object, such as mass, shape, and friction.

```
// Create a physics body for a sprite

auto sprite = Sprite::create("ball.png");

auto body = PhysicsBody::createCircle(sprite->getContentSize().width / 2);

sprite->setPhysicsBody(body);
```

1. **Collision Detection**: Define collision categories and masks to control which objects can collide with each other. Use collision event callbacks to handle collisions and apply custom logic.

```
// Set collision categories and masks

body1->setCategoryBitmask(0x01); // Category 1

body2->setCategoryBitmask(0x02); // Category 2

body1->setCollisionBitmask(0x02); // Collide with objects in Category 2
```

body2->setCollisionBitmask(0x01); *// Collide with objects in Category 1*

// Handle collision event

auto contactListener = EventListenerPhysicsContact::create();

contactListener->onContactBegin = [](PhysicsContact& contact) {

// Handle collision logic

return true; *// Return true to allow the collision to occur*

};

1. **Applying Forces and Impulses**: You can apply forces, impulses, and torque to physics bodies to simulate object movement and interactions.

// Apply a force to a physics body

body->applyForce(Vec2(100, 0)); *// Apply a force in the x-direction*

1. **Joints and Constraints**: Create joints to connect physics bodies and impose constraints on their movements. Cocos2d-x supports various joint types like distance joint, revolute joint, and more.

// Create a distance joint between two bodies

auto joint = PhysicsJointDistance::construct(body1, body2, Point::ZERO, Point::ZERO);

Custom Physics Behavior

While Cocos2d-x's Physics module provides a wide range of functionality, you may encounter scenarios where you need custom physics behavior. Custom physics can include non-standard collision responses, complex joint behaviors, or specialized physics simulations.

To implement custom physics behavior in Cocos2d-x, you can use the following approaches:

1. **Custom Forces and Constraints**: You can apply custom forces and constraints to physics bodies by directly manipulating their properties in your game's update loop. This allows you to implement custom physics logic outside the built-in physics engine.
2. **Extending the Physics Engine**: If your custom physics behavior requires more extensive changes, you can consider extending or modifying the underlying physics engine (Chipmunk) used by Cocos2d-x. However, this approach can be complex and may require in-depth knowledge of the physics engine's internals.
3. **Hybrid Systems**: In some cases, you can combine the built-in physics system with custom behavior. For example, you might use the physics engine for collision detection and resolution while implementing custom logic for character movement or specialized interactions.

Performance Considerations

Efficient physics simulation is critical for maintaining a smooth gaming experience. To optimize physics performance in Cocos2d-x, consider the following:

- **Use Simple Shapes**: Complex physics shapes can be computationally expensive. Whenever possible, use simpler shapes like circles or rectangles for collision detection.

- **Adjust Update Frequency**: You can control the update frequency of physics simulations to balance performance and accuracy. Reducing the update frequency may improve performance but can affect physics accuracy.

- **Minimize Object Count**: Limit the number of physics bodies and collisions in your game to avoid performance bottlenecks.

- **Profiling and Optimization**: Use profiling tools to identify performance bottlenecks within your physics simulations. Optimize code, reduce unnecessary calculations, and optimize collision detection to improve performance.

- **Collision Layers**: Carefully organize collision categories and masks to ensure that only necessary objects interact with each other. This reduces the number of collision checks.

In conclusion, integrating and customizing a physics engine in Cocos2d-x allows you to create dynamic and interactive gameplay experiences. Whether you rely on the built-in Physics module or implement custom physics behavior, understanding performance considerations and best practices will help you achieve smooth and realistic physics simulations in your games.

Section 3.3: Advanced User Input Handling

Efficient and responsive user input handling is a critical aspect of game development, as it directly affects the player's interaction with the game world. In this section, we'll explore advanced techniques for handling user input in Cocos2d-x games, covering touch and gesture recognition, virtual controls, and input customization.

Touch and Gesture Recognition

Cocos2d-x provides built-in support for handling touch events, which are essential for games on touch-enabled devices. You can capture touch events on individual nodes, allowing you to implement interactive elements like buttons, menus, and character movement controls.

Here's a basic example of touch event handling in Cocos2d-x:

```
// Enable touch events for a node

node->setTouchEnabled(true);

// Implement touch event callbacks

node->onTouchBegan = [](Touch* touch, Event* event) {

// Handle touch began event

return true; // Return true to indicate that the touch event was handled

};

node->onTouchMoved = [](Touch* touch, Event* event) {

// Handle touch moved event
```

```
};

node->onTouchEnded = [](Touch* touch, Event* event) {

// Handle touch ended event

};
```

Beyond basic touch events, you can implement gesture recognition for more complex interactions. Cocos2d-x supports gesture recognition libraries like *cocos2d-x-extra* for detecting gestures such as swipes, pinches, and rotations.

Virtual Controls

In many mobile and console games, virtual controls are used to provide a tactile interface for player input. Virtual controls can include on-screen buttons, joysticks, and directional pads. Implementing virtual controls effectively can enhance gameplay and accessibility.

To create virtual controls in Cocos2d-x, you can use the following approach:

1. **Create Control Nodes**: Design and create graphical control nodes, such as buttons or joysticks, as sprites or UI elements.
2. **Implement Touch Handling**: Attach touch event handlers to these control nodes to capture user input.
3. **React to Input**: In response to touch events on the control nodes, implement logic to interpret the input and translate it into game actions, character movement, or other gameplay interactions.

Here's an example of implementing a virtual joystick control in Cocos2d-x:

```
// Create a joystick sprite

auto joystick = Sprite::create("joystick.png");

joystick->setPosition(Vec2(100, 100));

addChild(joystick);

// Implement touch event handlers for the joystick

joystick->setTouchEnabled(true);

joystick->onTouchBegan = [](Touch* touch, Event* event) {

// Handle touch began event by showing the joystick's active state

};

joystick->onTouchMoved = [](Touch* touch, Event* event) {

// Handle touch moved event to update the joystick's position

};

joystick->onTouchEnded = [](Touch* touch, Event* event) {

// Handle touch ended event by resetting the joystick's state

};
```

Input Customization

Customizing input handling allows players to configure controls to their preferences and can improve the overall gaming experience. In Cocos2d-x, you can implement input customization by providing options for players to remap buttons, adjust sensitivity, or customize control layouts.

Here are some considerations for input customization:

- **Input Mapping**: Implement a system that allows players to map game actions to specific input events or buttons. Provide an in-game menu or settings screen for input configuration.

- **Sensitivity Settings**: Allow players to adjust the sensitivity of controls, such as the speed of character movement or camera rotation. Provide sensitivity sliders or options in the game's settings.

- **Control Layouts**: Offer multiple control layout presets to accommodate different player preferences and device orientations. For example, provide options for left-handed and right-handed layouts.

- **Button Remapping**: Allow players to remap buttons to their preferred keys or locations. This can be particularly important for players with accessibility needs.

Multitouch Handling

Modern mobile devices and some desktop platforms support multitouch input, allowing multiple simultaneous touch points. Handling multitouch can be useful for implementing complex gestures, multiplayer games, or interactions involving multiple fingers.

In Cocos2d-x, you can handle multitouch events by registering touch event handlers on different nodes and tracking individual touches.

```
// Enable multitouch for a node

node->setMultiTouchEnabled(true);

// Implement touch event callbacks

node->onTouchesBegan = [](const std::vector<Touch*>& touches, Event* event) {

// Handle multiple touch points

};

node->onTouchesMoved = [](const std::vector<Touch*>& touches, Event* event) {

// Handle touch movements

};

node->onTouchesEnded = [](const std::vector<Touch*>& touches, Event* event) {

// Handle touch releases

};
```

Testing and Debugging

Thorough testing and debugging of user input handling are crucial to ensure that controls are responsive and intuitive. Test your game on various devices and screen sizes to verify that controls work as expected. Use logging and debugging tools to diagnose and fix issues related to input responsiveness and accuracy.

In conclusion, advanced user input handling in Cocos2d-x games involves recognizing touch and gestures, implementing virtual controls, offering input customization, and addressing multitouch interactions. By providing responsive and customizable controls, you can enhance the player's experience and accessibility, leading to a more enjoyable gaming experience.

Section 3.4: Creating Dynamic Game Environments

Dynamic game environments add depth, immersion, and variety to gameplay experiences. In this section, we'll explore techniques for creating dynamic game environments in Cocos2d-x, including procedural generation, destructible terrain, weather systems, and day-night cycles.

Procedural Generation

Procedural generation is a powerful technique for creating dynamic and limitless game worlds. It involves generating game content, such as terrain, levels, or maps, algorithmically rather than manually. Procedural generation can result in unique and replayable game experiences.

In Cocos2d-x, you can implement procedural generation by defining algorithms to create terrain, dungeons, mazes, or other game elements. Consider the following approaches:

- **Random Generation**: Use random number generators to create terrain features, enemy placements, or item drops. Randomness adds unpredictability to the game.

- **Perlin Noise**: Perlin noise and its variants can be used to generate smooth and natural-looking landscapes. You can use Perlin noise to create terrain elevation, texture patterns, or cloud formations.

- **Cellular Automata**: Cellular automata rules can simulate growth processes and generate organic structures like forests, caves, or rivers.

- **L-Systems**: L-systems are formal grammars used to model branching structures like trees, rivers, or road networks. Implementing L-systems can add complexity and realism to your game environment.

Here's a simplified example of using Perlin noise for terrain generation in Cocos2d-x:

```
// Generate terrain heightmap using Perlin noise

int width = 100;

int height = 100;

std::vector<std::vector<float>> heightmap(width, std::vector<float>(height));

for (int x = 0; x < width; x++) {

for (int y = 0; y < height; y++) {

float noiseValue = SimplexNoise::noise(x * 0.1, y * 0.1);

heightmap[x][y] = noiseValue * maxHeight;

}

}
```

Destructible Terrain

Destructible terrain allows players to interact with and modify the game world. It's commonly used in games with environmental destruction, digging mechanics, or terrain deformation. Implementing destructible terrain in Cocos2d-x requires careful management of game objects and physics.

You can create destructible terrain by modeling the terrain as a grid of objects or tiles, where each tile can be modified or destroyed individually. Players can interact with the terrain by adding or removing tiles, causing changes in the game environment.

```
// Example: Digging a hole in the terrain

void digTerrain(Vec2 position) {

int tileX = position.x / tileSize;

int tileY = position.y / tileSize;

// Remove the tile at the specified position

terrainLayer->removeTileAt(Vec2(tileX, tileY));

}
```

Weather Systems

Weather systems can enhance the atmosphere and visual appeal of your game environment. Weather effects like rain, snow, fog, and dynamic lighting can create immersive and dynamic experiences. Cocos2d-x provides features and tools for implementing weather systems:

- **Particle Systems**: You can use Cocos2d-x's particle system to create various weather effects, such as raindrops, snowflakes, or falling leaves. Particle systems allow you to control the appearance, movement, and behavior of weather particles.

• **Dynamic Lighting**: Adjusting the lighting in your game based on weather conditions can add realism. For example, you can simulate darker skies and dimmer lighting during rain or thunderstorms.

• **Shader Effects**: Shaders can be used to create visual effects like water ripples, snow accumulation, or fog. Cocos2d-x supports shader programming, allowing you to implement custom weather-related shaders.

• **Sound Effects**: Consider adding audio effects to complement weather visuals. Rainfall sounds, thunder, or wind effects can significantly enhance the immersive quality of weather systems.

```
// Example: Creating a rain particle system

auto rain = ParticleRain::create();

rain->setTexture(Director::getInstance()->getTextureCache()->addImage("

rain->setPosition(Vec2(visibleSize.width / 2, visibleSize.height));

this->addChild(rain);
```

Day-Night Cycles

Day-night cycles introduce a sense of time and progression in your game. They can affect gameplay, visibility, and the behavior of in-game entities. Implementing a day-night cycle involves adjusting the lighting, sky visuals, and game mechanics over time.

In Cocos2d-x, you can create day-night cycles by gradually changing the game environment's appearance and lighting. You may also need to synchronize NPC behaviors, quests, or events with the time of day.

Here's a simplified example of a day-night cycle implementation:

```
// Update the time of day and adjust game visuals

void updateDayNightCycle(float deltaTime) {

// Increment the time of day

currentTime += deltaTime;

// Adjust lighting, sky visuals, and other game elements based on the time of day

if (currentTime >= nightfallTime) {

// It's night

adjustNighttimeVisuals();

} else {

// It's daytime

adjustDaytimeVisuals();

}

}
```

Testing and Balancing

When implementing dynamic game environments, thorough testing and balancing are essential to ensure that the gameplay remains enjoyable and fair. Test various scenarios, weather conditions, and time-of-day transitions to identify any issues with gameplay balance, performance, or visual glitches.

In conclusion, creating dynamic game environments in Cocos2d-x involves techniques like procedural generation, destructible terrain, weather systems, and day-night cycles

Section 3.5: Multiplayer Game Setup and Management

Adding multiplayer functionality to your game can significantly enhance its appeal and longevity. In this section, we will delve into the intricacies of setting up and managing multiplayer gameplay in Cocos2d-x, including network architectures, synchronization methods, and considerations for multiplayer game design.

Network Architectures

When developing multiplayer games, you must decide on a network architecture that suits your game's requirements and scale. Cocos2d-x supports both peer-to-peer (P2P) and client-server network architectures:

- **Peer-to-Peer (P2P)**: In P2P networking, each player's device communicates directly with other players' devices. P2P is suitable for small-scale multiplayer games, such as local multiplayer on a single Wi-Fi network. It's relatively simple to implement but may not be suitable for larger-scale online games due to connectivity limitations and synchronization challenges.

- **Client-Server**: In a client-server architecture, one player acts as the server, while others connect as clients. The server manages the game state, enforces rules, and synchronizes player actions. This architecture is suitable for online multiplayer games and offers more control and scalability. However, it requires a dedicated server infrastructure.

Synchronization Methods

Achieving smooth and fair multiplayer gameplay depends on effective synchronization of game states and player actions. Cocos2d-x provides several methods for synchronizing multiplayer games:

- **Remote Procedure Calls (RPCs)**: RPCs allow players to invoke functions on remote players' devices. They are commonly used for actions like shooting, chatting, or triggering events. Cocos2d-x's networking libraries can facilitate RPC implementation.

- **State Synchronization**: To keep all players in sync, you need to regularly update and broadcast the game state. You can use techniques like snapshot interpolation or delta compression to optimize state updates and minimize network traffic.

```
// Example: Sending and receiving game state updates

void sendGameState() {

// Serialize the game state into a data packet

NetworkData data = serializeGameState();

// Send the data packet to all connected players
```

```
sendToAllPlayers(data);
}
void receiveGameState(NetworkData data) {
// Deserialize and apply the received game state
gameState = deserializeGameState(data);
}
```

- **Latency Compensation**: Dealing with network latency is crucial for multiplayer games. Techniques like client-side prediction and server reconciliation can help mitigate the effects of latency, ensuring that player actions feel responsive and accurate.

Hosting and Matchmaking

For online multiplayer games, you'll need a system for hosting game sessions and matchmaking players. Cocos2d-x doesn't provide a built-in matchmaking system, but you can integrate third-party solutions or develop your own:

- **Third-Party Services**: Services like Google Play Games Services, Apple's Game Center, or dedicated matchmaking platforms offer matchmaking and hosting services, making it easier to find opponents and set up game sessions.

- **Custom Matchmaking**: If you prefer more control, you can implement custom matchmaking logic in your server infrastructure. This allows you to tailor matchmaking algorithms to your game's specific requirements.

Cheating Prevention

Multiplayer games are vulnerable to cheating and exploitation. To maintain fair gameplay, you should implement cheating prevention measures:

- **Server Authority**: Ensure that critical game logic and validation occur on the server rather than on the client. This prevents players from manipulating the game by modifying client-side code.

- **Anti-Cheat Measures**: Implement anti-cheat mechanisms to detect and prevent cheating behaviors. This may include cheat detection algorithms, automated banning systems, and regular audits of player actions.

- **Secure Communication**: Encrypt and secure network communication to prevent data manipulation and cheating through network traffic interception.

Player Experience

Consider the player experience when designing multiplayer games:

- **Matchmaking and Waiting**: Make the matchmaking and waiting experience enjoyable by providing feedback, animations, and social features like chat.

- **Player Progression**: Implement player progression systems, such as leveling, rewards, and achievements, to keep players engaged and motivated.

- **Communication Tools**: Include in-game communication tools like text chat, voice chat, or emotes to facilitate interaction and teamwork among players.

- **Fairness and Balance**: Ensure that multiplayer matches are fair and balanced. Implement ranking or skill-based matchmaking to match players of similar skill levels.

- **Server Scalability**: If your game gains popularity, be prepared to scale your server infrastructure to handle increased player loads.

In conclusion, setting up and managing multiplayer gameplay in Cocos2d-x involves choosing a network architecture, implementing synchronization methods, hosting game sessions, preventing cheating, and considering the player experience. Multiplayer games offer exciting social interactions and challenges but also require careful planning and development to deliver a seamless and enjoyable experience to players.

Chapter 4: Networking and Online Features

Section 4.1: Networking Basics in Cocos2d-x

Networking is a fundamental component of many modern games, enabling features like multiplayer gameplay, online leaderboards, and real-time interactions. In this section, we'll explore the basics of networking in Cocos2d-x, including communication protocols, client-server architecture, and common networking libraries.

Communication Protocols

Networking in games relies on communication protocols that define how data is exchanged between devices or servers. The choice of communication protocol depends on your game's requirements:

- **TCP (Transmission Control Protocol)**: TCP provides reliable, ordered, and error-checked data transmission. It's suitable for applications where data integrity is critical, such as turn-based games, chat systems, and data synchronization.

- **UDP (User Datagram Protocol)**: UDP offers low-latency, connectionless communication. It's commonly used for real-time multiplayer games, where low latency is essential, and occasional packet loss is acceptable. UDP is often preferred for fast-paced action games.

- **HTTP/HTTPS**: HTTP (Hypertext Transfer Protocol) and its secure variant, HTTPS, are used for web-based communication. They are suitable for features like downloading game assets, making web API requests, or implementing web-based features within your game.

Client-Server Architecture

Many multiplayer games follow a client-server architecture, where one device (the server) manages the game state and synchronizes player actions, while other devices (clients) interact with the server. The server enforces game rules, validates actions, and ensures fair gameplay.

Here's a simplified example of client-server communication in Cocos2d-x using TCP sockets:

```
// Server-side code

// Create a TCP server socket

auto server = TCPServer::create(IPAddress::create("127.0.0.1"), 12345);

server->onAccept = [](TCPClientSocket* client) {

// Handle a new client connection

log("Client connected: %s", client->getIPAddress().c_str());

};

server->onReceive = [](TCPClientSocket* client, const Data& data) {

// Handle data received from clients

log("Received data from client: %s", data.getBytes());

};
```

```
// Client-side code
// Create a TCP client socket
auto client = TCPClient::create();
client->onConnect = [](TCPClientSocket* socket) {
// Handle successful connection to the server
log("Connected to server");
};
client->onReceive = [](TCPClientSocket* socket, const Data& data) {
// Handle data received from the server
log("Received data from server: %s", data.getBytes());
};
client->connect("127.0.0.1", 12345);
```

Common Networking Libraries

Cocos2d-x provides networking capabilities through its own libraries and third-party libraries. Here are some common networking libraries used in Cocos2d-x game development:

- **Cocos2d-x Network Module**: Cocos2d-x includes its own networking module, which supports HTTP requests, socket communication, and WebSocket connections. It's suitable for basic networking tasks and can handle in-game communication.

- **Boost.Asio**: Boost.Asio is a C++ library that provides asynchronous I/O operations, including networking. It's a powerful choice for implementing custom network solutions in Cocos2d-x.

- **ENet**: ENet is a reliable UDP networking library that's well-suited for real-time multiplayer games. It offers features like packet sequencing, reliable data delivery, and bandwidth management.

- **WebSocket Libraries**: WebSocket libraries like libwebsockets and WebSocket++ are useful for implementing real-time communication in multiplayer games. They provide a convenient way to establish WebSocket connections between clients and servers.

Network Security

Security is a critical aspect of online gaming. When implementing networking in your game, consider the following security measures:

- **Encryption**: Encrypt sensitive data transmitted over the network to prevent eavesdropping and data tampering. Use secure protocols like HTTPS for web-based communication.

- **Authentication**: Implement player authentication to ensure that only authorized players can access your game's online features. Protect sensitive player data with authentication tokens or sessions.

- **Server-Side Validation**: Avoid relying solely on client-side validation for critical game logic. Implement server-side validation to prevent cheating and unauthorized actions.

- **Rate Limiting and Throttling**: Implement rate limiting and throttling mechanisms to prevent abuse of online services and protect against distributed denial-of-service (DDoS) attacks.

- **Data Validation**: Validate incoming data from clients to prevent injection attacks and exploits. Sanitize and validate user-generated content before processing it.

Testing and Debugging

Testing networking functionality is essential to ensure that your game works correctly in various network conditions. Conduct testing for different scenarios:

- **Local Testing**: Test networking functionality on a local network or on a single device to identify and fix issues early in development.

- **Simulated Latency**: Simulate network latency to assess the impact of latency on gameplay. Evaluate how the game handles delays in data transmission.

- **Stress Testing**: Perform stress tests to assess the scalability and stability of your server infrastructure. Ensure that it can handle a large number of concurrent players.

- **Security Testing**: Conduct security assessments and penetration testing to identify vulnerabilities and weaknesses in your network security.

Section 4.2: Implementing Multiplayer Systems

Implementing multiplayer systems in Cocos2d-x requires careful consideration of various aspects, including server architecture, synchronization, and communication. In this section, we will delve into the process of setting up and managing multiplayer systems for your game.

Server Architecture

The choice of server architecture is a critical decision when implementing multiplayer systems. The two primary server architectures for multiplayer games are peer-to-peer (P2P) and client-server:

- **Peer-to-Peer (P2P)**: In a P2P architecture, all players communicate directly with each other without a central server. P2P is suitable for small-scale local multiplayer games, where devices are on the same network. It's relatively simple to implement but has limitations in terms of scalability and reliability.

- **Client-Server**: In a client-server architecture, one device acts as the server, while others connect as clients. The server manages the game state, enforces rules, and synchronizes player actions. This architecture is suitable for online multiplayer games and offers more control, scalability, and security.

Synchronization Methods

Synchronizing game state and player actions is crucial for providing a consistent and fair multiplayer experience. Several synchronization methods can be employed:

- **Server Authority**: In a client-server architecture, the server has authoritative control over the game state. Clients send their actions to the server, which validates and broadcasts them to all connected clients. This ensures that all players have the same view of the game.

- **Remote Procedure Calls (RPCs)**: RPCs allow players to invoke functions on remote players' devices. RPCs are commonly used for actions like shooting, chatting, or triggering events. Cocos2d-x provides features to facilitate RPC implementation.

- **State Synchronization**: To maintain consistent game state across all clients, the server regularly broadcasts updates. Techniques like snapshot interpolation or delta compression can optimize state updates and reduce network traffic.

```
// Example: Sending and receiving game state updates

void sendGameState() {

// Serialize the game state into a data packet

NetworkData data = serializeGameState();

// Send the data packet to all connected players

sendToAllPlayers(data);
```

```
}

void receiveGameState(NetworkData data) {

// Deserialize and apply the received game state

gameState = deserializeGameState(data);

}
```

- **Latency Compensation**: Dealing with network latency is crucial for multiplayer games. Techniques like client-side prediction and server reconciliation can mitigate the effects of latency, ensuring that player actions feel responsive and accurate.

Hosting and Matchmaking

For online multiplayer games, you need systems for hosting game sessions and matchmaking players:

- **Matchmaking Services**: Third-party matchmaking services or platforms like Google Play Games Services and Apple's Game Center can simplify the process of finding opponents and setting up game sessions. These services often offer player matching, lobby management, and real-time messaging.

- **Custom Matchmaking**: If you prefer more control, you can implement custom matchmaking logic in your server infrastructure. This allows you to tailor matchmaking algorithms to your game's specific requirements.

Cheating Prevention

Preventing cheating and exploitation in multiplayer games is essential to ensure fair gameplay:

- **Server-Side Validation**: Critical game logic and validation should occur on the server rather than on the client. This prevents players from manipulating the game by modifying client-side code.

- **Anti-Cheat Measures**: Implement anti-cheat mechanisms to detect and prevent cheating behaviors. This may include cheat detection algorithms, automated banning systems, and regular audits of player actions.

- **Secure Communication**: Encrypt and secure network communication to prevent data manipulation and cheating through network traffic interception.

Player Experience

Consider the player experience when designing multiplayer games:

- **Matchmaking and Waiting**: Make the matchmaking and waiting experience enjoyable by providing feedback, animations, and social features like chat.

- **Player Progression**: Implement player progression systems, such as leveling, rewards, and achievements, to keep players engaged and motivated.

- **Communication Tools**: Include in-game communication tools like text chat, voice chat, or emotes to facilitate interaction and teamwork among players.

- **Fairness and Balance**: Ensure that multiplayer matches are fair and balanced. Implement ranking or skill-based matchmaking to match players of similar skill levels.

- **Server Scalability**: If your game gains popularity, be prepared to scale your server infrastructure to handle increased player loads.

In conclusion, implementing multiplayer systems in Cocos2d-x requires careful planning and consideration of server architecture, synchronization methods, matchmaking, cheating prevention, and the player experience. Multiplayer games offer exciting social interactions and challenges but also demand robust development practices to deliver a seamless and enjoyable experience to players.

Section 4.3: Online Data Storage and Retrieval

Online data storage and retrieval are essential components of many multiplayer and online games. In this section, we'll explore how to manage player data, scores, and other game-related information in an online environment using Cocos2d-x.

Player Profiles and Progress

Online games often require the ability to store and retrieve player profiles and progress. This includes information such as player names, avatars, achievements, and in-game currency balances. To implement player profiles and progress in Cocos2d-x, consider the following steps:

1. **User Authentication**: Implement a user authentication system to identify and authenticate players. This can be

achieved using a third-party authentication service or a custom solution.

2. **Database Integration**: Integrate a database system to store player data securely. Popular choices include SQL databases (e.g., MySQL) or NoSQL databases (e.g., MongoDB). Create tables or collections to store player profiles, progress, and related data.
3. **API Endpoints**: Develop API endpoints or server-side scripts that handle data retrieval and storage operations. These endpoints should enforce security measures to prevent unauthorized access.
4. **Data Serialization**: Serialize player data before sending it to the server and deserialize it when retrieving data. Use a common data format like JSON or Protobuf for compatibility.

```
// Example: Serializing and deserializing player data using JSON

// Serialization

PlayerData player;

player.name = "John";

player.level = 10;

player.gold = 500;

std::string serializedData = serializeToJson(player);

// Deserialization

PlayerData deserializedPlayer = deserializeFromJson<PlayerData>(serializedData);
```

1. **Data Storage**: Store player data securely on the server,

associating it with unique player IDs or usernames. Ensure that sensitive information like passwords is hashed and salted for security.

2. **Retrieval and Update**: Implement functions in your game client to retrieve player profiles and update progress. These functions should communicate with the server's API endpoints to fetch and send data.

Leaderboards and High Scores

Leaderboards and high scores add a competitive element to online games. Players can compare their performance with others and strive to reach the top of the rankings. To implement leaderboards and high scores in Cocos2d-x, follow these steps:

1. **Score Tracking**: Track player scores and achievements within your game client. Update these scores as players progress through the game.
2. **Server Integration**: Develop server-side scripts or API endpoints to receive and store player scores. Use a database to maintain a leaderboard that includes player IDs and scores.
3. **Submission and Retrieval**: Implement functions in your game client to submit player scores to the server and retrieve leaderboard data. Ensure that submitted scores are validated on the server to prevent cheating.

```
// Example: Submitting a player's score to the server

void submitScore(int score) {

// Send a request to the server to submit the score

// Include player ID or authentication token for identification
```

```
// Server validates and stores the score
}
```

1. **Leaderboard Display**: Create in-game UI elements to display the leaderboard to players. Retrieve leaderboard data from the server and update the UI accordingly.
2. **Security**: Implement security measures to prevent score manipulation or spoofing. Use server-side validation and encryption to protect leaderboard data.

Cloud Saves and Cross-Device Progress

Allowing players to save their game progress in the cloud and access it from multiple devices is a valuable feature. Here's how to implement cloud saves and cross-device progress in Cocos2d-x:

1. **Player Account**: Require players to create accounts or log in using existing accounts (e.g., Google Play Games, Apple Game Center). This ensures that their progress is associated with their identity.
2. **Cloud Storage**: Integrate cloud storage services like Google Cloud Storage or Amazon S3 to store player save data securely in the cloud. Serialize and upload game progress data to the cloud when players save their game.
3. **Synchronization**: Implement synchronization logic that retrieves the player's progress from the cloud when they log in from a new device. Ensure that conflicts are resolved correctly if progress has been updated on multiple devices.
4. **Privacy and Security**: Inform players about the data you collect and how it's used. Implement strong security measures to protect player data and privacy, including encryption of saved game data.

```
// Example: Synchronizing game progress with cloud storage

void synchronizeWithCloud() {

// Authenticate the player

if (authenticatePlayer()) {

// Retrieve saved game data from the cloud

SavedGameData savedData = retrieveFromCloud();

// Update the local game progress with the cloud data

updateLocalProgress(savedData);

}

}
```

1. **Offline Play**: Allow players to continue playing offline, but inform them that their progress will be synchronized with the cloud when they go online.

By implementing these features, you can enhance the player experience by providing a seamless and flexible way to save and retrieve game progress across devices and platforms.

Testing and Security

Thoroughly test the online data storage and retrieval features of your game to ensure data integrity, security, and reliability. Consider performing the following types of testing:

- **Functional Testing**: Test the end-to-end functionality of player profiles, leaderboards, cloud saves, and cross-device progress.

- **Security Testing**: Conduct security assessments and penetration testing to identify vulnerabilities and weaknesses in your data storage and retrieval mechanisms.

- **Performance Testing**: Evaluate the performance of data retrieval and storage operations under different loads and network conditions.

- **User Acceptance Testing**: Involve players in beta testing to gather feedback on the usability and reliability of online features.

In conclusion, online data storage and retrieval are crucial components of many multiplayer and online games. Implementing player profiles, leaderboards, cloud saves, and cross-device progress requires careful planning, server integration, and security measures to provide players with a seamless and secure gaming experience.

Section 4.4: Integrating with Third-Party Online Services

Integrating third-party online services into your Cocos2d-x game can enhance its functionality, improve player engagement, and simplify development. In this section, we'll explore the process of integrating various types of third-party online services, including social media, analytics, advertisements, and more.

Social Media Integration

Connecting your game to social media platforms can help players share their achievements, invite friends, and enhance the social aspect of your game. Common social media integration points include:

- **Sharing**: Allow players to share their in-game accomplishments, high scores, or custom messages on platforms like Facebook, Twitter, or Instagram. Implement share dialogs and APIs provided by social media platforms.

- **Invitations**: Enable players to invite friends to join the game, either through direct invitations or by posting invitations on their social media profiles.

- **Authentication**: Implement social media login options, such as "Login with Facebook" or "Login with Google." This simplifies the registration process for players and can help with user acquisition.

```
// Example: Implementing Facebook Login

void onFacebookLoginClicked() {

// Use the Facebook SDK to initiate the login process

FacebookSDK::login(callback);

}

void callback(FacebookLoginResult result) {

if (result.success) {

// User is successfully logged in with Facebook

// Fetch user data and proceed with the game

} else {

// Handle login failure
```

```
}
}
```

- **Leaderboards and Achievements**: Integrate social leaderboards and achievements so players can compare their progress with friends. Implement features like friend leaderboards and friend challenges.

Analytics and Player Engagement

Analyzing player behavior and engagement is crucial for improving your game and making data-driven decisions. Integration with analytics services allows you to track various metrics, such as player retention, in-game purchases, and user demographics. Common analytics services for game integration include:

- **Google Analytics for Firebase**: Firebase provides a comprehensive set of analytics tools tailored for mobile and web applications. It can help you track player engagement, monitor user journeys, and gain insights into your game's performance.

- **Game Analytics**: Game-specific analytics services like GameAnalytics offer features tailored to game development. They allow you to track events, monitor player progression, and analyze player behavior.

- **Custom Events**: Define custom events in your game and track them using analytics services. This can include events like level completion, in-game purchases, or specific player actions.

```
// Example: Tracking a custom event using Google Analytics for Firebase

void trackCustomEvent(const std::string& eventName, const std::string& eventParams) {

firebase::analytics::LogEvent(eventName, eventParams);

}
```

- **User Segmentation**: Segment your player base based on various criteria, such as player behavior, spending habits, or geographic location. This enables targeted marketing and game optimization.

Advertisements and Monetization

Integrating advertisements into your game can be a revenue source, especially in free-to-play games. Advertisements can include interstitial ads, rewarded video ads, and banner ads. Key steps for integrating ads into your Cocos2d-x game include:

- **Ad Networks**: Choose ad networks or mediation platforms compatible with Cocos2d-x. Popular options include AdMob, Unity Ads, and Chartboost.

- **Ad Placement**: Determine the appropriate placements for ads within your game. Consider user experience and ad frequency to avoid annoying players.

- **Rewarded Ads**: Implement rewarded video ads that offer in-game rewards, such as currency or power-ups, in exchange for watching an ad. This can improve player retention and monetization.

```
// Example: Implementing rewarded video ads with AdMob

void showRewardedAd() {

// Show a rewarded video ad to the player

AdMobSDK::showRewardedAd(callback);

}

void callback(RewardedAdResult result) {

if (result.success) {

// Player watched the ad and earned a reward

// Grant the reward in the game

} else {

// Ad was not watched or encountered an error

}

}
```

- **Monetization Strategy**: Determine your game's monetization strategy, which may include a combination of in-app purchases, ads, and premium versions. Balance revenue generation with player experience.

- **Ad Reporting**: Use reporting and analytics tools provided by ad networks to track ad performance, revenue, and user engagement. Optimize ad placements based on data.

Payment Gateways and In-App Purchases

Implementing in-app purchases (IAPs) allows you to sell virtual goods, currency, or premium content within your game. To integrate payment gateways and IAPs in Cocos2d-x, follow these steps:

- **Payment Processing**: Choose a payment gateway provider, such as Google Play Billing or Apple's StoreKit, and integrate it with your game. Implement functions to initiate purchases and handle payment responses.

```
// Example: Initiating an in-app purchase using Google Play Billing

void initiatePurchase(const std::string& productId) {

// Initiate the purchase process for the specified product

GooglePlayBilling::purchase(productId, callback);

}

void callback(PurchaseResult result) {

if (result.success) {

// Handle successful purchase and deliver the purchased item

} else {

// Handle purchase failure or cancellation

}

}
```

- **Virtual Goods**: Create virtual goods or

Section 4.5: Security Considerations in Online Play

Ensuring the security of your online game is paramount to protect both your players and your game's integrity. In this section, we will explore essential security considerations when developing online multiplayer games using Cocos2d-x.

Authentication and Authorization

1. **User Authentication**: Implement a robust user authentication system to verify the identity of players. Use secure protocols and techniques to safeguard sensitive information like passwords and authentication tokens.
2. **Authorization**: Control access to game features and data based on user roles and permissions. Ensure that only authorized players can perform certain actions, such as joining matches or modifying player profiles.

```
// Example: Authorization check before starting a multiplayer match

bool canStartMultiplayerMatch(Player user) {

if (user.hasPermission("start_match")) {

return true;

} else {

return false;

}

}
```

1. **Token Validation**: When communicating with the server,

validate authentication tokens to prevent unauthorized access to game resources. Implement token expiration and renewal mechanisms for added security.

Data Encryption

1. **Secure Communication**: Encrypt data transmitted between the game client and server using secure protocols like HTTPS or TLS. Protecting data in transit prevents eavesdropping and tampering with sensitive information.
2. **Client-Side Encryption**: If your game handles sensitive player data on the client side, consider encrypting that data. Use encryption libraries and techniques to secure data storage and transmission.

Server-Side Validation

1. **Server Authority**: Ensure that critical game logic and validation occur on the server side rather than relying solely on client-side checks. This prevents cheating and manipulation of game data.

```
// Example: Server-side validation of player movement

bool validatePlayerMove(ServerGameState state, PlayerMove move)
{

// Check if the move is valid based on the current game state

// Prevent invalid moves or cheating attempts

// Return true if the move is accepted, otherwise false

}
```

Cheat Detection and Prevention

1. **Anti-Cheat Measures**: Implement anti-cheat mechanisms to detect and prevent cheating behaviors. Use cheat detection algorithms, automated banning systems, and regular audits of player actions.
2. **Server Reconciliation**: Employ techniques like server reconciliation to resolve discrepancies between client and server states caused by network latency. This ensures that authoritative server data prevails.

Secure Storage

1. **Secure Player Data**: Store player data securely on the server, applying encryption and access controls. Protect player profiles, progress, and other sensitive information from unauthorized access.
2. **Cloud Storage Security**: If using cloud storage for player data or save games, apply strict access controls and encryption to safeguard data in the cloud.

Third-Party Services

1. **Third-Party Security**: When integrating third-party services such as authentication providers, analytics platforms, or advertisements, ensure that these services follow security best practices. Regularly update and monitor third-party libraries for security vulnerabilities.

Regular Security Audits

1. **Security Audits**: Conduct regular security audits of your game's codebase and infrastructure. Use security scanning

tools to identify vulnerabilities, and address any issues promptly.

Player Reporting

1. **Player Reporting**: Allow players to report suspicious or cheating behavior. Implement a reporting system that enables players to provide evidence of wrongdoing, and investigate and take appropriate action based on reports.

Compliance and Legal Considerations

1. **Privacy Regulations**: Comply with privacy regulations such as the General Data Protection Regulation (GDPR) and Children's Online Privacy Protection Act (COPPA). Inform players about data collection and obtain necessary consents.
2. **Terms of Service and Policies**: Establish clear terms of service and policies regarding player conduct, cheating, and use of third-party services. Enforce these policies consistently and transparently.
3. **Data Retention**: Define data retention policies and procedures. Regularly review and delete player data that is no longer needed for game operation.

Ongoing Security Monitoring

1. **Monitoring and Incident Response**: Implement security monitoring and incident response procedures. Continuously monitor server logs, player activities, and potential security threats. Develop a plan for responding to security incidents promptly.
2. **Updates and Patching**: Keep your game and server

software up to date with the latest security patches. Regularly update third-party libraries and dependencies to address known vulnerabilities.

Security is an ongoing concern in online game development, and a proactive approach is essential to protect your game and players. By implementing robust security measures, staying informed about emerging threats, and being responsive to incidents, you can create a safer and more enjoyable gaming experience for your players while preserving the integrity of your online game.

Chapter 5: Audio Engineering in Cocos2d-x

Section 5.1: Advanced Audio Techniques

Audio plays a crucial role in creating immersive gaming experiences. In this section, we will explore advanced audio techniques for enhancing the audio quality and realism of your Cocos2d-x game.

Audio Formats and Compression

Choosing the right audio formats and compression techniques is essential for optimizing audio quality and file size. Common audio formats for games include WAV, MP3, and Ogg Vorbis. Consider the following tips:

- **WAV**: Use WAV files for high-quality audio, especially for music and important sound effects. However, WAV files can be large, so consider compression for smaller file sizes.

- **MP3**: MP3 files are widely supported and offer good audio quality with compression. Use MP3 for background music and non-critical sound effects.

- **Ogg Vorbis**: Ogg Vorbis is an open-source audio format that provides good audio quality and smaller file sizes compared to MP3. It's a great choice for sound effects and voiceovers.

- **Compression Settings**: Adjust compression settings to balance audio quality and file size. Experiment with different bitrates and compression levels to find the right balance for your game.

Realistic Soundscapes

Creating realistic soundscapes involves spatial audio and environmental effects. These techniques can immerse players in the game world:

- **3D Audio**: Implement 3D audio spatialization to simulate sound sources' positions and movements in the game world. This adds depth to the audio experience as sounds come from specific directions.

- **Reverberation**: Add environmental reverb effects to simulate sound reflections in different in-game environments. Adjust reverb settings based on the environment, such as caves, forests, or indoor spaces.

```
// Example: Applying reverb to audio in Cocos2d-x

auto audioEngine = CocosDenshion::SimpleAudioEngine::getInstance();

audioEngine->setReverbPreset(ReverbPreset::Cave);
```

- **Doppler Effect**: Simulate the Doppler effect to change the pitch of sounds based on relative motion between the listener and sound source. This effect is especially useful for moving objects like vehicles.

Dynamic Audio Mixing

Dynamic audio mixing allows you to adjust audio levels and effects in real-time to respond to gameplay events. Here are some techniques:

- **Audio Ducking**: Implement audio ducking to lower the volume of background music or non-essential sounds when important voiceovers or dialogues occur. This ensures that players can hear critical information.

```
// Example: Implementing audio ducking in Cocos2d-x

auto audioEngine = CocosDenshion::SimpleAudioEngine::getInstance();

audioEngine->setEffectsVolume(0.5f); // Reduce sound effects volume

audioEngine->setBackgroundMusicVolume(0.2f); // Reduce background music volume
```

- **Dynamic Mixing**: Use audio middleware or engine features to dynamically mix audio layers based on the game's context. For example, increase intensity during action sequences or create tension with dynamic music changes.

Audio Synthesis and Effects

Creating unique sounds through synthesis and effects can set your game apart. Consider the following techniques:

- **Sound Synthesis**: Use audio synthesis techniques to generate procedural sound effects, such as footsteps, magic spells, or ambient sounds. Synthesized audio can be generated in real-time to respond to gameplay events.

- **Effects Processing**: Apply audio effects like equalization (EQ), filters, pitch modulation, and distortion to create unique and immersive soundscapes. Effects can be used to alter sound characteristics in real-time.

// Example: Applying audio effects in Cocos2d-x

auto audioEngine = CocosDenshion::SimpleAudioEngine::getInstance();

audioEngine->setEffectsVolume(0.8f); *// Adjust overall sound effects volume*

audioEngine->playEffect("explosion.mp3"); *// Apply effects to the explosion sound*

- **Dynamic Sound Generation**: Generate sound effects on-the-fly using scripting or procedural generation algorithms. This allows for endless variations of sound effects without the need for pre-recorded audio files.

Audio Performance Optimization

Optimizing audio performance is crucial for smooth gameplay experiences:

- **Streaming**: Stream audio files to reduce memory usage. Load and unload audio assets dynamically based on the player's location and progress in the game.

- **Polyphony Management**: Limit the number of simultaneous audio sources to avoid audio clutter and performance issues. Prioritize important sounds over less critical ones.

```
// Example: Managing polyphony in Cocos2d-x
auto audioEngine = CocosDenshion::SimpleAudioEngine::getInstance();
audioEngine->setMaxAudioInstance(16); // Limit the maximum number of concurrent audio instances
```

- **Memory Management**: Monitor and manage audio memory usage to prevent memory leaks or excessive resource consumption.

- **Audio Quality Levels**: Offer different audio quality settings in your game to accommodate various devices and player preferences. Allow players to adjust settings for better performance on lower-end devices.

By incorporating these advanced audio techniques into your Cocos2d-x game, you can create a more engaging and immersive experience for players. Whether it's enhancing audio quality, simulating realistic soundscapes, or dynamically adjusting audio based on gameplay events, audio engineering plays a vital role in crafting memorable gaming experiences.

Section 5.2: Incorporating Music and Sound Effects

Incorporating music and sound effects effectively into your Cocos2d-x game can greatly enhance its immersion and player engagement. In this section, we will explore the best practices and techniques for integrating music and sound effects.

Choosing the Right Sound

Selecting the appropriate sounds for your game is crucial. Each sound should serve a specific purpose and contribute to the overall experience:

- **Sound Design**: Invest time in sound design to create or select sounds that match your game's theme and atmosphere. Consider the emotions you want to evoke and choose sounds accordingly.

- **Variety**: Use a variety of sounds to avoid monotony. Differentiate between actions, objects, and environments with distinct sounds. For example, footsteps on different surfaces or variations in weapon fire.

Sound Effects Integration

Integrating sound effects effectively involves timing and precision:

- **Event-Based Sounds**: Trigger sound effects in response to specific in-game events. For example, play a "coin collected" sound when a player collects currency or a "footstep" sound when the character moves.

```
// Example: Playing a sound effect in Cocos2d-x

auto audioEngine = CocosDenshion::SimpleAudioEngine::getInstance();

audioEngine->playEffect("coin_collect.mp3");
```

• **Looping Ambience**: Create ambient audio loops that seamlessly repeat to set the mood for different game locations or scenarios. Ensure that the loops are long enough to avoid noticeable repetition.

• **3D Positional Audio**: Implement 3D positional audio to enhance immersion. Adjust the volume and panning of sounds based on the player's position and orientation within the game world.

Music Integration

Background music contributes significantly to the game's atmosphere and pacing:

• **Dynamic Music**: Use dynamic music systems that adapt to gameplay. Transition between different musical themes during combat, exploration, or suspenseful moments.

• **Layered Music**: Create layered music tracks with different instrument sets. Fade in or out specific layers to change the music's intensity or mood in response to gameplay events.

```
// Example: Fading in a new music layer in Cocos2d-x

auto audioEngine = CocosDenshion::SimpleAudioEngine::getInstance();

audioEngine->playBackgroundMusic("exploration_theme.mp3", true); // Start playing the base layer

audioEngine->setBackgroundMusicVolume(0.5f); // Set the volume of the base layer
```

```
// Later, during intense gameplay:

audioEngine->playBackgroundMusic("intense_theme.mp3", false); // Play an additional intense layer

audioEngine->setBackgroundMusicVolume(0.8f); // Increase the volume of the intense layer
```

- **Silence When Needed**: Allow moments of silence in your game's audio. Silence can enhance tension and anticipation, making sound effects and music more impactful when they do play.

Audio Resources Management

Managing audio resources efficiently is essential for performance:

- **Asset Compression**: Compress audio files appropriately to reduce storage and loading times. Use formats like Ogg Vorbis or MP3 with moderate compression to balance quality and size.

- **Memory Management**: Be mindful of audio memory usage, especially on mobile devices. Load and unload audio assets strategically to avoid memory exhaustion.

- **Streaming**: Stream audio data from disk when needed to minimize memory usage. Load only the portions of audio files required for immediate playback.

```
// Example: Streaming audio in Cocos2d-x

auto audioEngine = CocosDenshion::SimpleAudioEngine::getInstance();
```

```
audioEngine->preloadBackgroundMusic("background_music.mp3");
// Preload for streaming

audioEngine->playBackgroundMusic("background_music.mp3",
true); // Stream the music
```

- **Quality Settings**: Provide quality settings in your game to allow players to choose audio quality levels. Lower quality settings can conserve resources on older or less powerful devices.

Testing and Feedback

Always test your game's audio on various devices and platforms to ensure a consistent and enjoyable experience. Gather player feedback and be prepared to make adjustments based on their preferences and suggestions.

Incorporating music and sound effects effectively requires a keen understanding of your game's design and player experience. By choosing the right sounds, timing their integration, and managing audio resources efficiently, you can create a captivating auditory landscape that enhances your game's immersion and engagement.

Section 5.3: Audio Synchronization and Optimization

Audio synchronization and optimization are essential aspects of game development, ensuring that audio elements align seamlessly with gameplay while maintaining performance. In this section, we will delve into techniques for synchronizing audio and optimizing it for your Cocos2d-x game.

Synchronization with Gameplay

1. **Event-Driven Audio**: Sync audio events with specific gameplay actions. For instance, trigger the sound of a door opening precisely when the player interacts with it or play a character's voice lines during dialogues.

```
// Example: Triggering audio on player interaction in Cocos2d-x

auto audioEngine = CocosDenshion::SimpleAudioEngine::getInstance();

audioEngine->playEffect("door_open.mp3");
```

1. **Music Transitions**: Carefully plan transitions between different music tracks to match changes in gameplay intensity or environment. Smoothly fade between tracks to avoid abrupt shifts.

```
// Example: Smooth music transition in Cocos2d-x

auto audioEngine = CocosDenshion::SimpleAudioEngine::getInstance();

audioEngine->playBackgroundMusic("exploration_theme.mp3", true); // Start with exploration music

audioEngine->setBackgroundMusicVolume(0.5f);

// Later, when entering combat:

audioEngine->playBackgroundMusic("combat_theme.mp3", true); // Transition to combat music

audioEngine->setBackgroundMusicVolume(0.8f);
```

1. **Dialogue Timing**: Ensure that character dialogues align with character animations and facial expressions to create a realistic and immersive experience. Timing is crucial for character interactions.

Performance Optimization

Optimizing audio performance is vital to prevent lag and maintain a smooth gaming experience:

1. **Audio Pools**: Implement audio object pools to manage and reuse audio instances efficiently. Reusing objects reduces the overhead of creating and destroying audio elements.

```
// Example: Using an audio object pool in Cocos2d-x

std::vector<std::shared_ptr<SimpleAudioEngine>> audioPool;

const int poolSize = 10;

// Initialize the audio pool

for (int i = 0; i < poolSize; ++i) {

audioPool.push_back(std::make_shared<SimpleAudioEngine>());

}

// Reuse an audio engine from the pool when needed

auto audioEngine = audioPool[0];

audioEngine->playEffect("footstep.mp3");
```

1. **Polyphony Management**: Limit the number of concurrent audio sources, especially for sound effects.

Prioritize essential sounds and mute or reduce the volume of less critical ones when necessary.

// Example: Managing polyphony in Cocos2d-x

auto audioEngine = CocosDenshion::SimpleAudioEngine::getInstance();

audioEngine->setMaxAudioInstance(16); *// Limit the maximum number of concurrent audio instances*

1. **Audio Quality Settings**: Offer adjustable audio quality settings in your game. Lower quality settings can reduce the demand on CPU and memory, making the game accessible on a wider range of devices.
2. **Background Loading**: Preload and cache frequently used audio assets in the background to minimize delays during gameplay. Load assets during loading screens or idle moments.

// Example: Preloading audio assets in Cocos2d-x

auto audioEngine = CocosDenshion::SimpleAudioEngine::getInstance();

audioEngine->preloadEffect("explosion.mp3");

audioEngine->preloadBackgroundMusic("background_music.mp3");

1. **Memory Management**: Monitor and manage audio memory usage to prevent memory leaks or excessive resource consumption. Release audio resources that are no longer needed.

Cross-Platform Considerations

1. **Platform-Specific Optimization**: Optimize audio settings and configurations for different target platforms (e.g., iOS, Android, Windows). Each platform may have unique audio capabilities and requirements.
2. **Audio Drivers**: Be aware of the audio drivers and libraries used on various platforms. Test your game's audio performance on different devices to ensure compatibility.
3. **Latency**: Consider audio latency when developing for mobile devices. High latency can affect the timing of audio events, impacting gameplay and synchronization.
4. **Audio Formats**: Choose audio formats that are well-supported across different platforms to ensure consistent audio playback. Verify that your selected formats work seamlessly on all target devices.

By applying these audio synchronization and optimization techniques, you can create a more immersive gaming experience while maintaining optimal performance across various platforms. Synchronizing audio with gameplay events and optimizing audio performance are crucial steps in delivering a polished and engaging game to your players.

Section 5.4: Spatial Sound and 3D Audio

Spatial sound and 3D audio techniques can greatly enhance immersion in your Cocos2d-x game by creating a sense of depth and directionality in the audio experience. In this section, we will explore how to implement spatial sound and 3D audio.

Spatial Sound Principles

1. **Positional Audio**: Positional audio is the foundation of spatial sound. It simulates the perceived location of sound sources in the game world. Each sound source is associated with a specific position and orientation.
2. **Attenuation**: Sound attenuation refers to the decrease in volume as the listener moves away from the sound source. Implement attenuation calculations to make sounds quieter when they are farther from the player, creating a natural audio effect.
3. **Panning**: Adjust the stereo panning of audio sources to reflect their position relative to the player. Sounds on the left should be heard more from the left speaker, and vice versa, for realistic positioning.

```
// Example: Applying panning to audio in Cocos2d-x

auto audioEngine = CocosDenshion::SimpleAudioEngine::getInstance();

audioEngine->playEffect("monster_growl.mp3", false, 0.0f, 1.0f, 1.0f);
```

1. **Doppler Effect**: Implement the Doppler effect to change the pitch of sounds based on the relative motion between the listener and sound source. This effect is particularly useful for moving objects such as vehicles.

3D Audio Techniques

1. **3D Sound Sources**: Define audio sources as 3D objects with positions and orientations in the game world. The position of the listener is also crucial for calculating the

relative positions of sound sources.

// Example: Creating a 3D audio source in Cocos2d-x

auto audioEngine = CocosDenshion::SimpleAudioEngine::getInstance();

audioEngine->setListenerPosition(Vec2(0.0f, 0.0f)); *// Set the listener's position*

audioEngine->playEffect3D("bird_chirp.mp3", Vec3(10.0f, 0.0f, 0.0f)); *// Play a 3D sound*

1. **3D Sound API**: Use an audio engine or library that supports 3D audio, providing functions and settings to manipulate the spatial properties of audio sources and the listener. Cocos2d-x supports 3D audio features through certain plugins and extensions.
2. **Environmental Effects**: Enhance 3D audio with environmental effects such as reverb and occlusion. Apply these effects based on the listener's position and the presence of obstacles that can block sound.

Listener and Source Movement

1. **Dynamic Listener Position**: Update the listener's position in real-time to match the player's movements. This ensures that positional audio remains accurate as the player explores the game world.
2. **Moving Sound Sources**: For moving objects in the game, update the positions and orientations of sound sources accordingly. This is crucial for creating a convincing audio experience for dynamic objects.

```
// Example: Updating the position of a moving sound source in Cocos2d-x

auto audioEngine = CocosDenshion::SimpleAudioEngine::getInstance();

Vec3 monsterPosition(10.0f, 0.0f, 0.0f);

audioEngine->setEffectPosition(1, monsterPosition); // Update the position of the sound source
```

1. **Distance-Based Volume**: Adjust the volume of sound sources based on their distance from the listener. Use a distance attenuation formula that calculates volume reduction as the distance increases.

Testing and Tweaking

1. **Testing in 3D Environment**: Regularly test and fine-tune spatial audio in a 3D game environment. Ensure that audio positions and effects accurately match the game world's spatial layout.
2. **Player Feedback**: Gather feedback from players to ensure that spatial audio enhances immersion without causing distractions or discomfort. Make adjustments based on player preferences and comments.

Implementing spatial sound and 3D audio can significantly elevate the immersive qualities of your Cocos2d-x game. By considering principles such as positional audio, attenuation, panning, and the Doppler effect, you can create a more realistic and engaging auditory experience. Incorporate 3D audio techniques, update listener and source positions, and conduct thorough testing to fine-tune your spatial audio implementation for optimal player immersion.

Section 5.5: Dynamic Audio in Game Events

Dynamic audio in game events involves the real-time generation and manipulation of audio to respond to player actions and in-game events. This section explores the techniques and considerations for implementing dynamic audio in your Cocos2d-x game.

Dynamic Sound Generation

1. **Procedural Audio**: Procedural audio involves generating sound effects algorithmically rather than using pre-recorded audio files. This allows for on-the-fly audio generation, enabling unique and responsive soundscapes.

```
// Example: Procedural audio generation in Cocos2d-x (pseudocode)

function generateFootstepSound() {

var frequency = random(400, 800); // Randomize the frequency for variation

var duration = 0.2; // Set the duration of the footstep sound

var waveform = generateFootstepWaveform(frequency, duration);

playSound(waveform);

}
```

1. **Parameterized Audio**: Create sound effects with adjustable parameters. Modify pitch, volume, and other characteristics in real-time to match gameplay events. For example, altering the pitch of a magic spell based on its power level.

```
// Example: Adjusting sound parameters in Cocos2d-x
```

auto audioEngine = CocosDenshion::SimpleAudioEngine::getInstance();

audioEngine->setEffectsVolume(0.8f); *// Adjust overall sound effects volume*

audioEngine->playEffect("magic_spell.mp3"); *// Play a magic spell sound*

// Later, during gameplay:

audioEngine->setEffectsPitch(1.5f); *// Increase pitch for a more powerful spell*

Interactive Soundscapes

1. **Contextual Audio**: Implement contextual audio that adapts to the game's environment and events. For instance, the sound of rainfall could intensify during a thunderstorm or decrease when the player enters a sheltered area.
2. **Layered Soundscapes**: Create layered soundscapes with multiple audio tracks that can be toggled on and off based on gameplay conditions. These layers can represent different elements of the game world, such as wind, wildlife, or machinery.

// Example: Layered soundscapes in Cocos2d-x

auto audioEngine = CocosDenshion::SimpleAudioEngine::getInstance();

audioEngine->playBackgroundMusic("ambient_wind.mp3", **true**); *// Start with wind sounds*

```
audioEngine->playBackgroundMusic("birdsong.mp3", false); // Add birdsong layer

// Later, when entering a forest:

audioEngine->playBackgroundMusic("forest_ambience.mp3", false); // Add forest ambience layer
```

Event-Driven Audio

1. **Audio Queues**: Create queues or playlists of audio events triggered by in-game actions. These queues can contain sound effects, music tracks, or dialogue lines, allowing you to orchestrate audio sequences.

```
// Example: Audio event queue in Cocos2d-x

auto audioEngine = CocosDenshion::SimpleAudioEngine::getInstance();

std::vector<std::string> audioQueue = {"dialogue_1.mp3", "footstep.mp3", "dialogue_2.mp3"};

// Play audio events in the queue sequentially

for (const auto& audio : audioQueue) {

audioEngine->playEffect(audio);

}
```

1. **Dialogues and Voiceovers**: Integrate dynamic voiceover systems that respond to player choices and branching narratives. Ensure that dialogue lines align with character animations and interactions.

Real-time Mixing and Effects

1. **Real-time Mixing**: Use audio middleware or engine features to mix audio layers dynamically based on the game's context. Adjust the mix to emphasize or de-emphasize specific elements during gameplay events.
2. **Audio Effects**: Apply real-time audio effects, such as equalization (EQ), filters, reverbs, or distortion, to create dramatic audio changes in response to gameplay events. These effects can enhance immersion.

```
// Example: Applying real-time audio effects in Cocos2d-x

auto audioEngine = CocosDenshion::SimpleAudioEngine::getInstance();

audioEngine->setEffectsVolume(0.8f); // Adjust overall sound effects volume

audioEngine->playEffect("explosion.mp3"); // Apply effects to the explosion sound
```

1. **Adaptive Music**: Implement adaptive music systems that change the music's mood, tempo, or instrumentation in response to gameplay events. This dynamic music enhances the player's emotional engagement.

Dynamic audio in game events is a powerful tool for creating responsive and immersive gameplay experiences. By generating audio procedurally, adjusting sound parameters, crafting interactive soundscapes, and orchestrating event-driven audio sequences, you can captivate players and enhance their connection to your Cocos2d-x game world.

Chapter 6: UI/UX Design in Depth

6.1. Advanced UI Design Principles

In this section, we will delve into advanced UI design principles for creating engaging and user-friendly interfaces in your Cocos2d-x games. Effective UI design is crucial for providing a seamless and enjoyable player experience. Let's explore some key principles and strategies:

1. Consistency and Cohesion

Consistency in UI design helps users build mental models and navigate your game more intuitively. Ensure that your interface elements, such as buttons, fonts, and color schemes, maintain a cohesive visual style throughout the game. Consistency also extends to the layout and placement of UI elements across different screens.

2. User-Centered Design

Always prioritize the needs and preferences of your target audience. Conduct user research to understand their expectations and pain points. Design your UI elements with the user's perspective in mind, making interactions intuitive and efficient. Consider usability testing to gather feedback and refine your design.

3. Visual Hierarchy

Establish a clear visual hierarchy in your UI to guide users' attention. Use size, color, and positioning to emphasize important elements, such as buttons for primary actions. Ensure that less critical elements are visually subordinate to prevent clutter and confusion.

4. Responsiveness and Feedback

Make sure that UI elements respond promptly to user input. Provide visual and auditory feedback to acknowledge user actions. For example, highlight a button when it's tapped or play a sound effect when a menu option is selected. Responsive UI elements enhance the perceived quality of your game.

5. Accessibility

Consider the accessibility of your UI for players with disabilities. Provide alternative text for images, ensure readable fonts, and offer options for adjusting text size and color contrast. Accessibility features not only widen your player base but also demonstrate inclusivity.

6. Gesture-Based Interactions

Incorporate touch and gesture-based interactions for mobile platforms. Implement swipe, pinch, and tap gestures where appropriate. Ensure that these gestures are intuitive and well-documented within the game.

7. Animation and Transitions

Subtle animations and transitions can enhance the user experience by providing visual cues and smooth transitions between screens. Use animations sparingly and purposefully to avoid overwhelming the player.

8. Localization

If your game targets a global audience, invest in localization. Translate text, adapt cultural references, and adjust UI layouts to accommodate different languages and regions. Ensure that text expansion or contraction doesn't break your UI layout.

9. User Onboarding

Create a seamless onboarding experience for new players. Introduce game mechanics gradually and provide clear instructions through tooltips or tutorials. Avoid overwhelming beginners with too much information upfront.

10. A/B Testing

Consider conducting A/B testing to evaluate the effectiveness of different UI design variations. Compare user engagement and conversion rates to refine your UI based on real data.

Incorporating these advanced UI design principles will elevate the overall quality of your Cocos2d-x game and enhance player satisfaction. Keep in mind that UI/UX design is an iterative process, so gather feedback and make continuous improvements to optimize the user experience.

6.2. Creating Custom UI Components

In this section, we will explore the creation of custom UI components in Cocos2d-x. While the engine provides standard UI elements, there are scenarios where you may need unique or highly customized UI elements tailored to your game's specific requirements. Creating custom UI components allows you to have full control over their appearance and behavior.

Why Create Custom UI Components?

Custom UI components offer several advantages:

1. **Unique Visuals:** You can design UI elements that match your game's theme and aesthetics precisely.
2. **Functionality:** Custom UI components can incorporate specialized functionality that standard elements may not provide.
3. **Optimization:** Tailor UI elements for performance optimization to meet your game's requirements.
4. **Brand Identity:** Custom UI components can help reinforce your game's brand identity.

Steps to Create Custom UI Components

Let's walk through the steps to create a custom button as an example. We'll create a button with a unique appearance and behavior.

1. Extending Cocos2d-x Classes

To create a custom button, you typically extend existing Cocos2d-x classes. In this case, you might extend *cocos2d::Node* or *cocos2d::Sprite* to serve as the visual representation of the button.

```
class CustomButton : public cocos2d::Node {

public:

CREATE_FUNC(CustomButton);

// Constructor and methods for custom button behavior

};
```

2. Designing the Visuals

Design the visual appearance of your custom button. You can use an image as the button's background or draw it programmatically using Cocos2d-x's drawing functions.

```
bool CustomButton::init() {
if (!Node::init()) {
return false;
}
// Create and add button sprite or draw button graphics here
return true;
}
```

3. Handling User Interaction

Implement the logic to respond to user interactions, such as touch events or mouse clicks. You can use Cocos2d-x's event handling system for this.

```
bool CustomButton::onTouchBegan(cocos2d::Touch* touch, cocos2d::Event* event) {
// Handle touch events for button interactions
return true;
}
```

4. Adding Functionality

Customize the behavior of your button as needed. For example, you might trigger in-game actions when the button is pressed.

```
void CustomButton::performAction() {
// Implement button's functionality
}
```

5. Integrating into UI

Finally, integrate your custom button into your game's UI hierarchy by adding it to the appropriate layers or scenes.

```
auto customButton = CustomButton::create();
this->addChild(customButton);
```

Customizing UI Elements Further

Custom buttons are just one example. You can create custom labels, sliders, progress bars, or any other UI element using a similar approach. The key is to leverage Cocos2d-x's extensibility to create UI components tailored to your game's needs.

Remember to balance customization with maintainability and performance. Overly complex custom components can make your code harder to manage and may impact performance if not optimized properly. Always test and iterate to ensure that your custom UI components enhance the player experience in your Cocos2d-x game.

6.3. UX Considerations for Gamers

In this section, we will delve into the essential UX (User Experience) considerations for game developers using Cocos2d-x. A seamless and enjoyable user experience is paramount in keeping players engaged and satisfied with your game. Let's explore key principles and strategies to enhance the UX of your Cocos2d-x game.

1. Intuitive Controls

Ensure that the game controls are intuitive and responsive. Whether it's touch, keyboard, or gamepad input, players should be able to interact with your game effortlessly. Provide clear instructions or tutorials for new players to learn the controls.

2. Feedback and Feedback Loops

Feedback is crucial in gaming. Inform players about their progress, achievements, and the consequences of their actions. Use visual and auditory cues to provide feedback, such as health bars, score updates, or sound effects. Create a feedback loop where players' actions have meaningful consequences in the game world.

3. User Interface (UI) Clarity

Design a clear and uncluttered UI that doesn't overwhelm players with information. Display important information prominently, such as health and resources, and make less critical information accessible but not intrusive. Consider the placement and size of UI elements to avoid obscuring the gameplay.

4. Player Guidance

Guide players through the game's mechanics and objectives, especially in complex or story-driven games. Use tutorials, tooltips, or in-game hints to help players understand how to progress and overcome challenges. Avoid excessive hand-holding, allowing players to explore and discover on their own when appropriate.

5. Accessibility

Ensure your game is accessible to a wide range of players, including those with disabilities. Provide options for adjusting text size, color schemes, and audio settings. Consider compatibility with screen readers and other accessibility tools.

6. Performance Optimization

Optimize your game for smooth performance across various devices and platforms. Maintain a consistent frame rate and minimize loading times. Performance issues can disrupt the player's immersion and enjoyment.

7. Game Balancing

Achieve a balance between challenge and accessibility. Games should be challenging enough to engage players but not so difficult that they become frustrated. Implement difficulty levels or adaptive difficulty to cater to different player skill levels.

8. Save and Progression Systems

Include save and progression systems that allow players to continue their journey seamlessly. Autosave points, checkpoints, or manual save options can prevent players from losing progress and maintain their engagement.

9. Playtesting and Iteration

Regularly playtest your game with a diverse group of players. Collect feedback and make iterative improvements based on player experiences. Address usability issues and fine-tune gameplay mechanics to enhance the overall user experience.

10. Immersive Storytelling

If your game includes a narrative, focus on creating an immersive storytelling experience. Engage players emotionally through compelling characters, well-written dialogue, and a captivating plot. Ensure that gameplay and storytelling are integrated seamlessly.

11. Player Empowerment

Empower players by giving them choices and agency in the game world. Let their decisions have consequences and shape the narrative. This can increase player investment and emotional attachment to the game.

12. Emotional Engagement

Consider the emotional impact of your game. Design moments that evoke a range of emotions, from excitement and joy to tension and empathy. Emotional engagement can create memorable experiences for players.

By carefully addressing these UX considerations, you can create a more engaging and enjoyable experience for gamers in your Cocos2d-x game. Keep in mind that user experience is an ongoing process, and continuous refinement based on player feedback is essential to delivering a top-notch gaming experience.

6.4. Responsive Design Across Devices

In this section, we will explore the importance of responsive design in the context of Cocos2d-x game development. Responsive design ensures that your game adapts seamlessly to various screen sizes and resolutions, providing an optimal gaming experience across different devices, including smartphones, tablets, and desktop computers.

Why Responsive Design Matters

Responsive design is essential for the following reasons:

1. **Diverse Device Landscape:** Players use a wide range of devices to play games. From small smartphone screens to large desktop monitors, your game should look and perform well on all of them.
2. **User Expectations:** Players expect games to look and play smoothly, regardless of the device they are using. Inconsistent or poorly optimized layouts can lead to frustration.
3. **Market Reach:** By catering to different devices, you can expand your game's potential player base and reach a more extensive audience.

Key Principles of Responsive Design

To achieve responsive design in Cocos2d-x, consider these key principles:

1. Flexible Layouts

Design flexible layouts that can adapt to different screen sizes. Use relative positioning and sizing for UI elements instead of fixed values. Cocos2d-x provides tools for creating flexible UI components that scale gracefully.

```
auto screenSize = Director::getInstance()->getVisibleSize();

auto button = Button::create("button.png");

button->setPosition(Vec2(screenSize.width * 0.5, screenSize.height * 0.5));
```

2. Aspect Ratio Handling

Handle different aspect ratios by using letterboxing, pillarboxing, or content scaling. Ensure that essential gameplay elements are always visible, even on devices with unusual aspect ratios.

```
Director::getInstance()->getOpenGLView()->setDesignResolutionSize(1
1080, ResolutionPolicy::SHOW_ALL);
```

3. Asset Scaling

Provide multiple sets of assets (images and sprites) at different resolutions. Cocos2d-x supports asset loading based on device resolution, ensuring that the appropriate assets are used for each device.

```
Director::getInstance()->setContentScaleFactor(2.0f); // Set content scale factor for higher-resolution devices
```

4. Responsive UI Components

Create responsive UI components that adjust their layout and behavior based on screen size. For example, use scrollable lists for long menus on smaller screens and grid layouts for larger screens.

```
auto screenSize = Director::getInstance()->getVisibleSize();
if (screenSize.width < 768) {
// Use a scrollable list for smaller screens
} else {
// Use a grid layout for larger screens
}
```

5. User Input Adaptation

Consider how user input methods differ on various devices. Ensure that your game supports touch controls for mobile devices, keyboard and mouse for desktops, and gamepad input for consoles where applicable. Implement control schemes that feel natural on each platform.

6. Performance Optimization

Optimize your game's performance for different devices. Test your game on low-end and high-end devices to ensure smooth gameplay. Use performance profiling tools to identify and address performance bottlenecks.

Testing and Iteration

Responsive design requires thorough testing on a variety of devices and screen sizes. Use emulators, simulators, and physical devices to test your game across the target platforms. Solicit feedback from players using different devices to identify issues and areas for improvement.

Responsive design is an ongoing process. As new devices with different screen sizes and resolutions enter the market, continue to update and optimize your game to ensure it remains responsive and accessible to a broad audience. By following these principles and regularly testing your game on diverse devices, you can provide a consistent and enjoyable gaming experience to players on all platforms.

6.5. Accessibility in Game Design

In this section, we will focus on the crucial topic of accessibility in game design using Cocos2d-x. Accessibility ensures that your game can be enjoyed by players of all abilities, including those with disabilities. By making your game more accessible, you not only broaden your player base but also contribute to a more inclusive gaming community.

The Importance of Accessibility

Accessibility is essential for several reasons:

1. **Inclusivity:** It allows players with disabilities to enjoy your game, promoting inclusivity and diversity within the gaming community.
2. **Legal Compliance:** In some regions, there are legal requirements for digital content, including games, to be accessible to individuals with disabilities.
3. **Expanded Audience:** By considering accessibility, you can attract a broader audience, including those who might not otherwise be able to play your game.

Key Accessibility Considerations

To make your Cocos2d-x game more accessible, consider the following key accessibility considerations:

1. Text and Language Support

- Use readable fonts and allow players to adjust text size.
- Provide text-to-speech support for in-game text.
- Translate your game into multiple languages to reach a global audience.

2. Visual and Auditory Impairments

- Offer options for colorblind players, such as different color schemes or symbols.
- Include subtitles and closed captions for dialogues and audio cues.
- Provide adjustable audio settings, including volume and sound effects.

3. Motor and Mobility Disabilities

- Implement customizable control schemes, including alternative input methods.
- Allow players to adjust input sensitivity and timing.
- Minimize the need for rapid or precise inputs.

4. Cognitive Accessibility

- Offer clear and concise instructions, tutorials, and hints.
- Provide customizable difficulty levels or adaptive difficulty settings.
- Avoid complex puzzles or challenges that may be frustrating for some players.

5. Testing with Diverse Players

Regularly conduct playtesting with individuals who have disabilities. Gather feedback and make improvements based on their experiences and suggestions. Incorporate accessibility into your quality assurance process.

Implementation in Cocos2d-x

To implement accessibility features in your Cocos2d-x game, consider the following approaches:

1. Text-to-Speech (TTS)

Integrate text-to-speech functionality to read out in-game text for players with visual impairments. You can use platform-specific TTS APIs or third-party libraries that support Cocos2d-x.

```
#if CC_TARGET_PLATFORM == CC_PLATFORM_ANDROID

// Use Android TTS API

#elif CC_TARGET_PLATFORM == CC_PLATFORM_IOS
```

```
// Use iOS TTS API
#endif
```

2. *Subtitles and Closed Captions*

For dialogues and audio cues, add support for subtitles and closed captions. Provide options for players to enable or disable them as needed.

```
// Display subtitles or closed captions based on player preferences
if (Settings::isSubtitlesEnabled()) {
// Show subtitles
}
```

3. Input Customization

Implement customizable controls and input settings. Allow players to remap keys, adjust sensitivity, and choose input methods that suit their abilities.

```
// Customize input controls
if (Settings::isCustomControlsEnabled()) {
// Allow key remapping or input adjustments
}
```

4. User Interface Adjustments

Design a user interface (UI) that can adapt to different text sizes and color schemes. Avoid placing critical information in fixed positions or using color alone to convey meaning.

```
// Adapt UI to accommodate different text sizes and color schemes

auto label = Label::createWithTTF("Game Title", "fonts/arial.ttf", 24);

label->setDimensions(400, 100); // Adjustable dimensions based on text size
```

5. Inclusivity Features

Consider additional features, such as an "easy mode" for players who may have difficulty with certain aspects of the game. Allow players to toggle features like auto-aim, simplified controls, or hints.

```
// Provide an "easy mode" with simplified gameplay

if (Settings::isEasyModeEnabled()) {

// Enable simplified controls or other helpful features

}
```

Continued Learning and Improvement

Accessibility in game design is an ongoing process. Stay informed about best practices and evolving standards for accessibility in games. Regularly update your game to address accessibility issues and enhance the gaming experience for all players. By prioritizing accessibility, you can create a more inclusive and enjoyable gaming environment in your Cocos2d-x game.

Chapter 7: Scripting and Automation

7.1. Advanced Lua Scripting in Cocos2d-x

In this section, we will delve into advanced Lua scripting in Cocos2d-x, a powerful feature that allows you to add flexibility and extend the functionality of your game. Lua scripting enables you to create and manipulate game logic, implement complex behaviors, and even modify game content without recompiling your project. Let's explore how to leverage Lua scripting effectively in your Cocos2d-x game.

Why Use Lua Scripting?

Lua scripting offers several advantages for game development in Cocos2d-x:

1. **Flexibility:** Lua is a lightweight scripting language that provides flexibility in creating and modifying game logic and behavior without altering the core engine code.
2. **Rapid Prototyping:** You can quickly prototype and iterate on game mechanics and features using Lua scripts, saving development time.
3. **Separation of Concerns:** Scripting allows you to separate game logic from engine code, making it easier to maintain and modify game behavior.
4. **Live Updates:** You can update Lua scripts during runtime, allowing for live changes to the game without the need to rebuild and redeploy the entire project.

Integrating Lua in Cocos2d-x

To get started with advanced Lua scripting in Cocos2d-x, you'll need to integrate Lua into your project. Follow these steps:

1. Include Lua Libraries

Ensure that you have the Lua libraries integrated into your Cocos2d-x project. You can use Cocos2d-x's built-in Lua support or manually integrate the Lua runtime.

2. Create Lua Scripts

Write Lua scripts to define game logic, behaviors, and interactions. These scripts can be saved as separate .lua files or embedded directly within your C++ code.

—Example Lua script for character movement

function moveCharacter(character, direction)

—Implement character movement logic here

end

3. Execute Lua Scripts

Load and execute Lua scripts within your C++ code. You can call Lua functions and pass data between C++ and Lua.

// Load and execute a Lua script

lua_State* L = luaL_newstate();

luaL_openlibs(L);

```
luaL_dofile(L, "character.lua");

// Call a Lua function from C++

lua_getglobal(L, "moveCharacter");

lua_pushlightuserdata(L, characterPtr);

lua_pushstring(L, "right");

lua_pcall(L, 2, 0, 0);
```

4. Managing Lua State

Manage the Lua state carefully, ensuring proper initialization, execution, and cleanup. Consider using Lua's garbage collection to avoid memory leaks.

```
// Managing the Lua state

lua_close(L); // Close the Lua state when done
```

Advanced Lua Scripting Techniques

Now that you have integrated Lua scripting into your Cocos2d-x project, let's explore some advanced techniques:

1. Scripted Events

Use Lua scripts to define scripted events in your game. These events can control dialogues, cutscenes, and dynamic gameplay sequences.

```
—Example Lua script for a dialogue event

function startDialogue()

—Display dialogue text and choices
```

end

2. Modularization

Organize your Lua scripts into modules for better code organization and reusability. Lua modules can encapsulate related functionality.

—Example Lua module for enemy behaviors

local M = {}

function M.spawnEnemy()

—Spawn an enemy with specific behaviors

end

return M

3. Live Script Editing

Implement a system that allows for live script editing during runtime. This feature can be helpful for tweaking gameplay parameters without restarting the game.

4. Debugging and Profiling

Utilize Lua debugging and profiling tools to identify and resolve issues in your scripts. Cocos2d-x provides integration with debugging tools for Lua.

5. Data-Driven Design

Implement data-driven design by storing game parameters and content in Lua scripts or configuration files. This approach makes it easier to tweak game balance and content without recompiling.

Best Practices and Security

While Lua scripting provides great flexibility, it's important to follow best practices and consider security:

- Limit access to sensitive engine functions and data from Lua scripts.
- Avoid executing untrusted Lua code, as it can pose security risks.
- Profile and optimize Lua scripts to prevent performance bottlenecks.

By mastering advanced Lua scripting in Cocos2d-x, you can unlock the full potential of your game development, allowing for rapid prototyping, dynamic gameplay, and flexibility in creating engaging player experiences.

7.2. Scripting for Game Logic

In this section, we will explore the use of scripting for game logic in Cocos2d-x. Scripting allows you to define and control various aspects of your game's behavior, such as character movements, enemy AI, and game events. By scripting game logic, you can achieve greater flexibility and make your game more dynamic. Let's dive into how to effectively use scripting for game development in Cocos2d-x.

The Role of Scripting in Game Logic

Scripting plays a significant role in defining and managing game logic for the following reasons:

1. **Flexibility:** Scripts are versatile and can be modified without recompiling the entire game. This flexibility is crucial for rapid iteration and fine-tuning of game mechanics.
2. **Separation of Concerns:** Separating game logic from the engine's core code keeps the codebase organized and easier to maintain. Developers can work on scripts independently.
3. **Modularity:** Scripting allows you to create modular components of gameplay, making it easier to reuse and extend game logic across different parts of your project.

Choosing a Scripting Language

Cocos2d-x supports various scripting languages for game logic, including Lua, JavaScript, and Python. The choice of scripting language often depends on your team's familiarity and the specific requirements of your game.

Lua Scripting

Lua is a popular choice for scripting in Cocos2d-x due to its simplicity and performance. It provides a lightweight and efficient scripting environment that integrates well with C++.

JavaScript and Python

Cocos2d-x also offers support for JavaScript and Python, allowing developers with expertise in these languages to leverage their skills for game logic.

Implementing Game Logic with Scripts

To implement game logic using scripts in Cocos2d-x, follow these general steps:

1. Integration of Scripting Engine

Start by integrating the scripting engine of your chosen language into your Cocos2d-x project. Cocos2d-x provides built-in support for various scripting languages, making this step relatively straightforward.

2. Creating Script Files

Write scripts that define the desired game logic. These scripts can control character behaviors, enemy AI, item interactions, and more. Organize scripts into separate files for better organization.

—Example Lua script for character movement

function moveCharacter(character, direction)

—Implement character movement logic here

end

3. Interacting with C++ Code

Scripts can interact with C++ code by calling functions and accessing variables defined in the C++ codebase. This interaction allows you to bridge the gap between script-defined logic and the engine's functionality.

```
// Calling a C++ function from a script

lua_getglobal(L, "moveCharacter");

lua_pushlightuserdata(L, characterPtr);

lua_pushstring(L, "right");

lua_pcall(L, 2, 0, 0);
```

4. Event Handling

Scripts can respond to game events, such as collisions, user input, or timer events. Event handling in scripts allows you to create dynamic and responsive gameplay experiences.

```
—Example Lua script for handling collision events

function onCollisionEnter(self, other)

—Handle collision event logic here

end
```

5. Debugging and Testing

Use debugging tools provided by Cocos2d-x or the scripting language itself to identify and fix issues in your scripts. Testing game logic thoroughly is essential to ensure it behaves as intended.

6. Extending and Modifying Game Logic

One of the advantages of using scripts for game logic is the ability to extend or modify behavior without altering the engine's core code. This is particularly useful for adding new features, balancing gameplay, or creating mods for your game.

Best Practices and Considerations

When scripting game logic in Cocos2d-x, consider the following best practices and considerations:

- Maintain a clear structure and organization for your scripts to improve readability and maintainability.
- Document your scripts thoroughly, especially if multiple team members are working on them.
- Ensure that script execution does not introduce performance bottlenecks. Profile and optimize scripts as needed.
- Handle errors and exceptions in your scripts gracefully to prevent crashes or unexpected behavior.
- Be cautious when using global variables in scripts, as they can lead to unintended side effects and conflicts.

By effectively using scripting for game logic in Cocos2d-x, you can create dynamic and engaging gameplay experiences, empower modders and content creators, and streamline the development and iteration of your game's mechanics.

7.3. Automation Tools and Techniques

In this section, we will explore the importance of automation tools and techniques in the context of game development with Cocos2d-x. Automation plays a crucial role in streamlining various aspects of game development, from build and testing processes to content generation and deployment. Let's delve into how automation can enhance your game development workflow and the tools and practices to achieve it.

Why Automation in Game Development?

Automation offers several benefits for game development:

1. **Efficiency:** Automation tools can perform repetitive tasks faster and more accurately than manual processes, saving valuable development time.
2. **Consistency:** Automated processes ensure that tasks are executed consistently, reducing the risk of human errors.
3. **Quality Assurance:** Automation can help identify and address issues through automated testing, ensuring a higher level of quality and stability in your game.
4. **Scalability:** As your game project grows, automation tools can help manage complex tasks and workflows more effectively.

Key Areas of Automation

Let's explore some of the key areas in game development where automation can be applied:

1. Build and Deployment

Automate the build and deployment process to create game builds for different platforms quickly. Tools like CMake and CI/CD (Continuous Integration/Continuous Deployment) pipelines can help automate these tasks.

```
# Automating build using CMake

mkdir build

cd build

cmake ..

make
```

2. Testing and Quality Assurance

Automated testing frameworks allow you to run tests for various aspects of your game, including unit tests, integration tests, and performance tests. Tools like Google Test and Unity Test Framework can be integrated into your workflow.

```
// Example unit test using Google Test

TEST(MyGameTest, TestFunctionality) {

// Test game functionality here

}
```

3. Content Generation

Use procedural content generation techniques and tools to automate the creation of in-game content such as levels, textures, and audio. This can save time and add variety to your game.

```
# Procedural generation of terrain

def generate_terrain(size):

# Generate terrain data

pass
```

4. Version Control

Leverage version control systems like Git to automate code and asset versioning. This ensures that changes are tracked, and you can easily revert to previous states if needed.

```
# Automating version control with Git

git add .

git commit -m "Added new feature"

git push origin master
```

5. Documentation

Automate the generation of documentation for your game code using tools like Doxygen or Javadoc. This ensures that documentation stays up-to-date as your code evolves.

```
# Automating documentation generation with Doxygen
```

doxygen Doxyfile

6. Bug Tracking and Issue Management

Integrate bug tracking and issue management tools with your development workflow. Tools like Jira and Trello can help automate issue tracking and task management.

- *[X]* Fix game crash on level 3

- [ ] Implement new enemy behavior

Automation Practices

To effectively implement automation in your Cocos2d-x game development, consider the following practices:

- **Start Early:** Incorporate automation from the beginning of your project to reap its benefits throughout development.

- **Continuous Integration:** Set up CI/CD pipelines to automate build and testing processes on each code commit, ensuring early detection of issues.

- **Version Control Discipline:** Use branching and tagging in version control systems to manage code changes and ensure a stable main branch.

- **Documentation as Code:** Treat documentation as part of your codebase, and automate its generation to maintain consistency.

- **Feedback Loop:** Continuously collect feedback from automated tests and processes to improve the automation pipeline.

- **Security Considerations:** Ensure that automated processes do not compromise security or expose sensitive data.

Available Automation Tools

Various tools can help you implement automation in your Cocos2d-x game development:

- **CMake:** A versatile build automation tool that can generate project files for various development environments.

- **Continuous Integration Services:** Platforms like Jenkins, Travis CI, and GitHub Actions provide CI/CD capabilities for automating builds and testing.

- **Testing Frameworks:** Utilize testing frameworks like Google Test, Unity Test Framework, or custom test suites to automate testing.

- **Asset Pipelines:** Tools like Unity's Asset Pipeline or custom asset processing scripts can automate asset preparation and optimization.

- **Procedural Content Generation Libraries:** Libraries like libnoise or Perlin noise generators can automate terrain and world generation.

• **Version Control Systems:** Git, SVN, and Mercurial can automate versioning and collaboration.

• **Documentation Generators:** Tools like Doxygen, Javadoc, and Sphinx can automate code documentation.

• **Bug Tracking Tools:** Systems like Jira, Trello, or Redmine automate issue tracking and project management.

By embracing automation tools and techniques in your Cocos2d-x game development workflow, you can enhance productivity, improve game quality, and streamline the development process. Automation allows you to focus more on creative aspects and less on repetitive tasks, ultimately leading to a more efficient and enjoyable development experience.

7.4. Testing and Debugging Scripts

In this section, we will delve into the critical aspects of testing and debugging scripts in Cocos2d-x game development. Scripting is a powerful tool for implementing game logic, but it also introduces the potential for errors and unexpected behavior. To ensure the reliability and stability of your game, it's essential to have robust testing and debugging practices in place for your scripts.

The Importance of Script Testing

Effective script testing is crucial for the following reasons:

1. **Identifying Bugs:** Testing helps uncover bugs, errors, and logical issues in your scripts that could lead to gameplay problems or crashes.
2. **Ensuring Correct Behavior:** It ensures that your scripts

behave as intended, meeting the requirements of your game design.

3. **Performance Optimization:** Testing can reveal performance bottlenecks or inefficiencies in your scripts, allowing you to optimize them.
4. **Maintaining Quality:** Thorough testing contributes to the overall quality and reliability of your game, enhancing the player experience.

Types of Script Testing

Script testing in Cocos2d-x can encompass various types of testing:

1. Unit Testing

Unit testing involves testing individual functions or methods in your scripts in isolation. It verifies that specific parts of your code produce the correct output for a given set of inputs. Unit tests are valuable for validating the behavior of isolated script components.

```
// Example unit test using Google Test

TEST(MyScriptTests, TestFunctionA) {

// Arrange: Set up test data and conditions

// Act: Call the function to be tested

// Assert: Check if the result matches the expected outcome

}
```

2. Integration Testing

Integration testing focuses on the interactions between different script components. It ensures that various parts of your scripts work together correctly. Integration tests help uncover issues that may arise when different script modules interact.

3. Functional Testing

Functional testing assesses the functionality of entire script modules or systems within your game. It validates that the script components collectively perform their intended tasks and achieve the desired outcomes.

4. Regression Testing

Regression testing involves rerunning previously executed tests to ensure that new changes or updates to your scripts have not introduced new defects or broken existing functionality. It safeguards against unintended regressions.

5. Performance Testing

Performance testing evaluates the efficiency and speed of your scripts. It helps identify performance bottlenecks and resource-intensive operations, allowing you to optimize your scripts for smoother gameplay.

Debugging Scripts

Debugging is the process of identifying and fixing issues or defects in your scripts. Effective debugging practices are essential for resolving problems efficiently. Here are some debugging techniques you can use:

1. Logging

Logging is a valuable tool for understanding script behavior and identifying issues. You can use logging statements to output information, variable values, and debug messages to the console or log files during runtime.

—Lua script with logging

```
function myFunction()
print("Entering myFunction")
local result = someOperation()
print("Result:", result)
end
```

2. Breakpoints

Set breakpoints in your script code to pause execution at specific points. This allows you to inspect variable values, step through code, and identify the source of problems interactively using debugging tools provided by your development environment.

3. Exception Handling

Implement exception handling mechanisms in your scripts to gracefully handle errors and prevent crashes. This includes using try-catch blocks or error-handling functions to manage unexpected situations.

```
—Lua script with exception handling

function myFunction()

local success, result = pcall(someOperation)

if not success then

print("Error:", result)

else

print("Result:", result)

end

end
```

4. Debugging Tools

Leverage debugging tools and integrated development environments (IDEs) that support script debugging. These tools provide features like code stepping, variable inspection, and call stack navigation.

5. Unit Testing for Debugging

Unit tests can also serve as a debugging tool. When a unit test fails, it provides valuable information about the specific issue in your script, making it easier to pinpoint and fix the problem.

Best Practices for Script Testing and Debugging

To effectively test and debug your scripts in Cocos2d-x game development, consider the following best practices:

- **Automate Testing:** Implement automated testing for your scripts, including unit tests, integration tests, and functional tests, to ensure comprehensive coverage.

- **Test Early and Often:** Start testing your scripts early in the development process and continue testing as you make changes. Frequent testing reduces the likelihood of uncovering critical issues late in development.

- **Use Version Control:** Maintain version control for your scripts, allowing you to track changes, revert to previous states, and collaborate with team members while preserving script integrity.

- **Document Bugs:** Document identified script bugs and issues in a tracking system to ensure they are addressed in a systematic manner.

- **Collaboration:** Collaborate with scriptwriters, designers, and other team members to understand the intended script behavior and address issues effectively.

- **Continuous Improvement:** Continuously improve your testing and debugging processes based on lessons learned from previous projects.

By incorporating robust testing and debugging practices into your Cocos2d-x game development workflow, you can ensure the reliability and stability of your scripts, ultimately delivering a high-quality and enjoyable gaming experience to players.

7.5. Scripting Best Practices

In this section, we will discuss scripting best practices for Cocos2d-x game development. Effective scripting is essential for creating maintainable, performant, and bug-free game logic. By following these best practices, you can streamline your scripting workflow and improve the overall quality of your game.

1. Code Modularity

Organize your scripts into modular components. Each script should have a specific responsibility, making it easier to understand, maintain, and reuse. Avoid writing monolithic scripts that handle too many functionalities. Instead, break them down into smaller, focused modules.

```
—Example of modular scripting

—AI.lua

local AI = {}

function AI.update(enemy)

—Update AI logic for the enemy

end

return AI
```

2. Consistent Naming Conventions

Establish clear and consistent naming conventions for variables, functions, and classes in your scripts. This helps improve code readability and makes it easier for team members to understand and work with your code.

—Use descriptive variable and function names

local playerHealth = 100

function calculateDamage(attacker, target)

—Calculate damage here

end

3. Commenting and Documentation

Document your scripts with comments to explain complex logic, function purposes, and input/output expectations. Maintain up-to-date documentation to make it easier for other developers (including your future self) to understand and use your scripts.

—Comment your code for clarity

—This function handles player movement.

function movePlayer(direction)

—Implementation details

end

4. Error Handling

Implement error handling in your scripts to gracefully handle unexpected situations. Use try-catch or similar constructs to catch and handle errors, preventing crashes and improving the robustness of your game.

```
—Error handling example

function divide(a, b)

local success, result = pcall(function()

return a / b

end)

if not success then

print("Error:", result)

else

return result

end

end
```

5. Memory Management

Pay attention to memory management in your scripts, especially when dealing with resources like textures and objects. Ensure that you release resources when they are no longer needed to prevent memory leaks.

```
—Properly manage memory

local texture = cc.TextureCache:getInstance():addImage("sprite.png")

local sprite = cc.Sprite:createWithTexture(texture)
```

```
—When done with 'sprite,' remove it and release the texture

sprite:removeFromParent()

texture:release()
```

6. Performance Optimization

Optimize your scripts for performance by avoiding unnecessary computations and inefficient algorithms. Use profiling tools to identify bottlenecks and optimize critical parts of your code.

```
—Optimize code for better performance

local function expensiveOperation()

—Expensive computations

end

—Instead of calling 'expensiveOperation' multiple times, store the result

local result = expensiveOperation()
```

7. Version Control

Use version control systems like Git to track changes in your scripts. This allows you to collaborate with team members, revert to previous versions if needed, and maintain a history of your script modifications.

```
# Use Git for version control

git add script.lua

git commit -m "Implemented new enemy AI logic"

git push origin main
```

8. Testing

Implement comprehensive testing for your scripts. Unit tests, integration tests, and functional tests help ensure that your scripts behave as expected and catch issues early in development.

```
// Example unit test using Google Test

TEST(ScriptTests, TestFunctionality) {

// Test script functionality here

}
```

9. Code Reviews

Conduct code reviews with team members to get feedback on your scripts. Code reviews can help identify potential issues, promote best practices, and ensure consistency across your project's scripts.

10. Stay Informed

Stay up-to-date with scripting best practices and new developments in the scripting language you are using. Follow community guidelines and consider adopting improvements and best practices from the scripting community.

By adhering to these scripting best practices in Cocos2d-x game development, you can create scripts that are easier to maintain, less error-prone, and optimized for performance. Consistent, well-documented, and modular scripts contribute to a smoother development process and a higher-quality game.

Chapter 8: Data Management and Storage

8.1. Advanced Data Structures for Game Development

In this section, we will explore advanced data structures used in game development with Cocos2d-x. Efficient data management is crucial for optimizing performance and creating complex game systems. By choosing and implementing the right data structures, you can enhance your game's capabilities and maintainability.

The Importance of Data Structures

Data structures are fundamental components of game development, serving various purposes:

1. **Efficiency:** Well-designed data structures can significantly improve the efficiency of operations like searching, sorting, and retrieval, which are critical in games.
2. **Memory Management:** Data structures help manage memory allocation and deallocation, reducing the risk of memory leaks and fragmentation.
3. **Complexity Management:** Games often deal with complex relationships between entities and objects. Data structures help represent and manage these relationships.
4. **Performance Optimization:** The choice of data structure can impact the performance of your game, especially when dealing with large datasets.

Common Advanced Data Structures

Let's explore some advanced data structures commonly used in game development:

1. Quadtree and Octree

Quadtree and octree are hierarchical spatial data structures that partition space into smaller regions. They are useful for efficient collision detection, visibility culling, and terrain representation.

```
// Example of a quadtree node structure

struct QuadTreeNode {

// Node properties and data

std::vector<QuadTreeNode*> children;

};
```

2. Hash Maps and Hash Tables

Hash maps and hash tables are associative data structures that store key-value pairs. They provide fast access to values based on keys and are used for efficient data indexing and lookup.

```
// Example of a hash map in C++

std::unordered_map<std::string, int> playerScores;

playerScores["Alice"] = 100;

playerScores["Bob"] = 85;
```

3. Priority Queues

Priority queues are data structures that maintain a set of elements with associated priorities. They are commonly used in pathfinding algorithms and event handling systems.

```
// Example of a priority queue in C++

std::priority_queue<int, std::vector<int>, std::greater<int>> minHeap;

minHeap.push(5);

minHeap.push(2);

int smallest = minHeap.top(); // Retrieves the smallest element (2)
```

4. Graphs

Graphs are versatile data structures used for representing complex relationships between entities in games. They are essential for pathfinding, AI decision-making, and level design.

```
// Example of a graph node structure

struct GraphNode {

// Node properties and connections

std::vector<GraphNode*> neighbors;

};
```

Choosing the Right Data Structure

Selecting the appropriate data structure for your game depends on your specific needs and performance requirements. Consider the following factors:

- **Data Size:** Determine the size of your dataset and the expected growth. Some data structures are better suited for large datasets.

- **Access Patterns:** Understand how data will be accessed and modified in your game. Different data structures excel in different access patterns.

- **Complexity:** Assess the complexity of the operations you need to perform. Some data structures optimize specific operations but may be less efficient for others.

- **Memory Usage:** Consider memory constraints, especially in mobile and console game development. Some data structures consume more memory than others.

Custom Data Structures

In some cases, you may need to create custom data structures tailored to your game's requirements. Custom data structures allow you to optimize for specific use cases and can significantly impact your game's performance and functionality.

```
// Example of a custom data structure

class MyCustomDataStructure {

public:

// Custom methods and data members
```

```
private:
// Internal data representation
};
```

Memory Management

Proper memory management is crucial when using data structures. Always release memory when data structures are no longer needed to prevent memory leaks. Cocos2d-x provides memory management tools to help with this.

```
// Example of releasing memory in Cocos2d-x
auto sprite = Sprite::create("image.png");
this->addChild(sprite);
// When no longer needed
sprite->removeFromParentAndCleanup(true);
```

Data Serialization

To save and load game data, use data serialization techniques. Serialize complex data structures into a format that can be easily stored and retrieved, such as JSON, XML, or binary formats.

```
// Example of data serialization using JSON
{
"playerName": "Alice",
"score": 100
}
```

By understanding and effectively implementing advanced data structures in your Cocos2d-x game, you can optimize performance, manage complex game systems, and enhance the overall player experience. Careful consideration of data structure choices, memory management, and serialization is crucial for successful game development.

8.2. Efficient Data Storage and Retrieval

In this section, we will delve into the topic of efficient data storage and retrieval in Cocos2d-x game development. Efficiently managing game data is essential for optimizing performance and ensuring a smooth gaming experience. We will explore techniques and best practices for storing and retrieving data efficiently in your game.

Importance of Efficient Data Storage

Efficient data storage is crucial for several reasons:

1. **Performance:** Efficient data storage and retrieval directly impact your game's performance, especially when dealing with large datasets.
2. **Memory Usage:** Proper data storage helps manage memory efficiently, reducing the risk of memory leaks and improving overall stability.
3. **Load Times:** Efficient data retrieval ensures faster loading times, enhancing the player's initial experience.
4. **Scalability:** As your game evolves and grows, efficient data storage allows you to handle increasing amounts of data without performance degradation.

Common Data Storage Techniques

Let's explore some common techniques and data structures for efficient data storage and retrieval in game development:

1. Arrays and Lists

Arrays and lists are straightforward data structures for storing collections of items. They are suitable for storing data where direct access by index is required.

```
// Example of storing player scores in an array

std::vector<int> playerScores = {100, 85, 120, 75};

int aliceScore = playerScores[0]; // Accessing Alice's score
```

2. Dictionaries and Maps

Dictionaries and maps associate keys with values, allowing efficient data retrieval by key. They are ideal for storing data with a clear key-value relationship.

```
// Example of storing player scores in a map

std::map<std::string, int> playerScores;

playerScores["Alice"] = 100;

playerScores["Bob"] = 85;

int aliceScore = playerScores["Alice"]; // Retrieving Alice's score
```

3. Databases

Databases are powerful tools for storing and retrieving structured game data. They offer advanced querying capabilities and are commonly used for persistent game data storage.

```
// Example of using a SQLite database in Cocos2d-x

sqlite3* db;

int result = sqlite3_open("game_data.db", &db);

if (result == SQLITE_OK) {

// Perform database operations

sqlite3_close(db);

}
```

4. Binary Serialization

Binary serialization involves converting game data into binary format for efficient storage and retrieval. This method reduces data size and improves load times.

```
// Example of binary serialization in C++

struct PlayerData {

std::string playerName;

int score;

};

PlayerData player;
```

// Serialize player data to binary format and save to a file

Best Practices for Efficient Data Storage

To ensure efficient data storage and retrieval in your Cocos2d-x game, consider the following best practices:

1. **Data Compression:** Compress data when appropriate to reduce storage size and improve load times.
2. **Streaming Data:** Load data asynchronously and stream it into the game as needed to minimize initial loading times.
3. **Memory Pools:** Use memory pools to allocate and recycle memory efficiently, reducing memory fragmentation.
4. **Caching:** Implement data caching to store frequently accessed data in memory for faster retrieval.
5. **Optimized Queries:** When using databases, optimize database queries for efficient data retrieval.
6. **Data Sharding:** Divide data into smaller manageable chunks or shards for easier retrieval and loading.
7. **Data Cleanup:** Periodically clean up unused or outdated data to free up memory and storage resources.

Serialization and Deserialization

Serialization is the process of converting data into a format suitable for storage or transmission, such as binary, JSON, or XML. Deserialization is the reverse process of reconstructing data from its serialized form. Use serialization and deserialization techniques to save and load game data efficiently.

// Example of JSON serialization and deserialization

```
{
"playerName": "Alice",
```

```
"score": 100
}
```

By implementing efficient data storage and retrieval practices in your Cocos2d-x game, you can optimize performance, reduce memory usage, and create a seamless gaming experience for players. Careful consideration of data storage techniques and adherence to best practices are essential for successful game development.

8.3. Implementing Save Game Systems

In this section, we will discuss the implementation of save game systems in Cocos2d-x game development. Save game systems are essential for allowing players to save their progress and resume gameplay later. We will explore the key components and best practices for designing and implementing effective save game functionality.

Importance of Save Game Systems

Save game systems play a vital role in modern game development for several reasons:

1. **Player Convenience:** Save game functionality allows players to continue their progress, making games more accessible and enjoyable.
2. **Complexity Management:** In games with intricate storylines or character progress, save systems help manage and track the game state.
3. **Experimentation:** Players can experiment with different strategies or choices, knowing they can reload a previous save if needed.
4. **Player Engagement:** Save systems encourage players to

invest more time in your game, fostering engagement and loyalty.

Components of a Save Game System

A typical save game system consists of the following components:

1. Save Data

Save data includes information about the player's progress, such as their current level, character stats, inventory, and completed quests. This data is serialized and saved to a file.

```
// Example of save data structure in C++

struct SaveData {

int currentLevel;

std::string playerName;

// Additional game progress data

};
```

2. Save and Load Functions

Implement functions for saving and loading game data. These functions handle the serialization and deserialization of save data.

```
// Example of save and load functions in C++

bool saveGame(const SaveData& saveData) {

// Serialize saveData and save it to a file

}
```

```
bool loadGame(SaveData& saveData) {

// Load saved data from a file and deserialize it into saveData

}
```

3. User Interface (UI)

Design a user interface for players to interact with the save game system. This typically includes options to save, load, and delete saved games.

4. Save Slots

Save slots allow players to create multiple save files, enabling them to have different save points or experiment with different gameplay paths.

5. Auto-Save and Checkpoints

Implement auto-save functionality at specific checkpoints or milestones in your game. Auto-saves ensure that players don't lose progress in case of unexpected events, such as crashes.

Save Data Encryption

To protect save data from tampering or cheating, consider encrypting save files. Encryption ensures that save data remains secure and can only be accessed and modified by your game.

```
// Example of save data encryption in C++

void encryptSaveData(SaveData& saveData) {

// Encrypt saveData using a secure encryption algorithm
```

```
}

void decryptSaveData(SaveData& saveData) {

// Decrypt encrypted saveData to access its contents

}
```

Best Practices for Save Game Systems

To create an effective and reliable save game system in Cocos2d-x, follow these best practices:

1. **Backup and Recovery:** Implement backup mechanisms to prevent save data loss in case of corruption or errors during save operations.
2. **Version Compatibility:** Consider versioning your save data to ensure compatibility with future game updates and changes.
3. **Validation:** Validate save data integrity to detect and prevent corrupted save files.
4. **Cross-Platform Support:** If your game is multi-platform, ensure that save data is compatible across different platforms.
5. **Cloud Saves:** Consider integrating cloud save functionality to allow players to access their save data from multiple devices.
6. **Player Feedback:** Provide clear feedback to players regarding the status of their save operations, such as successful saves or loading errors.
7. **Testing:** Thoroughly test your save game system to identify and resolve issues related to saving, loading, and data integrity.

Save Game Services

For platforms like mobile devices and consoles, you can leverage platform-specific save game services provided by the platform's SDK. These services often offer cloud save functionality and simplify the implementation of save game systems.

By implementing a robust save game system in your Cocos2d-x game, you enhance the player experience, encourage engagement, and ensure that players can enjoy your game with confidence, knowing their progress is secure and easily accessible.

8.4. Cloud Storage Integration

In this section, we will explore the integration of cloud storage solutions into Cocos2d-x game development. Cloud storage allows you to securely store and retrieve game data on remote servers, providing several benefits for your game and players. We will discuss the advantages of cloud storage, integration methods, and best practices.

Advantages of Cloud Storage

Integrating cloud storage into your Cocos2d-x game offers numerous advantages:

1. **Cross-Device Progress:** Players can access their game progress and data across multiple devices seamlessly. This enhances the player experience and promotes player retention.
2. **Data Security:** Cloud storage solutions often employ encryption and security measures to protect player data, reducing the risk of data loss or theft.
3. **Backup and Recovery:** Player data is backed up in the

cloud, reducing the risk of data loss due to device failures or crashes.

4. **Multiplayer and Social Features:** Cloud storage can store game state and player profiles for multiplayer and social features, enabling real-time interaction and competition.

Popular Cloud Storage Services

Several cloud storage services are commonly used in game development:

1. Google Cloud Storage

Google Cloud Storage provides scalable, secure, and cost-effective object storage. It is often used in conjunction with other Google Cloud services for game backend development.

2. Amazon S3 (Simple Storage Service)

Amazon S3 is a widely used cloud storage service with excellent scalability and reliability. It offers various storage classes to optimize costs.

3. Firebase Realtime Database

Firebase Realtime Database, part of Google Firebase, is a NoSQL database that can be used for real-time data synchronization and storage of game data.

4. Microsoft Azure Blob Storage

Azure Blob Storage is Microsoft's cloud storage solution, suitable for storing binary and text data, including game assets and save data.

5. Custom Backend

For more control and customization, you can implement your custom backend using cloud services like AWS, Azure, or Google Cloud. This allows you to tailor the storage solution to your specific game requirements.

Integration Methods

Integrating cloud storage into your Cocos2d-x game involves the following steps:

1. Register for Cloud Service

Sign up for the cloud storage service of your choice and create a project or bucket to store your game data.

2. SDK Integration

Integrate the cloud storage SDK or library into your Cocos2d-x game project. Most cloud providers offer SDKs for various programming languages, including C++.

```
// Example of including a cloud storage SDK in C++
#include "cloud_storage_sdk.h"
```

3. Authentication

Implement authentication to secure access to your cloud storage. Players may need to log in or use API keys to access their data.

```
// Example of authentication in Cocos2d-x
```

CloudService.authenticate(userCredentials);

4. Data Storage

Use the SDK to store and retrieve game data in the cloud. This may include player profiles, save game data, leaderboards, and more.

// Example of storing and retrieving player data in Cocos2d-x

CloudService.storePlayerData(playerProfile);

PlayerData retrievedData = CloudService.retrievePlayerData(playerID);

5. Error Handling

Implement error handling to gracefully handle situations where cloud storage operations fail due to network issues or other reasons.

// Example of error handling in Cocos2d-x

try {

// Cloud storage operation

} **catch** (CloudStorageException& ex) {

// Handle the error

}

6. Testing

Thoroughly test your cloud storage integration to ensure that data is being stored and retrieved correctly. Pay special attention to edge cases and error scenarios.

Best Practices for Cloud Storage Integration

To make the most of cloud storage integration in your Cocos2d-x game, consider the following best practices:

1. **Data Validation:** Validate and sanitize data before storing it in the cloud to prevent unauthorized or malicious data manipulation.
2. **Data Versioning:** Implement data versioning to ensure compatibility as your game evolves and data structures change.
3. **Offline Support:** Provide offline functionality that allows players to continue playing and sync data with the cloud when an internet connection is available.
4. **Privacy Compliance:** Comply with data privacy regulations and inform players about data collection and usage in your game's privacy policy.
5. **Data Encryption:** Use encryption for sensitive data to protect it from unauthorized access.
6. **Data Segmentation:** Consider segmenting data storage based on user accounts or game instances to improve data organization and retrieval.
7. **Cost Optimization:** Optimize data storage costs by using the appropriate storage class and managing data retention policies.

Player Data Migration

When updating your game, consider player data migration strategies to ensure a smooth transition for existing players. Migration may be necessary when changing data structures or introducing new features.

By integrating cloud storage into your Cocos2d-x game, you can provide players with a seamless and secure experience, enable cross-device progress, and leverage cloud services' scalability and reliability. Careful planning, authentication, error handling, and data privacy considerations are essential for successful cloud storage integration.

8.5. Data Encryption and Security

In this section, we will delve into the critical topic of data encryption and security in Cocos2d-x game development. Protecting player data and sensitive information is paramount to maintain player trust and adhere to data privacy regulations. We will explore encryption techniques, best practices, and security measures to safeguard your game's data.

Importance of Data Encryption

Data encryption is essential for the following reasons:

1. **Player Privacy:** Encryption ensures that players' personal and sensitive data, such as login credentials and payment information, remains confidential.
2. **Data Integrity:** Encryption helps prevent unauthorized tampering with game data, ensuring its integrity and authenticity.
3. **Compliance:** Many regions have data protection regulations that require the encryption of sensitive information, and non-compliance can result in legal consequences.
4. **Player Trust:** Implementing robust security measures instills trust in players, reassuring them that their data is safe when playing your game.

Encryption Techniques

There are several encryption techniques and algorithms commonly used in game development:

1. Symmetric Encryption

Symmetric encryption uses a single key to both encrypt and decrypt data. It is efficient and suitable for encrypting large amounts of data. However, securely sharing the encryption key between parties can be challenging.

```
// Example of symmetric encryption in C++
std::string encryptedData = encryptSymmetric(data, encryptionKey);
std::string decryptedData = decryptSymmetric(encryptedData, encryptionKey);
```

2. Asymmetric Encryption (Public-Key Encryption)

Asymmetric encryption uses a pair of keys: a public key for encryption and a private key for decryption. This approach provides a secure way to exchange encryption keys but is less efficient for encrypting large data sets.

```
// Example of asymmetric encryption in C++
std::string encryptedData = encryptAsymmetric(data, publicKey);
std::string decryptedData = decryptAsymmetric(encryptedData, privateKey);
```

3. Hash Functions

Hash functions convert data into a fixed-size string of characters (hash) that is difficult to reverse. While not suitable for encryption, hash functions are essential for storing passwords securely by hashing and salting them.

// Example of hashing a password in C++

```
std::string hashedPassword = hashPassword(userPassword, salt);
```

Best Practices for Data Encryption and Security

To ensure robust data encryption and security in your Cocos2d-x game, follow these best practices:

1. **Use Strong Algorithms:** Choose well-established encryption algorithms and libraries with a strong track record of security.
2. **Secure Key Management:** Protect encryption keys and ensure they are not hard-coded in your game's source code. Use secure key management solutions.
3. **Data Minimization:** Collect and store only the necessary data from players, minimizing the risk of data breaches.
4. **HTTPS for Data Transmission:** When transmitting data over the internet, use HTTPS to encrypt data in transit between the player's device and your server.
5. **Authentication and Authorization:** Implement robust user authentication and authorization mechanisms to control access to sensitive data and game features.
6. **Regular Security Audits:** Conduct security audits and penetration testing to identify vulnerabilities and weaknesses in your game's security.
7. **Data Backup and Recovery:** Implement data backup and

recovery procedures to ensure data availability in case of data loss or system failures.

8. **Data Retention Policies:** Define and adhere to data retention policies, disposing of data that is no longer necessary.
9. **Regulatory Compliance:** Stay informed about data protection regulations in your target markets and ensure compliance with applicable laws.

Player Data and Consent

It is crucial to obtain explicit consent from players regarding the collection and use of their data. Clearly communicate your game's data privacy policy, detailing what data is collected, how it is used, and how it is protected.

```
// Example of requesting player consent in Cocos2d-x

bool getPlayerConsent() {

// Present a consent dialog to the player

// Record the player's consent preferences

return playerConsented;

}
```

Security Updates and Patches

Stay vigilant about security threats and vulnerabilities by regularly updating your game and its dependencies. Promptly address security issues by releasing patches and updates to protect player data.

```
// Example of releasing a security patch in Cocos2d-x
```

```
if (securityVulnerabilityDetected) {
// Develop and release a security patch
}
```

By implementing robust data encryption and security measures in your Cocos2d-x game, you can safeguard player data, protect their privacy, and build trust among your player community. Security should be an ongoing concern throughout the development lifecycle, and staying informed about emerging threats and best practices is crucial for maintaining a secure gaming environment.

Chapter 9: Leveraging C++ in Cocos2d-x

9.1. Advanced C++ Features in Cocos2d-x

In this section, we will explore advanced C++ features and techniques that can be leveraged in Cocos2d-x game development. While Cocos2d-x primarily uses C++ for game programming, understanding these advanced features can help you write more efficient and maintainable code. We will cover various aspects of C++ that are valuable for game development with Cocos2d-x.

Object-Oriented Programming (OOP)

Cocos2d-x is built around object-oriented programming principles. You can create game objects as classes, defining their properties and behaviors. Inheritance, encapsulation, and polymorphism are fundamental concepts in OOP that are beneficial in Cocos2d-x development.

```
// Example of an object-oriented approach in Cocos2d-x

class GameObject : public cocos2d::Node {

public:

// Constructor

GameObject();

// Member functions

void moveTo(float x, float y);

void update(float dt);
```

```
};
```

Smart Pointers

Smart pointers in C++ are essential for managing memory and preventing memory leaks. Cocos2d-x provides its smart pointer classes, such as *cocos2d::Ref*, to manage game objects' memory automatically. Using smart pointers helps ensure proper memory management and reduces the risk of crashes.

```
// Example of using cocos2d::Ref smart pointer

auto sprite = cocos2d::Sprite::create("image.png");

addChild(sprite);
```

RAII (Resource Acquisition Is Initialization)

RAII is a C++ programming idiom that associates the lifecycle of a resource with the scope of an object. Cocos2d-x's resource management often follows the RAII principle, making it easier to handle resources like textures, audio, and animations.

```
// Example of RAII in Cocos2d-x for loading a texture

cocos2d::Sprite* loadSprite(const std::string& filename) {

auto texture = cocos2d::Director::getInstance()->getTextureCache()->addImage(filenam

return cocos2d::Sprite::createWithTexture(texture);

}
```

Standard Template Library (STL)

The C++ Standard Template Library (STL) provides a rich collection of data structures and algorithms that can be useful in game development. You can leverage containers like *std::vector* and algorithms like *std::sort* to manage and manipulate game data efficiently.

```
// Example of using std::vector in Cocos2d-x

std::vector<int> scores = {100, 85, 120, 75};

std::sort(scores.begin(), scores.end()); // Sorting scores
```

Lambda Functions

Lambda functions in C++ allow you to create anonymous functions or closures. They are handy for defining small, inline functions for tasks like event handling or custom sorting algorithms.

```
// Example of a lambda function for custom sorting in Cocos2d-x

std::vector<int> scores = {100, 85, 120, 75};

std::sort(scores.begin(), scores.end(), [](int a, int b) {

return a > b; // Sort in descending order

});
```

Exception Handling

Exception handling in C++ is crucial for dealing with runtime errors gracefully. Cocos2d-x provides its exception handling mechanisms for handling errors in game code.

```
// Example of exception handling in Cocos2d-x
```

```
try {
// Code that may throw exceptions
} catch (const std::exception& e) {
// Handle the exception
}
```

Template Metaprogramming

Template metaprogramming is an advanced C++ technique where templates are used for compile-time computations and code generation. While it's not commonly used in Cocos2d-x game development, understanding the basics of metaprogramming can be beneficial for optimizing performance-critical code.

Advanced C++ Features for Game Optimization

Cocos2d-x games often require optimization for smooth performance. Understanding advanced C++ features like move semantics, custom memory allocators, and multithreading can help you optimize your game code.

```
// Example of using move semantics for resource optimization
std::vector<std::string> sourceData = getGameData();
std::vector<std::string> optimizedData = std::move(sourceData);
```

Effective Debugging and Profiling

Profiling and debugging tools are essential for identifying performance bottlenecks and bugs in your game. Familiarize yourself with Cocos2d-x's debugging and profiling features to diagnose and resolve issues efficiently.

```
// Example of using Cocos2d-x's debugging tools

CCLOG("Debug message: %d", variable);
```

Custom Memory Management

Custom memory management techniques, such as memory pools and object pools, can help optimize memory usage and reduce memory fragmentation in Cocos2d-x games.

```
// Example of implementing a memory pool in Cocos2d-x

class MemoryPool {

public:

void* allocate(size_t size);

void deallocate(void* ptr);

};
```

By exploring these advanced C++ features and techniques, you can write more efficient, maintainable, and performant code in your Cocos2d-x games. While not all of these concepts are required for every game, having a solid understanding of them can be valuable for tackling complex game development challenges and achieving optimal performance.

9.2. Memory Management and Optimization

Efficient memory management is crucial in Cocos2d-x game development to ensure your game runs smoothly and doesn't suffer from performance issues like memory leaks or excessive memory usage. In this section, we will explore memory management techniques and optimization strategies that can help you create memory-efficient games.

Automatic Reference Counting (ARC)

Cocos2d-x uses Automatic Reference Counting (ARC) to manage the memory of game objects. When you create a Cocos2d-x object, it is automatically reference-counted. When the reference count drops to zero, the object is deleted, freeing up memory.

```
// Example of creating and using a Cocos2d-x object

auto sprite = cocos2d::Sprite::create("image.png");

addChild(sprite); // Increase the reference count
```

However, it's essential to be mindful of circular references, where objects reference each other, preventing the reference count from reaching zero. To avoid memory leaks in such cases, use *cocos2d::RefPtr* or *std::weak_ptr* to break circular references.

Object Pools

Object pools are a memory optimization technique where you preallocate a pool of objects and reuse them instead of creating and destroying objects frequently. This can significantly reduce memory allocation and deallocation overhead.

```
// Example of an object pool in Cocos2d-x

class ObjectPool {

public:

ObjectPool(int initialSize) {

// Initialize and store a pool of objects
```

```
}

GameObject* acquire() {

// Get an object from the pool

}

void release(GameObject* obj) {

// Return an object to the pool

}

private:

std::vector<GameObject*> objectPool;

};
```

Texture Atlases

Texture atlases are a way to optimize memory usage for game sprites and textures. By combining multiple images into a single texture atlas, you can reduce the number of texture swaps and improve rendering performance.

```
// Example of using a texture atlas in Cocos2d-x

auto spriteFrame = cocos2d::SpriteFrameCache::getInstance()->getSpriteFrameByName("sprit

auto sprite = cocos2d::Sprite::createWithSpriteFrame(spriteFrame);

addChild(sprite);
```

Dynamic Memory Allocation

Dynamic memory allocation, such as using *new* and *delete*, should be minimized in real-time games as it can lead to memory fragmentation and performance overhead. Prefer stack memory and object pools whenever possible.

```
// Example of dynamic memory allocation in Cocos2d-x

auto enemy = new Enemy(); // Avoid frequent use in game loops
```

Resource Unloading

Unload unused game resources, such as textures, audio, and assets, when they are no longer needed. Cocos2d-x provides mechanisms to preload and unload resources efficiently.

```
// Example of unloading resources in Cocos2d-x

cocos2d::Director::getInstance()->getTextureCache()->removeUnusedTe
```

Profiling and Monitoring

Use profiling and memory monitoring tools to identify memory bottlenecks and leaks. Cocos2d-x provides built-in tools and third-party profilers can also be useful.

```
// Example of using Cocos2d-x's built-in profiling tools

cocos2d::Director::getInstance()->getScheduler()->schedule([](float
dt) {

// Check memory usage and report it

}, this, 1.0f, false, "memory_profiler");
```

Custom Memory Allocators

In some cases, implementing custom memory allocators can improve memory allocation and deallocation performance. This is an advanced technique that can be beneficial in highly performance-critical scenarios.

```
// Example of implementing a custom memory allocator in Cocos2d-x

void* customAllocate(size_t size) {

// Custom memory allocation logic

}

void customDeallocate(void* ptr) {

// Custom memory deallocation logic

}
```

Release Builds and Optimization Flags

When building your game for release, use optimization flags provided by your compiler to generate more efficient code. These flags can significantly reduce memory and CPU usage.

```
// Example of optimization flags for a release build

// -O2: Moderate optimization

// -O3: Aggressive optimization

// -Os: Optimize for code size
```

Continuous Testing and Profiling

Regularly test and profile your game, especially on target devices, to identify and address memory-related issues. Continuous testing ensures that your game remains memory-efficient throughout development.

```
// Example of profiling memory usage during development
if (isDebugBuild) {
// Log memory usage and detect leaks
}
```

Efficient memory management is vital for creating high-performance games in Cocos2d-x. By applying these memory optimization techniques, monitoring memory usage, and profiling your game, you can ensure that your game runs smoothly, even on resource-constrained devices, and provides a great player experience.

9.3. C++ Best Practices in Game Development

In this section, we will explore best practices for using C++ effectively in Cocos2d-x game development. Following these practices can help you write clean, maintainable, and efficient code that enhances your game's performance and reduces the likelihood of bugs.

Consistent Code Style

Maintain a consistent and well-documented code style throughout your Cocos2d-x project. Adhering to a coding standard, such as Google's C++ Style Guide or the Cocos2d-x coding style, makes your code more readable and ensures that team members can collaborate seamlessly.

```
// Example of code style in Cocos2d-x using Google's C++ Style Guide

class GameScene : public cocos2d::Scene {

public:

void onEnter() override {

// Use meaningful variable and function names

int playerScore = 0;

updatePlayerScore(playerScore);

// Use consistent indentation and formatting

if (playerScore >= 100) {

// Perform actions

}

}

private:

void updatePlayerScore(int score) {

// ...

}

};
```

Avoid Global Variables

Minimize the use of global variables as they can make your code less maintainable and prone to bugs. Instead, encapsulate data in classes and pass necessary information through function parameters.

```
// Example of avoiding global variables in Cocos2d-x

class GameManager {

public:

int getPlayerScore() const {

return playerScore;

}

void setPlayerScore(int score) {

playerScore = score;

}

private:

int playerScore = 0;

};
```

RAII for Resource Management

Adopt the RAII (Resource Acquisition Is Initialization) principle for resource management. Use smart pointers and Cocos2d-x's built-in resource management to handle memory and resource cleanup automatically.

```
// Example of RAII for resource management in Cocos2d-x
```

```
auto sprite = cocos2d::Sprite::create("image.png"); // Automatic resource cleanup
addChild(sprite);
```

Effective Use of Const

Use the *const* keyword to declare variables, member functions, and parameters as constant when appropriate. This helps prevent unintentional modification of data and can improve code clarity.

```
// Example of using const in Cocos2d-x
class Player {
public:
void takeDamage(int damage) {
health -= damage;
}
int getHealth() const {
return health;
}
private:
int health = 100;
};
```

Avoid Manual Memory Management

Prefer using smart pointers like *std::shared_ptr* and *cocos2d::RefPtr* over manual memory management with *new* and *delete*. Smart pointers help prevent memory leaks and make your code more reliable.

```
// Example of using smart pointers in Cocos2d-x

auto sprite = std::make_shared<cocos2d::Sprite>("image.png");

addChild(sprite);
```

Error Handling

Implement robust error handling mechanisms, such as exceptions or error codes, to gracefully handle unexpected situations and failures. Avoid using exceptions for control flow; they should be reserved for exceptional circumstances.

```
// Example of error handling in Cocos2d-x using error codes

bool loadGameLevel(int level) {

if (level < 0 || level >= maxLevels) {

return false; // Invalid level

}

// Load the game level

return true;

}
```

Modularize Code

Divide your game code into smaller, modular components and classes. Each class or module should have a single responsibility, making your code easier to understand, test, and maintain.

```
// Example of modularization in Cocos2d-x

class Player {

public:

void move(float x, float y) {

// Move the player character

}

void attack() {

// Perform an attack

}

};

class Enemy {

public:

void update() {

// Update enemy behavior

}

void takeDamage(int damage) {

// Handle damage
```

```
}

};
```

Code Comments and Documentation

Document your code using comments and documentation comments (e.g., Doxygen or Javadoc) to explain the purpose and usage of classes, functions, and variables. Well-documented code is easier for you and others to understand and maintain.

```
// Example of code comments in Cocos2d-x

class GameManager {

public:

/**

* Constructor for GameManager.

* @param initialScore The initial player score.

*/

GameManager(int initialScore) : playerScore(initialScore) {}

// ...

};
```

Unit Testing

Implement unit testing for critical game components and logic. Unit tests help catch bugs early and ensure that changes to your code do not introduce regressions.

```
// Example of unit testing in Cocos2d-x using a testing framework
```

```
void testPlayerHealth() {

Player player;

player.takeDamage(20);

ASSERT_EQUAL(player.getHealth(), 80);

}
```

By adhering to these C++ best practices, you can write high-quality, maintainable code for your Cocos2d-x game. Clean code not only reduces the likelihood of bugs but also makes it easier to collaborate with other developers, maintain and extend your game, and deliver a great player experience.

9.4. Integrating C++ with Other Languages

In Cocos2d-x game development, you may need to integrate C++ code with other programming languages like JavaScript or Lua. This can be useful for various purposes, such as scripting game logic, creating plugins, or achieving platform-specific functionality. In this section, we will explore how to seamlessly integrate C++ with other languages in your Cocos2d-x project.

JavaScript Integration

Cocos2d-x provides a JavaScript binding mechanism that allows you to write game logic and scripts in JavaScript while utilizing C++ for the underlying engine functionality. This integration enables you to take advantage of JavaScript's flexibility and ease of use for scripting.

Here's a basic example of how to create a JavaScript script and call it from C++:

```
// C++ code to call a JavaScript function
```

```
JSContext* cx = ScriptingCore::getInstance()->getGlobalContext();

JSObject* global = ScriptingCore::getInstance()->getGlobalObject();

JS::RootedObject jsObj(cx, global);

JS::RootedValue rval(cx);

JS_CallFunctionName(cx, jsObj, "myJavaScriptFunction", JS::HandleValueArray::empty(), &rval);
```

You can expose C++ classes and functions to JavaScript using the Cocos2d-x JavaScript bindings. This allows you to access C++ functionality directly from JavaScript.

Lua Integration

Lua is another scripting language often used for game development. Cocos2d-x provides a Lua binding mechanism that allows you to write game logic in Lua scripts and interact with C++ code.

Here's a simple example of calling a Lua function from C++:

```
// C++ code to call a Lua function

lua_State* L = LuaEngine::getInstance()->getLuaStack()->getLuaState();

lua_getglobal(L, "myLuaFunction");

lua_call(L, 0, 0);
```

You can also register C++ functions and classes with Lua using Cocos2d-x's Lua binding system, making them accessible from Lua scripts.

Platform-Specific Functionality

In some cases, you may need to access platform-specific functionality that is not available in the Cocos2d-x engine. You can achieve this by creating platform-specific C++ extensions or plugins and calling them from the shared C++ game code.

For example, if you need to access the device's camera on iOS and Android, you can create C++ extensions for each platform that provide camera access. Then, you can call the appropriate extension based on the platform.

```
// C++ code to call platform-specific extensions

#if CC_TARGET_PLATFORM == CC_PLATFORM_IOS

// Call iOS camera extension

iOSCameraExtension::openCamera();

#elif CC_TARGET_PLATFORM == CC_PLATFORM_ANDROID

// Call Android camera extension

AndroidCameraExtension::openCamera();

#endif
```

Error Handling

When integrating C++ with other languages, pay attention to error handling. Ensure that your error-handling mechanisms can propagate errors between C++ and the scripting language. Proper error handling helps diagnose and fix issues that may arise during integration.

Performance Considerations

While integrating C++ with scripting languages provides flexibility, it may introduce some performance overhead, especially for computationally intensive tasks. Keep this in mind when deciding which parts of your game logic to implement in C++ and which to script.

Consider profiling and optimizing critical sections of code to maintain good performance.

Third-Party Libraries

When integrating C++ with other languages, be aware of third-party libraries and tools that can simplify the process. Cocos2d-x offers built-in support for JavaScript and Lua scripting, but you may find external libraries or frameworks that provide additional features or ease of use.

Testing and Debugging

Thoroughly test and debug your integration code to ensure that C++ and the scripting language work seamlessly together. Pay attention to memory management and resource cleanup, as mixing languages can sometimes lead to memory leaks or resource conflicts.

By effectively integrating C++ with other languages in your Cocos2d-x project, you can harness the power and flexibility of multiple languages to create dynamic and feature-rich games while maintaining a high level of performance and stability.

9.5. Debugging and Profiling C++ Code

Debugging and profiling are essential processes in game development to identify and resolve issues, optimize performance, and ensure the quality of your Cocos2d-x game. In this section, we'll explore various debugging and profiling techniques and tools that can help you effectively debug and optimize your C++ code.

Debugging Tools

1. Logging: Logging is a fundamental tool for debugging. Cocos2d-x provides a built-in logging system through **CCLOG** ***and*** **CCLOGERROR*****, which allows you to print messages to the console.***

```
// Example of logging in Cocos2d-x

CCLOG("Debug message: %d", variable);

CCLOGERROR("Error message: %s", errorMessage.c_str());
```

2. Breakpoints: Debuggers like Visual Studio, Xcode, or CLion offer breakpoint functionality. You can set breakpoints in your C++ code to pause execution at specific points and inspect variables and call stacks.

3. Assertions: Assertions are checks that you can place in your code to validate assumptions. They are helpful for catching bugs during development.

```
// Example of using assertions in C++

assert(someCondition && "Assertion message");
```

4. Debug Builds: Compile your C++ code in debug mode to enable additional debugging information. Debug builds may run slower but provide more detailed error messages.

5. Integrated Development Environments (IDEs): IDEs like Visual Studio and Xcode come with debugging tools that allow you to step through code, examine variables, and inspect memory.

Profiling Tools

1. Cocos2d-x Profiler: Cocos2d-x offers built-in profiling tools that help you monitor aspects of your game's performance, such as frame rate, memory usage, and rendering time.

```
// Example of using Cocos2d-x's built-in profiling tools

cocos2d::Director::getInstance()->getScheduler()->schedule([](float dt) {

// Check memory usage and report it

}, this, 1.0f, false, "memory_profiler");
```

2. External Profilers: External profiling tools like Instruments (for iOS), Android Profiler (for Android), or Perf (for Linux) can provide in-depth performance analysis. These tools can help you identify bottlenecks in your code.

3. Memory Profilers: Memory profilers such as Valgrind (for Linux) or Memory Diagnostic Tools (for Windows) can help detect memory leaks and other memory-related issues.

4. Graphics Profilers: Graphics profiling tools like NVIDIA Nsight or Intel Graphics Performance Analyzers are useful for optimizing rendering performance and identifying GPU-related bottlenecks.

Optimization Techniques

1. Frame Rate Optimization: Maintain a consistent frame rate by optimizing rendering and logic code. Avoid unnecessary rendering calls and complex calculations within the game loop.

2. Memory Optimization: Regularly check for memory leaks and optimize memory usage. Profile your game to identify areas where memory can be optimized, such as texture management or object pooling.

3. Multithreading: Utilize multithreading to distribute computational tasks across multiple cores, improving performance. Be cautious when implementing multithreading to avoid race conditions and synchronization issues.

4. Data Structures: Use efficient data structures and algorithms to store and manipulate game data. Consider the performance characteristics of different data structures when choosing one for a specific purpose.

5. Asset Loading: Optimize asset loading by using texture atlases, asynchronous loading, and caching. Minimize the loading time during gameplay to provide a smoother player experience.

6. Batch Rendering: Use batch rendering to reduce the number of draw calls, especially for objects with the same texture or shader. Combining rendering calls can significantly improve performance.

7. Profiler Analysis: Regularly analyze profiler data to identify performance bottlenecks. Focus your optimization efforts on the most critical areas to achieve the best results.

Continuous Testing

Continuous testing is vital throughout the development process. Regularly test your game on target devices and simulate real-world scenarios to identify performance issues early. Use automated testing frameworks when possible to catch regressions.

Player Feedback

Player feedback is invaluable for optimizing your game. Pay attention to user reviews, ratings, and feedback on forums or social media. Player feedback can highlight issues you might have missed during testing.

By integrating debugging and profiling techniques into your Cocos2d-x game development workflow and following optimization best practices, you can create high-performance, stable games that provide an enjoyable experience for players. Debugging and profiling are ongoing processes that should be part of your development cycle from start to finish to ensure your game meets its performance and quality goals.

Chapter 10: Effective Game Testing Strategies

10.1. Unit Testing in Cocos2d-x

Unit testing is a crucial component of ensuring the reliability and correctness of your Cocos2d-x game code. Unit tests allow you to test individual units or components of your code in isolation to verify that they function as expected. In this section, we'll explore how to perform unit testing in Cocos2d-x and discuss best practices for effective testing.

Setting Up a Testing Environment

Before you can start writing unit tests for your Cocos2d-x game, you need to set up a testing environment. Cocos2d-x provides support for testing through various testing frameworks, including Google Test and Catch2. Here's how to set up Google Test for your Cocos2d-x project:

1. **Add the Testing Framework:** Download and integrate the testing framework into your project. You can typically do this by including the framework's header files and linking to its libraries.
2. **Configure the Build System:** Modify your project's build configuration to include the necessary flags and settings for the testing framework.
3. **Create Test Cases:** Write test cases by creating C++ test files that contain test functions. Each test function should verify a specific aspect of your code.
4. **Run Tests:** Use the testing framework's runner to execute your test cases. This will execute the tests and report the

results.

Writing Testable Code

To facilitate unit testing, it's essential to write code that is easily testable. Here are some best practices for writing testable Cocos2d-x code:

- **Separation of Concerns:** Divide your code into small, focused functions or classes that have well-defined responsibilities. This makes it easier to isolate and test individual units.

- **Dependency Injection:** Use dependency injection to provide dependencies (such as services or data) to your classes instead of hardcoding them. This allows you to substitute dependencies with mock objects during testing.

- **Avoid Global State:** Minimize the use of global variables and mutable global state in your code. Global state can make it challenging to isolate units for testing.

- **Mocking:** When testing a unit that depends on external resources (e.g., file system, network), consider using mocking frameworks to simulate these dependencies and control their behavior during tests.

Writing Test Cases

When writing test cases for your Cocos2d-x game, consider the following guidelines:

- **Test One Thing at a Time:** Each test case should focus on testing a single aspect of your code. Avoid combining multiple tests into one test case.

- **Use Descriptive Test Names:** Give your test cases and test functions descriptive names that indicate what aspect of your code they are testing.

- **Setup and Teardown:** Use setup and teardown methods provided by the testing framework to set up and clean up test fixtures. This ensures that each test starts in a known state.

- **Assertions:** Use assertions provided by the testing framework to check that the actual results of your code match the expected results. Common assertions include *EXPECT_EQ*, *EXPECT_TRUE*, and *EXPECT_FALSE*.

Running Tests

Running unit tests in a Cocos2d-x project typically involves invoking the testing framework's test runner, which executes your test cases and reports the results. The testing framework provides detailed information about which tests passed and which ones failed.

You can integrate test execution into your build process or use dedicated testing tools to run tests automatically whenever code changes are made.

Continuous Integration

To maintain a robust testing process, consider setting up continuous integration (CI) for your Cocos2d-x project. CI systems like Jenkins,

Travis CI, or GitHub Actions can automatically build your project and run unit tests whenever changes are pushed to your code repository. CI ensures that tests are regularly executed, helping catch regressions early.

Benefits of Unit Testing

Unit testing offers several benefits in Cocos2d-x game development:

- **Bug Prevention:** Writing tests forces you to think about how your code should behave and can help identify issues before they reach production.

- **Code Quality:** Testable code tends to be more modular and well-structured, making it easier to maintain and extend.

- **Regression Detection:** Unit tests can catch regressions (unexpected side effects) when you make changes to your code.

- **Documentation:** Tests serve as documentation for how your code is expected to work, making it easier for developers to understand and use your code.

- **Confidence:** Having a comprehensive suite of passing tests gives you confidence that your code works as intended.

In conclusion, unit testing is a vital practice in Cocos2d-x game development. It helps ensure the reliability and correctness of your code, reduces the risk of introducing bugs, and contributes to overall code quality. By following best practices and integrating testing into your development workflow, you can create more stable and robust Cocos2d-x games.

10.2. Integration and System Testing

Integration testing and system testing are essential phases in the game testing process that focus on evaluating the interactions between various components and the overall functionality of your Cocos2d-x game. In this section, we'll explore these testing phases, their goals, and best practices for conducting effective integration and system testing.

Integration Testing

Integration testing is the process of testing how individual components of your game work together when integrated. The primary goal of integration testing is to identify any issues that arise when combining different modules, systems, or services. This ensures that the integrated parts of your game function correctly as a whole.

Key points to consider for integration testing:

- **Test Component Interfaces:** Focus on testing the interactions and interfaces between different components, such as game systems, classes, and libraries.

- **Data Flow Testing:** Verify that data flows correctly between components, and that inputs and outputs are handled as expected.

- **Stress Testing:** Test how your game handles high loads, such as a large number of simultaneous players or complex in-game scenarios.

- **Dependency Testing:** Ensure that dependencies, including third-party libraries and plugins, are integrated correctly and don't cause conflicts.

- **Automated Testing:** Implement automated integration tests that can be run regularly during development to catch integration issues early.

System Testing

System testing is a higher-level testing phase that evaluates the entire game as a system. It focuses on verifying that your game functions correctly in its intended environment, including different platforms, devices, and network conditions. The goal of system testing is to assess the game's overall functionality and performance.

Considerations for system testing:

- **Platform Testing:** Test your game on various target platforms, including desktop, mobile devices, and consoles, to ensure compatibility and identify platform-specific issues.

- **Performance Testing:** Evaluate your game's performance under different conditions, such as low and high-end devices, various screen resolutions, and network connectivity scenarios.

- **Usability Testing:** Assess the user experience, including user interfaces, controls, and overall game flow, to ensure it meets player expectations.

- **Network Testing:** If your game has multiplayer or online features, conduct network testing to ensure smooth online gameplay and identify potential latency or synchronization issues.

- **Compatibility Testing:** Test your game on a range of devices, screen sizes, and operating system versions to ensure it works consistently across different configurations.

- **Security Testing:** Assess the security of your game to identify vulnerabilities that could be exploited by malicious users.

- **Localization Testing:** If your game supports multiple languages, verify that localization is accurate and culturally sensitive.

Test Environments

To conduct effective integration and system testing, it's essential to set up dedicated test environments that closely mimic the production environment. These test environments should replicate the target platforms, devices, and network conditions as closely as possible. Consider using virtual machines, emulators, or cloud-based testing services to create diverse testing environments.

Regression Testing

As your game evolves, it's crucial to continuously perform regression testing during integration and system testing. Regression tests ensure that new features or changes to your game do not introduce new bugs or break existing functionality. Automated regression testing can help streamline this process by running a suite of predefined tests whenever code changes are made.

Reporting and Documentation

During integration and system testing, maintain detailed test documentation and reports. This documentation should include the test plan, test cases, test results, and any issues or defects discovered during testing. A well-organized test suite and documentation provide valuable insights into the quality and reliability of your game and help track progress in resolving issues.

In conclusion, integration and system testing are critical phases in the game development process that ensure the proper functioning of your Cocos2d-x game when all components are combined. These testing phases help identify issues related to component interactions, platform compatibility, performance, and user experience. By following best practices and conducting thorough integration and system testing, you can deliver a polished and reliable game to players on various platforms and devices.

10.3. Performance Testing and Optimization

Performance testing is a critical aspect of game testing, especially for Cocos2d-x games, as it directly impacts the player's experience. In this section, we will explore performance testing strategies, tools, and optimization techniques to ensure that your game runs smoothly and efficiently.

The Importance of Performance Testing

Performance testing focuses on assessing the speed, responsiveness, and stability of your game under various conditions. It's essential because a poorly performing game can lead to player frustration, negative reviews, and a decrease in user retention. Here are key reasons why performance testing is crucial:

• **User Experience:** Players expect smooth gameplay with consistent frame rates and minimal lag. Performance issues can disrupt immersion and enjoyment.

• **Platform Compatibility:** Your game should run well on a wide range of devices and platforms. Performance testing helps identify issues specific to different hardware configurations.

• **Resource Efficiency:** Performance testing can highlight areas where your game may be using excessive memory, CPU, or GPU resources, leading to battery drain on mobile devices and potential overheating.

• **Network Performance:** For online games, network performance is crucial. Testing helps ensure that online gameplay is lag-free and responsive.

Performance Testing Strategies

To conduct effective performance testing for your Cocos2d-x game, consider the following strategies:

1. **Baseline Testing:** Establish performance benchmarks for your game on various devices and platforms. This provides a reference point for measuring improvements and identifying regressions.
2. **Load Testing:** Simulate high player loads to assess how your game handles stress. This includes testing multiplayer servers, if applicable, to ensure they can handle the expected number of concurrent players.
3. **Stress Testing:** Push your game to its limits by creating extreme scenarios, such as rendering a large number of objects or simulating complex AI. Stress testing helps

identify performance bottlenecks.

4. **Continuous Testing:** Integrate performance testing into your development pipeline. Run tests regularly as you make changes to catch performance regressions early in the development cycle.

Performance Testing Tools

Several tools can help with performance testing and profiling in Cocos2d-x:

- **Cocos2d-x Profiler:** Cocos2d-x includes built-in profiling tools that allow you to monitor performance metrics such as frame rate, memory usage, and rendering time. Use these tools to identify performance bottlenecks.

- **External Profilers:** Third-party profiling tools like Instruments (for iOS), Android Profiler (for Android), and graphics profilers for specific GPU vendors can provide detailed insights into your game's performance.

- **Network Simulation Tools:** If your game relies on network functionality, consider using network simulation tools to emulate various network conditions and test how your game performs under different scenarios.

- **Memory Profilers:** Tools like Valgrind (for Linux) or Memory Diagnostic Tools (for Windows) can help detect memory leaks and memory-related performance issues.

Optimization Techniques

Once you've identified performance bottlenecks, you can apply optimization techniques to improve your game's performance:

1. **Graphics Optimization:** Optimize rendering by reducing the number of draw calls, using sprite batching, and implementing level-of-detail (LOD) techniques.
2. **Asset Optimization:** Compress textures and audio files, use texture atlases, and implement asset streaming to reduce memory usage.
3. **Code Profiling:** Profile your code to identify CPU-intensive functions and optimize critical sections. Use profiling data to prioritize optimizations.
4. **Multithreading:** Implement multithreading to distribute CPU-intensive tasks across multiple cores, improving performance on multi-core devices.
5. **Memory Management:** Carefully manage memory by avoiding unnecessary allocations and releasing resources when they are no longer needed.
6. **Network Optimization:** Optimize network communication to reduce latency and improve the synchronization of multiplayer games.
7. **Battery Efficiency:** Implement power-saving techniques, such as reducing the frame rate during periods of inactivity, to improve battery life on mobile devices.

Performance Testing Metrics

When conducting performance testing, consider the following key metrics:

- **Frame Rate:** Measure and monitor the frame rate to ensure it meets your target frame rate (e.g., 60 frames per second). Consistent frame rates provide a smooth gameplay experience.

- **Memory Usage:** Track memory consumption to avoid excessive memory leaks and ensure your game remains within acceptable memory limits.

- **CPU Usage:** Monitor CPU utilization to identify CPU-bound areas of your game that may require optimization.

- **GPU Usage:** Profiling the GPU usage helps identify rendering bottlenecks and inefficiencies in your graphics pipeline.

- **Network Latency:** For online multiplayer games, measure network latency to ensure that interactions between players are responsive.

Conclusion

Performance testing and optimization are ongoing processes in Cocos2d-x game development. Regularly test your game's performance, profile critical code sections, and apply optimization techniques to create a responsive, efficient, and enjoyable gaming experience for your players. By prioritizing performance testing, you can deliver a high-quality game that runs smoothly across various devices and platforms.

10.4. Beta Testing and User Feedback

Beta testing is a crucial phase in the game development process that involves releasing your Cocos2d-x game to a limited audience of players before the official launch. This testing phase allows you to gather valuable user feedback, identify issues, and make necessary improvements to ensure a successful game launch. In this section, we'll explore the importance of beta testing, how to conduct it effectively, and ways to collect and utilize user feedback.

The Importance of Beta Testing

Beta testing serves several essential purposes:

1. **Bug Identification:** Beta testers help uncover bugs, glitches, and gameplay issues that might not have been detected during internal testing. Their diverse experiences can reveal unexpected problems.
2. **Game Balance:** Beta testing provides insights into game balance, helping you fine-tune difficulty levels, character abilities, and other gameplay elements.
3. **Performance Optimization:** Testing on a wide range of devices and configurations helps identify performance issues specific to different hardware.
4. **Usability and User Experience:** Beta testers provide feedback on the game's user interface, controls, and overall player experience, helping you make improvements.
5. **Stress Testing:** Beta tests simulate real-world player loads and help identify server-related issues for online multiplayer games.

Conducting Effective Beta Testing

Here are steps to conduct effective beta testing for your Cocos2d-x game:

1. **Select a Diverse Group of Testers:** Choose beta testers who represent your target audience, including different devices, platforms, and playstyles. This diversity helps uncover a wider range of issues.
2. **Define Clear Objectives:** Set specific goals for the beta

test, such as finding critical bugs, balancing gameplay, or assessing server stability for online games.

3. **Provide Clear Instructions:** Give testers clear guidelines on how to provide feedback, report issues, and use any testing tools or platforms you provide.
4. **Version Control:** Ensure that you can easily distribute new versions of the game to testers, incorporating bug fixes and improvements based on their feedback.
5. **Feedback Mechanisms:** Implement easy-to-use mechanisms for testers to report issues, provide feedback, and share their experiences. This can include in-game feedback forms or dedicated communication channels.
6. **Test Phases:** Consider running multiple beta test phases, starting with a closed beta with a small group of trusted testers and gradually expanding to an open beta with a wider audience.
7. **Incentives:** Provide incentives or rewards for participation to motivate testers to provide valuable feedback. This can include in-game items, early access, or other perks.

Collecting User Feedback

Effective feedback collection is crucial during beta testing. Here are methods to gather feedback from beta testers:

1. **Feedback Forms:** Implement in-game feedback forms that allow testers to report bugs, suggest improvements, or share their thoughts directly from within the game.
2. **Testing Forums:** Create dedicated testing forums or community platforms where testers can discuss issues, share experiences, and collaborate with other testers.
3. **Surveys:** Conduct surveys to gather structured feedback on specific aspects of the game, such as gameplay

mechanics, graphics, or user interface.

4. **Bug Tracking System:** Use a bug tracking system to manage and prioritize reported issues. Provide a system where testers can submit bug reports with detailed information.
5. **Player Data Analysis:** Analyze player data to gain insights into player behavior, progression, and pain points. Tools like analytics platforms can help you identify trends and areas for improvement.

Utilizing User Feedback

Once you've collected feedback from beta testers, it's essential to use this information effectively:

1. **Bug Fixes:** Prioritize and address critical bugs and gameplay issues identified by testers. Regularly release updated versions of the game with bug fixes.
2. **Game Balance:** Adjust game balance based on feedback to ensure a fair and enjoyable experience for all players.
3. **Usability Improvements:** Make user interface and control improvements based on user feedback to enhance the overall player experience.
4. **Performance Optimization:** Use feedback to identify and address performance-related issues on different devices and platforms.
5. **Community Engagement:** Foster a positive relationship with your beta testing community. Show appreciation for their efforts, acknowledge their contributions, and keep them informed about the game's progress.
6. **Transparency:** Communicate with beta testers transparently about your plans for addressing their feedback and any changes made as a result.

Conclusion

Beta testing and user feedback play a pivotal role in shaping the final quality of your Cocos2d-x game. By engaging a diverse group of testers, collecting feedback effectively, and using that feedback to make necessary improvements, you can increase the chances of a successful game launch. Beta testing not only helps you identify and resolve issues but also builds a community of engaged players who can become advocates for your game.

10.5. Continuous Integration and Delivery

Continuous Integration (CI) and Continuous Delivery (CD) are essential practices in modern game development that streamline the development process, improve code quality, and ensure a more reliable release pipeline. In this section, we'll explore the concepts of CI/CD, their benefits, and how to implement them effectively for your Cocos2d-x game.

Understanding CI/CD

- **Continuous Integration (CI):** CI is a development practice where developers regularly integrate their code changes into a shared repository. Each integration triggers an automated build and a series of tests to check the quality and correctness of the code. CI aims to catch integration issues early and maintain a consistent codebase.

- **Continuous Delivery (CD):** CD extends CI by automating the deployment and release process. With CD, changes that pass CI tests can be automatically deployed to various environments, including testing, staging, and production. CD ensures that code changes are always in a deployable state.

Benefits of CI/CD in Game Development

Implementing CI/CD practices in your Cocos2d-x game development process offers several advantages:

1. **Faster Development:** CI/CD streamlines the development cycle, enabling rapid iteration and faster feature delivery.
2. **Improved Code Quality:** Automated testing and code analysis tools identify and prevent the introduction of bugs and issues into the codebase.
3. **Reliable Builds:** CI ensures that your game builds successfully, reducing the likelihood of broken builds that can slow down development.
4. **Consistency:** CD ensures that builds are consistent across different environments, reducing the "it works on my machine" problem.
5. **Automated Testing:** Automated tests run consistently and catch regressions early, allowing for more confident code changes.
6. **Deployment Automation:** CD automates the deployment process, reducing the risk of human error during releases.

Implementing CI/CD for Cocos2d-x Games

Here are steps to implement CI/CD for your Cocos2d-x game:

1. **Version Control:** Use a version control system like Git to manage your game's source code. Hosting platforms like GitHub, GitLab, or Bitbucket provide features for collaboration and integration.

2. **Automated Builds:** Set up automated build pipelines using CI/CD services like Jenkins, Travis CI, CircleCI, or GitLab CI/CD. Configure these pipelines to build your game whenever changes are pushed to the repository.
3. **Testing Suites:** Implement comprehensive test suites that cover different aspects of your game, including unit tests, integration tests, performance tests, and UI tests.
4. **Code Analysis:** Use code analysis tools to enforce code quality standards and catch issues early. Tools like Clang Static Analyzer and cppcheck can help identify potential problems.
5. **Artifact Management:** Store build artifacts, such as executables and assets, in a central repository for easy access during deployment.
6. **Deployment Scripts:** Create scripts or configurations for deploying your game to different environments, such as local testing, staging, and production servers.
7. **Release Pipelines:** Set up release pipelines that automate the deployment of your game to various platforms and app stores. Ensure that the process includes testing on target devices.
8. **Feedback Loops:** Establish feedback loops to monitor the health of your CI/CD pipeline and receive notifications of failed builds or deployments.
9. **Security Scanning:** Implement security scanning tools to identify vulnerabilities in your game's dependencies and code.
10. **Rollback Mechanism:** Plan for rollbacks in case of deployment failures, ensuring that you can quickly revert to a stable version.

Continuous Deployment vs. Continuous Delivery

While Continuous Deployment and Continuous Delivery are related concepts, they differ in their approach to releasing new features and updates:

- **Continuous Delivery (CD):** In CD, changes are automatically deployed to a staging environment for testing and validation. Once the changes are approved, they can be manually or automatically promoted to production. CD ensures that code is always deployable but gives you control over when changes go live.

- **Continuous Deployment (CD):** In CD, every code change that passes tests is automatically deployed to production without manual intervention. This approach is common for web applications but may require more caution in game development, where player experience and compatibility are critical.

The choice between Continuous Delivery and Continuous Deployment depends on your game's requirements and the level of control you want over releases.

Conclusion

Implementing Continuous Integration and Continuous Delivery practices in your Cocos2d-x game development process can significantly improve the efficiency, quality, and reliability of your game releases. By automating builds, testing, and deployments, you can streamline development, catch issues early, and deliver a better gaming experience to your players. CI/CD is a valuable investment that can lead to more successful and sustainable game development projects.

Chapter 11: Deployment and Distribution

11.1 Packaging and Exporting Games

When it comes to releasing your game to the world, packaging and exporting it correctly is crucial. This section will guide you through the process of preparing your game for distribution across various platforms. Whether you're targeting mobile devices, desktop computers, or consoles, understanding the nuances of packaging and exporting is essential for a successful game launch.

Understanding Packaging

Packaging refers to the process of bundling all the necessary assets and code required to run your game into a deployable package. This package typically includes the game executable, assets such as graphics and audio files, configuration files, and any necessary libraries or dependencies. The exact contents of the package may vary depending on the target platform.

In Cocos2d-x, packaging involves creating platform-specific builds of your game. Each platform (e.g., iOS, Android, Windows, macOS) may have its own requirements and specifications for packaging. Here are some key considerations for packaging your game:

1. **Platform-Specific Requirements**: Different platforms have unique guidelines for packaging and distribution. It's essential to familiarize yourself with these requirements and follow them diligently.
2. **Build Configuration**: You may need to adjust your build configuration settings to ensure that the game is compiled

correctly for the target platform. This might include specifying the target architecture, compiler options, and more.

3. **Asset Management**: Ensure that all game assets are included in the package and are correctly referenced in your code. Pay attention to file paths and naming conventions that may differ across platforms.
4. **Permissions and Certificates**: Some platforms require specific permissions or certificates to run applications. For example, mobile platforms often require code-signing certificates to ensure the integrity of the app.
5. **Localization**: If your game supports multiple languages, consider how localization is handled during packaging. Different platforms may have specific mechanisms for managing localized content.
6. **Testing**: Thoroughly test your packaged game on the target platform to identify and address any issues that may arise during deployment.
7. **Versioning**: Implement a versioning system to keep track of different releases of your game. This helps users and platform stores identify which version they are downloading or purchasing.
8. **File Compression**: Compressing files within the package can reduce download sizes and improve installation times. Choose appropriate compression methods based on the platform's recommendations.

Let's dive into platform-specific considerations for packaging and exporting games in the following subsections.

Packaging for Mobile Platforms

When packaging your game for mobile platforms such as iOS and Android, you'll encounter platform-specific processes and requirements.

iOS Packaging

iOS game packaging involves several steps, including:

1. **Xcode Project Configuration**: Create and configure an Xcode project for your game. Ensure that the project settings match your game's requirements.
2. **Provisioning Profiles**: Obtain the necessary provisioning profiles for development and distribution. These profiles ensure that your app can be installed on iOS devices.
3. **Code Signing**: Sign your game's executable with a valid code signing certificate. This step is essential for app distribution on iOS.
4. **App Store Submission**: If you plan to release your game on the App Store, follow Apple's guidelines for app submission. Prepare promotional materials and store listings.

Android Packaging

Packaging for Android involves the following steps:

1. **Android Studio Configuration**: Set up your Android Studio project and configure the necessary build settings, such as the AndroidManifest.xml file.
2. **Keystore and Signing**: Create or obtain a keystore for

signing your APK (Android Package) files. Signing is crucial for app integrity and distribution.

3. **Google Play Console**: If you intend to publish your game on the Google Play Store, create a developer account and set up your game listing. Provide assets, descriptions, and pricing details.
4. **APK Generation**: Generate signed APK files for distribution. Different APKs may be required for various device configurations.

These are the basic steps for packaging games on mobile platforms, but each platform may have additional requirements and considerations. Be sure to refer to platform-specific documentation and guidelines for comprehensive instructions.

Exporting for Desktop Platforms

Packaging games for desktop platforms like Windows and macOS involves creating standalone executable files that users can install and run on their computers.

Windows Packaging

When targeting Windows, you'll typically create an installer package (e.g., .msi or .exe) that guides users through the installation process. Here's a high-level overview of the steps involved:

1. **Compile Executable**: Compile your game code into a Windows executable file. Ensure that any necessary libraries and assets are bundled.
2. **Installer Creation**: Use an installer creation tool to package your game into an installer package. You can customize installation options, create shortcuts, and

specify installation directories.

3. **Testing**: Thoroughly test the installer to ensure that it correctly installs the game on different versions of Windows.
4. **Distribution**: Distribute your game installer through various channels, such as your website, digital distribution platforms, or physical media.

macOS Packaging

Packaging games for macOS typically involves creating a macOS application bundle (.app) that users can drag into their Applications folder. Here are the key steps:

1. **Application Bundle**: Organize your game files and resources into a macOS application bundle structure. This includes creating a .app directory with the necessary components.
2. **Code Signing**: Sign your macOS application to ensure its integrity and compatibility with Gatekeeper, macOS's security feature.
3. **Testing**: Test the macOS application bundle on different versions of macOS to ensure compatibility and functionality.
4. **Distribution**: Distribute your macOS game through platforms like the Mac App Store, your website, or other distribution channels.

Conclusion

Packaging and exporting games is a critical step in the game development process. Whether you're targeting mobile devices or desktop computers, understanding the platform-specific requirements and following best practices for packaging and distribution is essential for reaching your audience and ensuring a smooth gaming experience. In the next sections of this chapter, we'll explore additional considerations, such as platform-specific deployment considerations, managing game updates, digital distribution platforms, and licensing and intellectual property.

Stay tuned for more insights on successfully deploying and distributing your game to players worldwide.

11.2 Platform-Specific Deployment Considerations

When deploying your game to various platforms, it's crucial to consider platform-specific deployment considerations. Each platform has its own ecosystem, requirements, and best practices for distribution. In this section, we'll explore some key aspects to keep in mind when deploying your game to different platforms.

Target Platforms and Ecosystems

Before diving into platform-specific considerations, you need to decide which platforms you want to target. Common platforms for game deployment include:

- **Mobile Platforms**: iOS, Android
- **Desktop Platforms**: Windows, macOS, Linux
- **Console Platforms**: PlayStation, Xbox, Nintendo Switch
- **Web**: Browser-based games

Each of these platforms has its own audience and ecosystem, so your choice should align with your target audience and game genre.

Platform-Specific Deployment Tools

To deploy your game on various platforms, you'll often need to use platform-specific deployment tools and services. Here are some examples:

- **Xcode (iOS/macOS)**: For iOS and macOS development and distribution, you'll use Xcode, Apple's integrated development environment.

- **Android Studio (Android)**: Android Studio is the official IDE for Android app development. It's used for building and deploying Android games.

- **Visual Studio (Windows)**: For Windows game development, Microsoft Visual Studio is a popular choice. It offers tools for building and packaging Windows applications.

- **Steamworks (Steam)**: If you plan to release your game on Steam, you'll use Steamworks, Valve's suite of tools and services for game developers. It provides features for DRM, multiplayer, and more.

- **Unity and Unreal Engine**: If you're using game engines like Unity or Unreal Engine, they provide built-in deployment tools for multiple platforms, simplifying the process.

Platform-Specific Requirements

Each platform has its own set of requirements for deploying and distributing games. Here are some platform-specific considerations:

App Store Guidelines

- **iOS App Store**: Apple has strict guidelines for apps published on the App Store. Your game must meet these guidelines to be accepted. Ensure that your game's content and functionality comply with Apple's policies.

- **Google Play Store**: Google Play also has guidelines for app submissions. Pay attention to content restrictions, in-app purchases, and user data handling.

Compatibility

- **Cross-Platform Compatibility**: Ensure that your game is compatible with various screen sizes, resolutions, and device configurations. Test your game on multiple devices to identify and fix compatibility issues.

- **Operating System Versions**: Be aware of the minimum operating system versions supported by each platform. Older devices may not run your game if it requires a newer OS version.

Performance Optimization

- **Performance Profiling**: Use platform-specific profiling tools to identify performance bottlenecks. Optimize your game to run smoothly on the target platform's hardware.

- **Resource Management**: Consider platform-specific resource limitations, such as memory and storage. Efficiently manage resources to prevent crashes or performance degradation.

Input Methods

- **Input Handling**: Different platforms may have varying input methods, such as touch screens, controllers, or keyboard and mouse. Implement appropriate input handling for each platform to ensure a seamless player experience.

Certification and Testing

- **Certification Processes**: Many platforms require games to go through a certification process before they can be published. This process involves testing and verifying that your game meets platform-specific requirements. Be prepared for certification timelines.

- **Beta Testing**: Some platforms offer beta testing programs that allow you to gather feedback from a select group of users before the official release. Consider participating in beta testing to identify and address issues.

Distribution Channels

- **Digital Distribution Platforms**: If you plan to distribute your game digitally, research and choose the appropriate digital distribution platforms. Examples include Steam, the App Store, Google Play, and Epic Games Store.

- **Retail Distribution**: If you intend to release physical copies of your game, coordinate with retail partners and distribution channels. This involves manufacturing physical copies and packaging.

Platform-Specific Updates

After your game is deployed, you'll need to manage updates and patches for each platform. Be aware of the platform-specific processes for releasing updates and ensure that players receive bug fixes and new features in a timely manner.

In conclusion, successfully deploying your game to different platforms involves careful planning, adherence to platform-specific guidelines, and optimization for each target environment. By understanding the nuances of each platform's ecosystem, you can reach a broader audience and provide an enjoyable gaming experience across various devices and platforms.

11.3 Managing Game Updates and Patches

Managing game updates and patches is a crucial aspect of maintaining a successful game after its initial release. Players expect ongoing support, bug fixes, and new content. In this section, we'll explore the best practices for effectively managing updates and patches for your game.

Continuous Improvement

Game development doesn't end with the initial release. It's an ongoing process of improvement and refinement. Here's why managing updates is essential:

1. **Bug Fixes**: Even with thorough testing, some bugs may slip through the cracks. Updates allow you to address these issues promptly.
2. **Balancing**: Player feedback may reveal balance issues or exploits. Updates enable you to tweak gameplay mechanics to create a more enjoyable experience.
3. **New Content**: To keep players engaged, consider adding new content such as levels, characters, items, or features. Regular updates can inject freshness into your game.
4. **Performance Optimization**: As new devices and platforms emerge, optimizing your game for improved performance becomes crucial. Updates can help you stay compatible with evolving hardware.
5. **Security**: Addressing security vulnerabilities is vital. Updates should include security patches to protect player data and maintain the integrity of your game.

Planning Updates

Effective update management starts with a well-defined plan. Consider the following aspects when planning updates:

Prioritization

Identify which issues or improvements should be prioritized. Critical bugs, performance bottlenecks, or game-breaking issues should be addressed first. Player feedback can help you determine priorities.

Patch Notes

Create detailed patch notes for each update. These notes inform players about changes, bug fixes, and new content. Clear communication builds trust with your player community.

Versioning

Implement a versioning system for your game. Use semantic versioning (e.g., MAJOR.MINOR.PATCH) to convey the significance of updates. For example, a "1.0.0" release signifies the initial version, while "1.1.0" indicates a minor update with new features or improvements.

Release Schedule

Define a release schedule based on your game's development capacity. Frequent updates can keep players engaged, but avoid overwhelming your team with too many updates too quickly.

Player Feedback

Listen to player feedback through forums, social media, or support channels. Player insights can help you identify issues and prioritize updates effectively.

Updating the Game

Once you've planned an update, it's time to execute the process. Here's a general workflow:

1. **Development**: Work on the update's features, bug fixes, or content additions. Use version control to manage code changes and collaborate with your team.
2. **Testing**: Thoroughly test the update internally to catch any regressions or new issues. Consider setting up a test environment that mimics your production environment.
3. **Beta Testing**: If possible, engage with a group of trusted players or testers to conduct beta testing. They can provide valuable feedback and help you identify issues before the public release.
4. **Staging Deployment**: Deploy the update to a staging environment that closely resembles the production environment. Verify that the update works as expected in this controlled setting.
5. **Production Deployment**: Once you're confident in the update's stability, deploy it to the production environment. Ensure that the update process is smooth and doesn't disrupt gameplay for existing players.
6. **Communication**: Inform players about the update through various channels, including in-game notifications, social media, and your website. Share detailed patch notes to keep players informed.
7. **Monitoring**: After the update is live, closely monitor the game for any unexpected issues or player feedback. Be prepared to address any critical issues quickly.
8. **Player Support**: Provide support channels for players to report issues or seek assistance. Promptly respond to player inquiries and issues.

Handling Rollbacks

Sometimes, updates may introduce unforeseen issues or negatively impact the player experience. In such cases, you should be prepared to perform a rollback, reverting the game to a previous stable version. Rollbacks should be executed with caution and clear communication to players.

Post-Update Analysis

After an update, it's essential to analyze its impact on the game and player engagement. Consider the following:

- **Player Feedback**: Collect feedback from players regarding the update's changes. This can inform future updates and improvements.

- **Metrics**: Analyze game metrics, such as player retention, user acquisition, and in-game purchases, to assess the update's impact on player behavior.

- **Bug Tracking**: Continue to monitor for any new issues introduced by the update and address them promptly.

- **Community Engagement**: Engage with your player community to acknowledge their feedback and demonstrate your commitment to improving the game.

Managing updates and patches is an ongoing process that requires careful planning, testing, and communication. By maintaining a proactive approach to update management, you can keep your game fresh, engaging, and responsive to player needs.

11.4 Digital Distribution Platforms

Digital distribution platforms have become a cornerstone of the modern gaming industry. These platforms provide a convenient and efficient way to distribute and sell your game to a global audience.

In this section, we'll explore digital distribution platforms, their benefits, and considerations for releasing your game on them.

What Are Digital Distribution Platforms?

Digital distribution platforms are online marketplaces where developers can publish, sell, and distribute their games directly to players. These platforms have gained immense popularity due to several advantages:

1. **Global Reach**: Digital platforms enable developers to reach players worldwide without the need for physical distribution channels.
2. **Accessibility**: Games are easily accessible for download or purchase, making it convenient for players to acquire new titles.
3. **Updates and Patches**: Developers can release updates, patches, and downloadable content (DLC) seamlessly through these platforms, keeping games up-to-date and engaging.
4. **Community and Social Features**: Platforms often offer community forums, reviews, and social interaction features that can help promote games and foster player engagement.
5. **Analytics and Insights**: Developers can access valuable data and analytics on player behavior, which can inform future updates and improvements.

Popular Digital Distribution Platforms

Several digital distribution platforms dominate the gaming market. Here are some of the most prominent ones:

1. Steam

- **Description**: Steam is one of the largest and most well-known digital distribution platforms for PC gaming. It offers a vast catalog of games, including indie titles and AAA releases.

- **Benefits**: Steam provides developers with access to a massive player base, extensive developer tools, and features like Steam Workshop for mod support.

- **Considerations**: Competition on Steam is fierce, and visibility can be a challenge. Developers should invest in marketing and community engagement.

2. Epic Games Store

- **Description**: The Epic Games Store is another major player in the digital distribution space. Known for its exclusivity deals and free game giveaways, it has quickly gained a substantial user base.

- **Benefits**: Epic Games Store offers developers a competitive revenue share model and support for cross-platform play.

- **Considerations**: The store has strict curation standards, and developers may need to negotiate exclusivity deals with Epic Games.

3. Apple App Store

- **Description**: The Apple App Store is a digital distribution platform for iOS and macOS apps, including mobile games.

- **Benefits**: It provides access to a massive user base of Apple device owners and offers in-app purchases and subscriptions for monetization.

- **Considerations**: Developers must adhere to Apple's guidelines and policies, and a revenue share applies to in-app purchases and subscriptions.

4. Google Play Store

- **Description**: Google Play is the counterpart to the Apple App Store, serving Android users.

- **Benefits**: It offers a broad audience of Android device users, and developers can monetize through ads, in-app purchases, and subscriptions.

- **Considerations**: Like Apple, Google enforces guidelines and policies for apps on its platform, and a revenue share applies to certain transactions.

5. Xbox Live Marketplace and PlayStation Store

- **Description**: These platforms cater to console gaming, with Xbox Live Marketplace for Xbox consoles and the PlayStation Store for PlayStation consoles.

• **Benefits**: Access to console gaming audiences, online multiplayer capabilities, and a trusted payment ecosystem.

• **Considerations**: Developers need to meet platform-specific requirements and may need partnerships with Microsoft or Sony.

Publishing on Digital Distribution Platforms

Publishing your game on a digital distribution platform involves several steps:

1. **Developer Account**: Create a developer account on the platform of your choice. This often involves providing necessary information and agreeing to terms and conditions.
2. **Game Submission**: Prepare your game build according to platform-specific requirements. This includes packaging, code signing, and compliance with guidelines.
3. **Content Review**: Platforms typically review submitted games for quality, content, and compliance with their policies. Be prepared for this evaluation process.
4. **Pricing and Monetization**: Set pricing and choose monetization methods, such as selling the game, in-app purchases, or ads.
5. **Marketing and Promotion**: Develop a marketing strategy to promote your game on the platform. Utilize platform-specific tools and features for visibility.
6. **Launch and Updates**: Once approved, launch your game. Regularly release updates and engage with the player community to maintain interest.

Key Considerations

While digital distribution platforms offer numerous advantages, developers should also be aware of the challenges:

- **Competition**: The sheer volume of games available can make it challenging to stand out. Effective marketing and community engagement are crucial.

- **Revenue Share**: Most platforms take a percentage of revenue from game sales. Be aware of these fees and plan your pricing strategy accordingly.

- **Policies and Guidelines**: Each platform has its own rules and guidelines. Violations can lead to consequences, including removal of your game from the platform.

- **Customer Support**: Be prepared to provide customer support for your game. Respond to player inquiries and address issues promptly.

- **Platform-Specific Features**: Utilize platform-specific features and tools to enhance your game's visibility and engagement.

Digital distribution platforms provide an excellent opportunity to showcase and monetize your game. By understanding the unique aspects of each platform and tailoring your approach, you can maximize your game's success in the digital marketplace.

11.5 Licensing and Intellectual Property

Licensing and intellectual property (IP) considerations are fundamental aspects of game development, especially when distributing games on digital platforms. In this section, we'll explore the importance of licensing, protecting your intellectual property, and navigating legal aspects related to game development.

Understanding Licensing

Licensing is a legal agreement that defines how your game can be used, distributed, and accessed by others. It establishes the terms and conditions under which players, distributors, and other parties can interact with your game. Here are some key aspects of licensing in game development:

End-User License Agreements (EULAs)

An EULA is a contract between you (the developer or publisher) and the end user (the player). It outlines the rights and restrictions associated with using your game. Common EULA provisions include:

- **License Grant**: Specify the rights granted to the player, such as the right to install and play the game.

- **Restrictions**: Detail the limitations on the player's use, such as prohibiting reverse engineering, modifying the game, or using it for commercial purposes.

- **Termination**: Describe the conditions under which the license can be terminated, such as violating the EULA or engaging in prohibited activities.

- **Warranty and Liability**: Clarify the extent of your responsibility for game defects and limitations on liability.

- **Dispute Resolution**: Define the procedures for resolving disputes, which may include arbitration or litigation.

Digital Distribution Platforms

When distributing your game through platforms like Steam, the platform provider may have its own licensing terms. These terms may impact how your game is sold and used on the platform. Ensure that your EULA aligns with the platform's terms and doesn't violate them.

Protecting Your Intellectual Property

Intellectual property encompasses the unique creations and assets in your game, such as characters, artwork, music, and code. Protecting your IP is essential to prevent unauthorized use and potential legal disputes. Here are methods for safeguarding your intellectual property:

Copyright

Copyright automatically protects original creative works, including your game and its components. As the copyright holder, you have exclusive rights to reproduce, distribute, and adapt your game. To strengthen copyright protection:

- Include copyright notices in your game's credits and documentation.

- Register your copyright with the appropriate government agency, which may provide additional legal benefits.

Trademarks

Trademarks protect distinctive names, logos, and symbols associated with your game. Registering trademarks for your game's branding can prevent others from using similar marks. This includes the game's title, logo, and any recognizable characters or symbols.

Licensing Agreements

When collaborating with others, such as artists, composers, or writers, create clear licensing agreements that specify the terms of their contributions and the rights you acquire. This prevents disputes over ownership and usage rights.

Non-Disclosure Agreements (NDAs)

When sharing confidential information about your game's development, consider using NDAs to protect sensitive information. NDAs legally bind recipients to maintain confidentiality.

Patents

While less common in game development, patents can protect unique gameplay mechanics or technical innovations. Consult with a legal expert to determine if patent protection is relevant to your game.

Dealing with Infringements

If you discover that someone is infringing on your intellectual property, take appropriate action to protect your rights. This may involve sending cease-and-desist letters, filing a lawsuit, or pursuing alternative dispute resolution methods.

Legal Consultation

Seek legal counsel from professionals experienced in intellectual property and entertainment law. They can provide guidance on protecting your rights, drafting contracts, and addressing legal issues that may arise during game development and distribution.

In conclusion, licensing and intellectual property protection are vital aspects of game development, especially when distributing games on digital platforms. Understanding the legal framework, creating clear agreements, and seeking legal counsel can help you safeguard your intellectual property and navigate legal complexities in the gaming industry.

Chapter 12: Marketing and Monetization

12.1 Marketing Strategies for Indie Developers

Marketing is a critical aspect of game development, and for indie developers, it's often the key to success. Effective marketing can help you reach a wider audience, generate buzz, and drive sales. In this section, we'll explore marketing strategies specifically tailored for indie game developers.

Define Your Unique Selling Proposition (USP)

Every game needs a unique selling proposition (USP) that sets it apart from the competition. As an indie developer, you have the creative freedom to explore unique ideas and niches. Consider the following when defining your USP:

- **Gameplay Innovation**: Does your game offer innovative gameplay mechanics or a fresh twist on a genre?

- **Artistic Style**: Is your game's art style distinctive and visually appealing?

- **Storytelling**: Does your game have a compelling narrative or unique storytelling approach?

- **Mechanical Depth**: Does your game offer depth and complexity that hardcore gamers will appreciate?

- **Accessibility**: Is your game designed to be accessible and enjoyable for a wide range of players?

Identifying your USP is crucial because it forms the foundation of your marketing efforts. It's what makes your game stand out in a crowded market.

Build an Engaging Online Presence

Establishing a strong online presence is essential for indie developers. Here's how to do it effectively:

Create a Website

Set up a professional website for your game. It should showcase gameplay videos, screenshots, developer blogs, and contact information. A well-designed website builds credibility.

Utilize Social Media

Engage with your audience on social media platforms like Twitter, Facebook, Instagram, and TikTok. Share development updates, behind-the-scenes content, and interact with followers.

Developer Blogs and Dev Diaries

Regularly publish developer blogs and dev diaries on your website or platforms like Medium. These provide insights into your development process, creating a sense of transparency and community.

Email Marketing

Build an email list of interested players and fans. Send regular newsletters with updates, announcements, and exclusive content. Email marketing can be a powerful tool for building anticipation.

Create a Captivating Trailer

A well-crafted game trailer is a marketing cornerstone. It's often the first impression players have of your game. When creating a trailer:

- Keep it concise and engaging, aiming for a length of 1-2 minutes.
- Highlight your game's unique features and USP.
- Use high-quality gameplay footage and capture the essence of the game.
- Incorporate music and sound effects that complement the visuals.
- Include call-to-action elements, such as links to your website or social media.

Build Hype with Teasers and Demos

Generate excitement around your game through teasers and demos. Teasers are short video snippets that offer a sneak peek of your game's atmosphere or story. Demos provide players with a hands-on experience. Utilize platforms like Steam, itch.io, and Game Jolt to distribute demos to a broad audience.

Engage with Gaming Communities

Participate in gaming communities and forums relevant to your game's genre. Engage in discussions, share your development journey, and seek feedback. Platforms like Reddit, Discord, and indie game forums can be valuable for connecting with potential players.

Collaborate and Cross-Promote

Consider collaborating with other indie developers or content creators who align with your game's genre or style. Cross-promotion can help you reach each other's audiences and expand your reach.

Leverage Crowdfunding and Early Access

Crowdfunding platforms like Kickstarter and Indiegogo can provide financial support for your game while building a community of backers. Early access on platforms like Steam allows players to play and provide feedback during development, creating a sense of ownership and investment in your game's success.

Prepare for Launch

As your game's launch date approaches, ensure you have a well-defined marketing plan in place. This plan should include:

- A specific launch date and time.
- A coordinated marketing blitz, including social media posts, emails to your list, and press releases.
- A strategy for engaging with gaming influencers and reviewers to secure coverage.

- A contingency plan for addressing unexpected issues or delays.

Remember that marketing is an ongoing effort. Continue to engage with your audience post-launch, provide updates and patches, and maintain a vibrant online presence to nurture your game's community.

In conclusion, indie developers face unique challenges and opportunities when it comes to marketing. By defining your game's USP, building an engaging online presence, and utilizing various promotional strategies, you can increase your game's visibility and chances of success in the competitive gaming industry.

12.2 Monetization Models in Game Development

Monetization is a crucial aspect of game development that determines how you generate revenue from your game. There are various monetization models available to developers, each with its advantages and considerations. In this section, we'll explore common monetization models in game development.

1. Premium/Paid Games

In the premium or paid model, players purchase the game upfront, typically through a one-time payment. This model is straightforward and provides an immediate source of revenue. Here are some key points to consider:

- **Advantages**: Premium games offer a clear revenue stream and often provide a higher income per player compared to free-to-play games. They can also avoid some of the ethical concerns associated with other monetization models.

- **Considerations**: Success in the premium model depends on creating a game that justifies the upfront cost. Players expect a high-quality experience with no hidden fees. Marketing and pricing strategies are critical to attracting players.

2. Free-to-Play (F2P) with In-App Purchases (IAP)

In the F2P model, the game is free to download and play, but revenue is generated through in-app purchases. Players can buy virtual items, currency, power-ups, or other enhancements. Key points to consider:

- **Advantages**: F2P games have a low barrier to entry, attracting a large player base. The model encourages ongoing player engagement and spending over time.

- **Considerations**: Designing fair and balanced monetization systems is crucial to avoid pay-to-win scenarios or alienating non-paying players. Ethical implementation is essential to maintain player trust.

3. Ads and Ad-Supported Games

Ad-supported games generate revenue through in-game advertisements. Players see ads during gameplay, typically in the form of banners, interstitials, rewarded videos, or native ads. Consider the following:

- **Advantages**: Ads provide a continuous stream of income and can be implemented in free games without requiring IAPs. Rewarded ads offer players incentives for viewing.

- **Considerations**: Balancing ad frequency and player experience is crucial. Overloading with ads can drive players away. Ads should be non-intrusive and offer value to players.

4. Subscription Models

Subscription models require players to pay a recurring fee to access the game or premium features. These models often offer exclusive content or benefits to subscribers. Here's what to keep in mind:

- **Advantages**: Subscriptions provide predictable, recurring revenue. They can foster player loyalty and ongoing engagement.

- **Considerations**: Offering enough value to justify the subscription cost is essential. Players must see the benefits of subscribing, such as exclusive content or ad-free gameplay.

5. DLCs and Expansions

Downloadable content (DLC) and expansions are additional game content that players can purchase after the initial game release. These may include new levels, characters, storylines, or cosmetic items. Consider:

- **Advantages**: DLCs and expansions can extend the game's lifespan and generate additional revenue from existing players.

- **Considerations**: Balancing the pricing of DLCs and ensuring they complement the base game without feeling like cut content is crucial. Communication with the player community about upcoming DLC is essential.

6. Loot Boxes and Gacha Mechanics

Loot boxes and gacha mechanics involve players spending money to obtain randomized virtual items or characters. This model has faced criticism and regulatory scrutiny due to potential gambling-like elements. Consider:

- **Advantages**: Loot boxes can create a sense of excitement and engagement, driving player spending.

- **Considerations**: Ethical implementation is critical. Developers must disclose odds, avoid predatory practices, and be transparent about the potential costs associated with these mechanics.

7. Pay-Per-Play and Token Systems

Some games use a pay-per-play or token system, where players purchase tokens or energy to access gameplay sessions. This model is common in mobile puzzle games. Key points include:

- **Advantages**: It can encourage players to spend more time in the game while providing revenue opportunities.

- **Considerations**: Balancing token costs and session lengths is crucial to avoid frustration. Players should feel that their spending is providing fair value.

8. Crowdfunding and Donations

Crowdfunding platforms like Kickstarter allow developers to secure funding directly from players interested in a game's concept. This model can be suitable for indie developers seeking initial support. Consider:

- **Advantages**: Crowdfunding can provide upfront capital without sacrificing creative control to publishers.

- **Considerations**: Meeting backer expectations, managing rewards, and delivering on promises are essential for a successful crowdfunding campaign.

9. Sponsorships and Partnerships

Some games secure sponsorships or partnerships with brands, advertisers, or influencers. These collaborations may involve in-game branding or sponsored content.

- **Advantages**: Sponsorships can provide additional revenue streams and exposure to a broader audience.

- **Considerations**: Ensure that partnerships align with your game's values and target audience. Maintain transparency with players about sponsored content.

Choosing the Right Monetization Model

Selecting the appropriate monetization model depends on your game's genre, target audience, and design. Consider player satisfaction, ethical considerations, and long-term sustainability when deciding on a model. It's also essential to remain adaptable and open to adjusting your monetization strategy based on player feedback and industry trends.

In conclusion, game monetization models are diverse, and each has its advantages and challenges. Successful monetization requires a deep understanding of your game's audience, ethical considerations, and a commitment to delivering value to players while generating revenue to support ongoing development.

12.3 Implementing In-App Purchases

In-app purchases (IAPs) are a widely used monetization strategy in mobile games and apps. They allow developers to offer additional content, features, or virtual items for sale within a free or paid app. When implementing IAPs, it's essential to strike a balance between generating revenue and providing value to players. In this section, we'll explore the process of implementing in-app purchases in your game.

1. Platform Integration

To implement IAPs, you'll need to integrate the platform's IAP system into your game. The major platforms, such as iOS (App Store) and Android (Google Play), provide SDKs and documentation for this purpose. Here's a high-level overview of the process:

- **Developer Account**: Set up a developer account on the platform's developer portal.
- **App Registration**: Register your app and configure IAP settings, including product names, descriptions, prices, and regions where they are available.
- **SDK Integration**: Integrate the platform's IAP SDK into your game's codebase. This involves initializing the SDK, handling purchase requests, and verifying receipts.

- **Testing**: Test IAPs thoroughly in sandbox or test environments provided by the platform. Ensure that purchases are processed correctly and that players receive the expected items or features.

2. Types of In-App Purchases

There are several common types of in-app purchases you can implement in your game:

- **Consumable**: These are items or currency that players can purchase and use, but they are depleted after use. Examples include health potions, virtual coins, or energy refills.

- **Non-Consumable**: Non-consumable IAPs are permanent and typically unlock a feature or content in the game. For example, a level pack or an ad-free version of the game.

- **Subscriptions**: Subscriptions grant access to premium features or content for a limited time, usually on a recurring basis (e.g., monthly or annually). This model is common for apps with ongoing services.

- **DLC (Downloadable Content)**: DLC IAPs provide players with additional content, such as new levels, characters, or storylines.

- **Cosmetic Items**: Cosmetic IAPs offer purely visual enhancements, such as skins, costumes, or avatar customization options. These items don't affect gameplay.

3. Pricing and Value Proposition

Determining the pricing of your in-app purchases is a crucial decision. Consider the following factors:

- **Player Perception**: Ensure that the price aligns with the perceived value of the item or feature. Players should feel that they are getting their money's worth.

- **Competitive Analysis**: Research similar games and their IAP pricing to gauge market standards. Don't price your items significantly higher unless they offer substantial value.

- **Sales and Promotions**: Offer occasional discounts or promotions to incentivize purchases and attract budget-conscious players.

- **Bundle Offers**: Consider bundling related items or content at a discounted price. Bundles can encourage players to spend more.

- **Localization**: Adjust pricing based on the region to accommodate different economic conditions and currencies.

4. User Experience

A seamless and user-friendly IAP experience is crucial for player satisfaction and monetization success:

- **Clarity**: Clearly present IAP options to players. Use concise and informative descriptions. Avoid misleading or deceptive practices.

- **Purchase Flow**: Make the purchase process simple and intuitive. Minimize the number of clicks or steps required to complete a purchase.

- **Confirmation**: Always confirm purchases with a confirmation dialog to prevent accidental or unauthorized transactions.

- **Refunds and Customer Support**: Provide accessible customer support for inquiries, refunds, or issues related to IAPs. Follow platform guidelines for handling refunds.

5. Analytics and A/B Testing

Implement analytics to track the performance of your IAPs. Analyze data on conversion rates, revenue per user, and player behavior to make informed decisions. Consider A/B testing different pricing strategies, bundles, or promotional offers to optimize your monetization approach.

6. Fairness and Ethical Considerations

Maintaining player trust is paramount. Ensure that your IAP system is fair and transparent. Avoid pay-to-win mechanics that provide unfair advantages to paying players. Clearly communicate the benefits of IAPs and their impact on gameplay.

7. Regular Updates and Content

To sustain monetization through IAPs, provide a consistent stream of updates, content, and reasons for players to engage with your game. New levels, characters, events, or cosmetic items can incentivize continued spending.

8. Compliance and Platform Guidelines

Adhere to the platform's guidelines and policies regarding IAPs, including pricing transparency, disclosure of subscription terms, and handling of refunds. Non-compliance can lead to penalties or removal from app stores.

In summary, implementing in-app purchases requires careful planning, integration, and consideration of player value and fairness. When executed ethically and transparently, IAPs can be an effective monetization strategy for your mobile game, providing a revenue stream while enhancing the player experience.

12.4 Analytics and Player Engagement

Analytics play a crucial role in game development and monetization. They provide valuable insights into player behavior, preferences, and engagement patterns. By analyzing this data, developers can make informed decisions to improve their games and enhance monetization strategies. In this section, we'll explore the significance of analytics and strategies for fostering player engagement.

The Importance of Analytics

Analytics help answer fundamental questions about your game and its players:

- **Player Retention**: Are players returning to the game after the initial install, and if not, why?
- **Monetization**: Which in-game purchases or ads are generating the most revenue, and how can this be optimized?

• **Gameplay Patterns**: How are players progressing through the game, and where do they encounter challenges or drop out?

• **Player Segmentation**: Are there distinct player segments with different behaviors and preferences?

• **Bug Identification**: Are there recurring bugs or issues that need addressing?

Key Metrics to Track

Several key metrics are essential for understanding player behavior and engagement:

1. **Daily Active Users (DAU)**: The number of unique players who engage with the game on a daily basis. DAU is a crucial indicator of player retention.
2. **Monthly Active Users (MAU)**: Similar to DAU, but measured on a monthly basis. MAU provides insights into long-term player engagement.
3. **Player Churn Rate**: The percentage of players who stop playing the game over a specific period. High churn rates may indicate problems with player retention.
4. **Conversion Rate**: The percentage of players who make in-app purchases or engage with ads. A high conversion rate indicates effective monetization.
5. **Average Revenue Per User (ARPU)**: The average revenue generated from each player. ARPU helps evaluate the game's overall monetization performance.
6. **Session Length**: The average duration of a player's gaming session. Longer sessions may indicate high player engagement.

7. **Retention Rate**: The percentage of players who continue playing the game over time. Retention rate measures player loyalty.
8. **Funnel Analysis**: Tracking how players move through specific stages of the game, such as onboarding, completing tutorials, or making a purchase.
9. **Abandoned Carts**: In the context of in-app purchases, this metric measures how many players add items to their cart but don't complete the purchase.

Implementing Analytics

To gather meaningful data, you'll need to implement analytics tools into your game. Popular analytics platforms for game development include Firebase Analytics, GameAnalytics, and Unity Analytics. Here's how to integrate analytics effectively:

1. **Choose the Right Tools**: Select an analytics platform that suits your game's development environment and requirements.
2. **Instrumentation**: Integrate the analytics SDK or library into your game code. Set up event tracking for relevant actions, such as level completion, in-app purchases, or tutorial progress.
3. **User Identification**: Implement user identification to track individual player behavior across sessions and devices.
4. **Testing**: Test the analytics implementation thoroughly to ensure it accurately captures events and data. Use testing or sandbox environments provided by the analytics platform.
5. **Privacy Compliance**: Ensure that your analytics implementation complies with privacy regulations, such as GDPR or COPPA. Inform players about data collection and obtain their consent where necessary.

6. **Data Visualization**: Use the analytics platform's dashboard or reporting tools to visualize and analyze the collected data. Look for trends, anomalies, and opportunities for improvement.

Player Engagement Strategies

Analyzing player engagement data is valuable, but it's equally important to take actionable steps to enhance player engagement. Here are some strategies:

1. **Regular Updates**: Continuously add new content, features, or events to keep players engaged and excited.
2. **Community Engagement**: Foster a strong community around your game through social media, forums, and in-game chat. Engage with players, listen to feedback, and respond to their needs.
3. **Rewards and Incentives**: Offer rewards, achievements, or daily bonuses to incentivize players to return to the game.
4. **Live Events**: Host time-limited events, challenges, or tournaments that encourage active participation.
5. **Personalization**: Use player data to personalize the gaming experience, such as suggesting content based on player preferences.
6. **Feedback Loops**: Implement feedback loops that allow players to provide input or report issues directly within the game.
7. **Social Features**: Incorporate social sharing, multiplayer modes, or collaborative gameplay to encourage players to involve friends.
8. **Optimize Monetization**: Use analytics to optimize the placement and frequency of ads or in-app purchase offers, ensuring they enhance the player experience.

Ethical Considerations

While analytics are powerful tools for understanding and improving player engagement, it's essential to use them ethically. Avoid invasive data collection, respect player privacy, and be transparent about the information you gather. Additionally, prioritize the player experience over excessive monetization tactics that may alienate or frustrate players.

In conclusion, analytics and player engagement are intertwined aspects of successful game development and monetization. By implementing analytics effectively, tracking key metrics, and using data to inform your decisions, you can create a more engaging gaming experience and optimize your monetization strategies while maintaining ethical standards.

12.5 Community Building and Management

Building and managing a community around your game is a vital aspect of game development, especially in the age of online and social gaming. A strong and engaged community can lead to increased player retention, valuable feedback, and word-of-mouth marketing. In this section, we'll explore strategies for community building and effective community management.

Why Build a Community?

A thriving community benefits both developers and players:

- **Player Retention**: Engaged communities help retain players for longer periods, reducing churn.

- **Feedback and Testing**: Communities provide a valuable source of feedback during development, helping identify and address issues.

- **Word-of-Mouth Marketing**: Happy community members are more likely to recommend your game to others.

- **Content Creation**: Enthusiastic community members may create content, such as fan art, mods, or guides, that extends the life of your game.

- **Brand Loyalty**: A strong community fosters brand loyalty, which can lead to continued support for your games and future projects.

Building Your Community

Here are strategies for building a strong gaming community:

1. **Social Media Presence**: Create and maintain active social media profiles for your game on platforms like Twitter, Facebook, Instagram, and TikTok. Share development updates, engage with players, and use relevant hashtags to reach a wider audience.
2. **Official Forums and Websites**: Set up official forums or a website where players can discuss the game, report issues, and provide feedback. Ensure that you have moderators to maintain a positive atmosphere.
3. **Developer Blogs and Dev Diaries**: Publish regular developer blogs and dev diaries that provide insights into your development process. Share behind-the-scenes stories, challenges, and milestones to connect with players.
4. **Email Newsletters**: Collect email addresses from

interested players and send newsletters with updates, announcements, and exclusive content. Email marketing can be a powerful tool for community engagement.

5. **Streaming and Let's Play**: Encourage streamers and content creators to play your game on platforms like Twitch and YouTube. Provide review copies or keys to facilitate coverage.
6. **Community Events**: Organize in-game events, contests, or tournaments to bring players together and foster a sense of community. Prizes or recognition for winners can incentivize participation.
7. **Feedback Channels**: Create dedicated channels for feedback and bug reporting within your community spaces. Actively listen to player concerns and acknowledge their input.

Effective Community Management

Once you've built a community, effective management is crucial to maintaining a positive and productive environment:

1. **Moderation**: Appoint moderators or community managers to enforce community guidelines and ensure respectful interactions. Address toxic behavior promptly.
2. **Transparency**: Be transparent about development progress, upcoming changes, and known issues. Honest communication builds trust.
3. **Engagement**: Actively engage with the community by responding to comments, participating in discussions, and acknowledging fan creations.
4. **Feedback Incorporation**: Show that player feedback matters by incorporating valuable suggestions and addressing legitimate concerns in updates.

5. **Regular Updates**: Maintain a regular update schedule to keep players engaged and excited about the game's future.
6. **Community Building Tools**: Consider using community-building tools like Discord servers, subreddit communities, or dedicated fan websites to provide spaces for players to connect.
7. **Events and Contests**: Continuously host community events, contests, or challenges to maintain activity and excitement.
8. **Treat All Players Equally**: Avoid showing favoritism or bias toward specific players or groups within the community.
9. **Conflict Resolution**: Develop protocols for handling conflicts and disputes within the community, including appeals processes.
10. **Feedback Loops**: Establish clear channels for players to provide feedback, whether through surveys, in-game feedback forms, or forums.

Ethical Considerations

While building and managing a community, it's essential to maintain ethical standards:

- **Privacy**: Respect player privacy and data protection regulations. Clearly communicate data handling practices.

- **Inclusivity**: Foster an inclusive community that welcomes players of all backgrounds and identities. Address harassment and discrimination promptly.

- **Transparency**: Be transparent about your affiliations, sponsorships, and conflicts of interest when interacting with the community.

- **Fairness**: Treat all community members fairly and avoid bias or favoritism.

- **Respect**: Encourage respectful and constructive discussions while discouraging hate speech, harassment, or toxicity.

In conclusion, community building and management are integral to the success of modern game development. A thriving community can lead to increased player engagement, retention, and positive word-of-mouth marketing. By following ethical guidelines, actively engaging with players, and maintaining transparent communication, you can build a strong and loyal gaming community around your game.

Chapter 13: Advanced Physics and Collision Detection

13.1 Complex Physics Simulations

Physics simulations are a fundamental component of many games, providing realistic movement, collision detection, and interactions between objects. In advanced game development, you may encounter scenarios where complex physics simulations are required to achieve specific gameplay mechanics or visual effects. In this section, we will delve into the realm of complex physics simulations and explore techniques to implement them effectively.

Understanding Complex Physics Simulations

Complex physics simulations involve more than basic rigid body dynamics or simple collision detection. They often require handling intricate physical behaviors such as fluid dynamics, soft-body deformation, or advanced vehicle physics. Here are some common scenarios where complex physics simulations are applied:

1. **Fluid and Liquid Simulation**: Games with underwater environments, fluid puzzles, or realistic water dynamics may require fluid simulations. Techniques like Smoothed Particle Hydrodynamics (SPH) or Navier-Stokes equations can simulate fluid behavior.
2. **Soft-Body Physics**: Soft-body simulations are used to model deformable objects like cloth, rubber, or organic materials. These simulations involve complex mathematical models and physics equations.
3. **Advanced Vehicle Physics**: Racing games or vehicle simulations often demand realistic vehicle physics. This

includes simulating tire friction, suspension dynamics, and aerodynamics.

4. **Ragdoll Physics**: To achieve lifelike character animations and reactions to in-game events, ragdoll physics simulate the dynamics of a character's limbs and body.

Implementing Complex Physics Simulations

Implementing complex physics simulations requires a solid understanding of physics principles and mathematical modeling. Here are steps to get started:

1. **Physics Engine Selection**: Choose a physics engine or library that supports the type of simulation you need. Popular options include NVIDIA PhysX, Bullet Physics, and open-source libraries.
2. **Mathematical Modeling**: Develop or adapt mathematical models that describe the behavior of the physical system you want to simulate. This may involve differential equations, numerical methods, or custom algorithms.
3. **Integration with Game Logic**: Integrate the physics simulation seamlessly with your game logic. Ensure that the simulation updates in sync with the game's frame rate.
4. **Collision Detection**: Implement precise collision detection algorithms suitable for your simulation type. This may involve techniques like bounding volume hierarchies (BVH), spatial partitioning, or custom collision detection methods.
5. **Realistic Materials and Parameters**: Fine-tune material properties like friction, elasticity, and mass to match the desired physical behavior. Experimentation and testing are crucial for achieving realism.
6. **Optimization**: Complex physics simulations can be

computationally intensive. Implement optimization techniques such as multithreading, culling, and spatial partitioning to maintain performance.

7. **Debugging and Visualization**: Create debugging tools and visualizations to help understand and fine-tune the simulation. Tools for visualizing physics properties and collision shapes can be invaluable.

Case Studies

Let's explore a few case studies of complex physics simulations:

1. Fluid Dynamics in an Underwater Game

In an underwater adventure game, you need to simulate realistic fluid dynamics to create convincing underwater environments. Smoothed Particle Hydrodynamics (SPH) can be employed to model water behavior accurately. SPH involves approximating fluid properties at discrete particles and applying forces like pressure, viscosity, and surface tension to simulate fluid movement.

2. Cloth Simulation in a Costume Designer Game

In a game where players design costumes, soft-body physics can be used to simulate the behavior of fabrics and clothing. Implementing a mass-spring system can model the cloth's deformation and movement realistically as players interact with it.

3. Realistic Vehicle Physics in a Racing Game

A racing game aiming for realism requires advanced vehicle physics. This involves modeling tire grip, suspension dynamics, aerodynamics, and vehicle weight distribution. Implementing a physics engine with support for these features can create a lifelike driving experience.

Challenges and Considerations

Complex physics simulations come with challenges:

- **Performance**: High-fidelity simulations can be computationally expensive. Optimizing the simulation to run smoothly on target hardware is a constant concern.
- **Integration**: Ensuring that the physics simulation integrates seamlessly with game logic and player interactions can be complex.
- **Debugging**: Debugging complex physics simulations can be challenging. Visual debugging tools and logging are essential for identifying issues.
- **Realism vs. Gameplay**: Balancing realism with gameplay is crucial. In some cases, simplifications may be necessary to create an enjoyable gaming experience.

In conclusion, complex physics simulations add depth and realism to games, enhancing player immersion and gameplay. When implementing these simulations, a combination of physics knowledge, mathematical modeling, and the right tools is essential. Be prepared for challenges in terms of performance optimization and integration, but the results can greatly enrich your game's dynamics and interactions.

13.2 Custom Collision Detection Techniques

Collision detection is a fundamental aspect of game physics that determines when and how objects in a game world interact. While many game engines provide built-in collision detection systems, there are scenarios where custom collision detection techniques are necessary. In this section, we'll explore the concept of custom collision detection and various techniques to implement it effectively.

When to Use Custom Collision Detection

Custom collision detection becomes necessary when the built-in collision detection system of your game engine lacks the flexibility or precision required for specific game mechanics or scenarios. Here are some situations where custom collision detection may be needed:

1. **Complex Shapes**: When dealing with objects with irregular or complex shapes that cannot be accurately represented by basic collision primitives like spheres, boxes, or capsules.
2. **Penetration Resolution**: When you need fine-grained control over how objects react when they overlap or penetrate each other, which may not be achievable with the default collision resolution methods.
3. **Efficiency**: In scenarios where performance is critical, and you want to optimize collision detection for specific types of objects or interactions.

Techniques for Custom Collision Detection

Implementing custom collision detection requires a good understanding of geometry, mathematics, and the specific requirements of your game. Here are some techniques commonly used for custom collision detection:

1. Polygon Collision Detection:

- **Separating Axis Theorem (SAT)**: SAT is a popular technique for detecting collisions between convex polygons. It checks if there exists a line (axis) along which the projections of two polygons do not overlap. If such a line exists, the polygons are not colliding.

- **Minkowski Sum**: By creating a new shape called the Minkowski sum, you can simplify collision detection between two convex polygons to point-in-polygon tests. This technique is especially useful when dealing with concave polygons.

2. Continuous Collision Detection:

- **Swept AABB**: When objects move at high speeds, simple discrete collision detection can miss collisions. Swept AABB involves checking the swept volume of objects over a time interval, allowing detection of fast-moving collisions.

- **Time of Impact (TOI)**: TOI algorithms determine when and where two objects will collide along their trajectories. This is crucial for accurate and realistic collision resolution, especially in fast-paced games.

3. Raycasting and Line-Segment Intersection:

- **Ray-Cylinder Intersection**: For games involving raycasting and cylindrical objects, implementing custom collision detection for ray-cylinder intersections can be necessary.

- **Line-Segment Intersection**: When you need to detect intersections between line segments, custom algorithms based on vector math can provide precise results.

4. Swept Volume Collision Detection:

- **Bounding Volume Hierarchy (BVH)**: BVHs are hierarchical structures used to optimize collision detection for complex scenes. They partition objects into bounding volumes, reducing the number of collision checks needed.

- **Octrees and Quad Trees**: These spatial partitioning structures divide 3D or 2D space into smaller regions, enabling efficient collision detection for objects within each region.

5. Collision Callbacks and Event Handling:

- Implement callback functions or event handlers to respond to custom collision detection results. This allows you to define specific reactions or behaviors when collisions occur, such as triggering animations, applying forces, or resolving complex interactions.

Implementing Custom Collision Detection

The implementation of custom collision detection involves several steps:

1. **Geometry Representation**: Ensure that the objects involved in the collision detection are represented accurately. This may involve creating custom geometry classes or structures to describe object shapes.
2. **Collision Detection Algorithms**: Implement the chosen collision detection algorithm based on the requirements of your game. Pay attention to edge cases and optimizations.
3. **Collision Response**: Define how objects should react when a collision is detected. This may involve resolving penetration, calculating forces, or triggering game events.
4. **Testing and Debugging**: Thoroughly test the custom collision detection system to ensure accuracy and performance. Implement debugging tools to visualize collision shapes and detect issues.
5. **Integration with Game Logic**: Integrate custom collision detection seamlessly with your game's logic and physics simulation. Ensure that collision events are processed correctly.

Performance Considerations

Custom collision detection can be computationally expensive, especially for complex shapes and large numbers of objects. To maintain performance:

- Implement efficient algorithms and data structures.

- Use spatial partitioning techniques like BVHs, octrees, or grids.

- Implement broad-phase and narrow-phase collision detection to reduce the number of detailed checks.

- Profile and optimize your code to identify bottlenecks.

In conclusion, custom collision detection is a valuable tool for game developers when the built-in collision systems of game engines are not sufficient for specific game mechanics or scenarios. By understanding the mathematics and geometry involved, choosing appropriate algorithms, and optimizing for performance, you can implement custom collision detection effectively and achieve the precise collision interactions your game requires.

13.3 Physics-Based Game Mechanics

Physics-based game mechanics leverage the principles of physics to create engaging and realistic interactions within video games. These mechanics simulate the behavior of objects and characters in response to physical forces, gravity, friction, and other natural phenomena. In this section, we'll explore the concept of physics-based game mechanics and how they can be implemented to enhance gameplay.

The Role of Physics in Games

Physics simulations play a crucial role in modern video games. They contribute to the realism and immersion of gameplay by providing:

1. **Realistic Motion**: Physics simulations allow objects to move and interact with each other in a way that mimics the real world. This includes realistic character animations, object dynamics, and environmental interactions.
2. **Emergent Gameplay**: Physics-based interactions can lead

to emergent gameplay, where unexpected outcomes and interactions occur organically. This adds depth and replayability to games.

3. **Puzzle Mechanics**: Physics-based puzzles challenge players to solve problems by understanding and manipulating the physical properties of objects in the game world. Games like "Portal" and "Angry Birds" are prime examples.
4. **Dynamic Environments**: Physics simulations enable dynamic environments where structures can be destroyed, objects can be moved, and the world can react realistically to player actions.

Implementing Physics-Based Game Mechanics

To implement physics-based game mechanics effectively, follow these steps:

1. **Choose a Physics Engine**: Most game engines come with built-in physics engines or support integration with popular physics libraries like NVIDIA PhysX or Bullet Physics. Choose the one that aligns with your game's requirements.
2. **Object Representation**: Define the physical properties of objects in your game, such as mass, shape, friction, and elasticity. These properties determine how objects behave in the physics simulation.
3. **Physics Interactions**: Implement interactions between objects based on real-world physics principles. This includes handling collisions, applying forces (e.g., gravity or user input), and calculating responses like bouncing or sliding.
4. **Character Physics**: If your game involves characters, implement character physics to control their movement

and animations realistically. This includes handling walking, jumping, and collisions with the environment.

5. **Environmental Physics**: Consider how the game world itself can react to physics. This might involve destructible environments, dynamic weather, or objects that can be manipulated by the player.
6. **Testing and Tweaking**: Thoroughly test and fine-tune the physics-based mechanics to ensure they provide a satisfying and balanced gameplay experience. Players should feel in control but still face challenges.

Examples of Physics-Based Mechanics

Let's explore some common examples of physics-based mechanics in games:

1. Ragdoll Physics:

- Ragdoll physics simulate the behavior of characters' limbs and bodies realistically. This allows characters to react dynamically to in-game events, like falling, explosions, or impacts.

2. Projectile Physics:

- Games with ranged combat often use projectile physics to model the trajectory and behavior of projectiles like bullets, arrows, or spells. Factors like gravity, wind, and speed affect the path of projectiles.

3. Vehicle Physics:

- Racing games and vehicle simulations rely on realistic vehicle physics to provide a convincing driving experience. This includes simulating tire grip, suspension dynamics, and vehicle weight distribution.

4. Rigid Body Physics:

- Rigid body simulations allow objects to collide, bounce, and slide off each other realistically. This is used in various games for puzzles, stacking objects, or simulating physical interactions.

5. Fluid Dynamics:

- Games set underwater or in fluid environments use fluid dynamics to model water behavior accurately. This adds realism to underwater exploration and swimming mechanics.

Challenges and Considerations

While physics-based game mechanics can enhance gameplay, they come with challenges:

- **Performance**: Physics simulations can be computationally expensive, especially in complex scenes. Optimizing physics calculations and using efficient data structures is crucial.

- **Integration**: Integrating physics-based mechanics seamlessly with game logic and controls can be complex.

Consistency and predictability are essential for player satisfaction.

- **Balancing Realism**: Striking a balance between realism and gameplay is crucial. Sometimes, realism can make a game overly complex or frustrating.

- **Debugging**: Debugging physics-related issues can be challenging. Implement debugging tools and visualizations to assist in identifying and resolving problems.

In conclusion, physics-based game mechanics are a powerful tool for creating realistic, engaging, and interactive gameplay experiences. By understanding the principles of physics, choosing the right physics engine, and implementing mechanics that enhance gameplay without sacrificing performance, you can leverage physics to create compelling gaming experiences that captivate players and immerse them in your game world.

13.4 Realistic Movement and Interaction

Realistic movement and interaction are essential components of game development, contributing to the immersion and authenticity of the gaming experience. In this section, we will explore techniques and considerations for achieving lifelike movement and interactions within video games.

The Importance of Realism

Realistic movement and interactions enhance player engagement and create a more immersive gameplay experience. Whether it's the way characters walk and run, the physics of objects in the environment, or the responsiveness of controls, realism adds depth and authenticity to games.

1. Character Animation:

- Realistic character animations encompass movements like walking, running, jumping, and interacting with the environment. Motion-capture technology and advanced animation techniques contribute to lifelike character behavior.

2. Physics-Based Interactions:

- Objects and characters should interact with the game world based on physical principles. Realistic collisions, forces, and reactions contribute to a more believable game environment.

3. Environmental Dynamics:

- Dynamic environments that respond to player actions, such as destructible objects or interactive elements, add realism and unpredictability to gameplay.

Techniques for Realistic Movement

Achieving realistic movement in games involves various techniques and considerations:

1. Character Animation:

- Use motion-capture data or advanced animation systems to create lifelike character movements. Blend animations seamlessly to ensure smooth transitions between different actions.

2. Inverse Kinematics (IK):

- IK algorithms are used to calculate the positions and orientations of a character's limbs and joints in response to user input or environmental constraints. This adds realism to movements like reaching for objects or climbing.

3. Ragdoll Physics:

- Implement ragdoll physics to simulate the dynamic behavior of characters when they fall, get hit, or interact with the environment. This adds realism to character reactions.

4. Animation Blending:

- Blend animations based on player input or environmental factors to create responsive and context-aware character movements. This ensures that characters adapt to different situations convincingly.

5. Motion Smoothing:

- Apply motion smoothing techniques to reduce the jitteriness of character movements. Techniques like motion warping or temporal smoothing can enhance the visual quality of animations.

Techniques for Realistic Interaction

Achieving realistic interactions involves ensuring that objects and characters respond believably to the player's actions:

1. Physics Simulations:

- Use physics engines to simulate the behavior of objects, including collisions, gravity, friction, and object dynamics. This ensures that objects in the game world interact realistically with each other and with the player.

2. Environmental Interactivity:

- Design game environments with interactive elements that respond to the player's actions. This could include destructible objects, levers, buttons, and physics-based puzzles.

3. Sound Feedback:

- Audio feedback is crucial for enhancing the perception of realism. Implement sound effects that match the physical interactions in the game, such as footsteps, object collisions, or environmental sounds.

4. Haptic Feedback:

- If the game platform supports it, incorporate haptic feedback (e.g., controller vibrations) to provide tactile feedback that aligns with in-game interactions.

Challenges and Considerations

Achieving realism in movement and interactions can be challenging:

- **Performance**: Realistic animations and physics simulations can be computationally intensive. Optimization is crucial to maintain smooth gameplay.

- **Balance**: Striking a balance between realism and gameplay is essential. Realistic movement and interactions should enhance, not hinder, the player's experience.

- **Consistency**: Ensure that the level of realism is consistent throughout the game. Sudden shifts in realism can break immersion.

- **Testing**: Extensive testing and iteration are necessary to fine-tune animations, physics, and interactions to achieve the desired level of realism.

In conclusion, realistic movement and interactions are integral to creating engaging and immersive gaming experiences. Leveraging advanced animation techniques, physics simulations, and interactivity can enhance player engagement and contribute to the overall quality of a game. While achieving realism presents challenges, the rewards in terms of player immersion and satisfaction are well worth the effort.

13.5 Performance Considerations in Physics

Physics simulations play a vital role in modern video games, providing realistic movement, interactions, and dynamic environments. However, achieving realistic physics can be computationally intensive and impact game performance. In this section, we'll explore performance considerations when implementing physics in games and techniques to optimize physics simulations.

The Impact of Physics on Game Performance

Physics simulations involve complex calculations, such as collision detection, rigid body dynamics, and object interactions. These calculations can strain a game's performance, especially in scenes with many objects or complex physics interactions. Here are some ways physics can impact game performance:

1. **Frame Rate**: Physics simulations are typically updated at a fixed rate, often tied to the game's frame rate. If physics calculations take too long, the frame rate can drop, resulting in a less smooth gameplay experience.
2. **CPU Usage**: Physics calculations are CPU-intensive. Excessive CPU usage on physics can leave less processing power for other game systems, including AI, rendering, and gameplay logic.
3. **Memory Usage**: Physics simulations may require significant memory for data storage and buffering. High memory usage can lead to performance issues on systems with limited RAM.

Techniques for Optimizing Physics

Optimizing physics in games is essential to maintain smooth performance while preserving the realism of physics-based interactions. Here are techniques and considerations for optimizing physics simulations:

1. Bounding Volume Hierarchies (BVH):

- Implement BVH data structures to reduce the number of collision checks. BVHs organize objects into hierarchical bounding volumes, allowing for efficient culling of potential collisions.

2. Spatial Partitioning:

- Divide the game world into smaller regions using spatial partitioning techniques like grids, octrees, or quad trees. This reduces the number of objects that need to be considered for physics interactions.

3. Broad-Phase and Narrow-Phase Collision Detection:

- Use broad-phase collision detection techniques to quickly identify potential collision pairs before performing detailed narrow-phase checks. Broad-phase checks help filter out unlikely collisions, improving performance.

4. Collision Resolution Simplifications:

- In some cases, you can simplify collision resolution to reduce computational overhead. For example, using simplified collision shapes or approximations for distant objects can speed up calculations.

5. Asynchronous Physics Updates:

- Decouple physics updates from the rendering frame rate by updating physics at a lower rate (e.g., fixed physics time step). Interpolate rendering between physics updates to maintain smooth visual motion.

6. Multithreading:

- Utilize multi-core processors to parallelize physics calculations. Offloading physics to separate threads can significantly improve performance, especially on CPUs with multiple cores.

7. Level of Detail (LOD):

- Implement LOD techniques for physics objects. Reduce the complexity of physics calculations for objects that are farther from the player's viewpoint or not currently in focus.

8. Use Physics Engine Profiling:

- Many physics engines offer profiling tools to identify performance bottlenecks. Use these tools to pinpoint areas of physics simulation that require optimization.

9. Caching and Memoization:

- Cache or memoize results of expensive calculations when possible. For example, if an object's physics state hasn't changed since the last frame, there's no need to recompute its physics interactions.

Adaptive Quality Settings

Consider allowing players to adjust the quality settings for physics in your game. This allows players with different hardware capabilities to tailor the physics simulation to their systems. Options for adjusting physics quality can include reducing the number of objects with physics, simplifying collision shapes, or lowering the physics time step.

Physics and Game Design Balance

Maintaining a balance between realism and performance is crucial. While realistic physics can enhance immersion, it's essential to ensure that the physics simulation does not overwhelm the hardware or negatively impact gameplay. Be willing to make trade-offs and simplifications in the physics simulation to achieve the best performance without sacrificing the overall gaming experience.

In conclusion, optimizing physics simulations is a critical aspect of game development, as it directly impacts game performance and player experience. By employing techniques such as spatial partitioning, multithreading, and LOD, and by allowing players to adjust physics quality settings, developers can strike a balance between realism and performance, delivering engaging gameplay experiences while ensuring smooth performance across a variety of hardware configurations.

Chapter 14: AI and Machine Learning Integration

14.1 Implementing AI in Games

Artificial Intelligence (AI) plays a significant role in shaping the behaviors and interactions of non-player characters (NPCs) and entities within video games. It enables NPCs to make decisions, respond to player actions, and create challenging and engaging gameplay experiences. In this section, we will explore the implementation of AI in games, including key concepts, techniques, and considerations.

The Role of AI in Games

AI in games serves various purposes, enhancing both single-player and multiplayer experiences. Here are some fundamental roles of AI in gaming:

1. **Enemy Behavior**: AI is responsible for controlling enemy behavior, allowing them to pursue, attack, take cover, and react to the player's movements and actions strategically.
2. **Non-Player Character (NPC) Interaction**: AI-driven NPCs can engage in dialogue, trade, or provide quests, contributing to the narrative and immersion of the game world.
3. **Pathfinding and Navigation**: AI algorithms enable characters to navigate complex environments, avoid obstacles, and follow optimal paths.
4. **Procedural Content Generation**: AI can generate procedural content, such as terrain, levels, quests, and even music, to create dynamic and varied gameplay experiences.

5. **Adaptive Difficulty**: AI can adjust the game's difficulty based on the player's performance, ensuring that the game remains challenging and enjoyable.

Implementing AI in Games

Implementing AI in games involves a combination of techniques, algorithms, and design considerations. Here are the key steps to implement AI in a game:

1. Define AI Goals and Behaviors:

- Start by defining the goals and behaviors you want the AI to exhibit. Consider the role of AI characters in the game and how they should interact with players and the environment.

2. Select AI Algorithms:

- Choose appropriate AI algorithms based on the defined goals. Common AI techniques include finite state machines (FSMs), behavior trees, neural networks, and decision-making algorithms like A* for pathfinding.

3. Data Collection and Training (Machine Learning):

- For machine learning-based AI, collect data and train AI models using techniques such as supervised learning, reinforcement learning, or deep learning. This is common for NPCs that need to learn and adapt to player behavior.

4. Implement AI Logic:

- Write the code that governs AI behavior based on the chosen algorithms. This includes defining states, transitions, actions, and decision-making processes.

5. Sensory Input:

- Provide AI entities with sensory input, such as vision, hearing, and touch, to enable them to perceive the game world. Implement sensors and perception models to simulate how AI entities "sense" their surroundings.

6. Decision-Making:

- Implement decision-making algorithms that allow AI entities to choose actions based on their goals and sensory input. This may involve using utility-based systems, finite state machines, or custom decision-making logic.

7. Testing and Iteration:

- Thoroughly test AI behavior in various game scenarios and iterate on the AI logic to fine-tune and improve performance. AI debugging tools and visualizations can assist in identifying and resolving issues.

Types of AI in Games

AI in games can take on various forms and roles:

1. Scripted AI:

- Scripted AI follows predetermined scripts or sequences, making it suitable for simple, predictable behaviors. It is often used for basic enemy movements or scripted events.

2. Rule-Based AI:

- Rule-based AI uses sets of predefined rules and conditions to determine AI behavior. It is suitable for creating deterministic AI, such as puzzle-solving NPCs.

3. Machine Learning-Based AI:

- Machine learning-based AI learns and adapts from data and player interactions. It can create dynamic and challenging AI opponents by continuously improving their strategies.

4. Navigation AI:

- Navigation AI focuses on pathfinding and movement in the game world. It ensures that characters and entities can navigate environments intelligently, avoiding obstacles and taking optimal routes.

Challenges and Considerations

Implementing AI in games comes with challenges and considerations:

- **Performance**: AI computations can be resource-intensive. Efficient algorithms and optimization are essential to maintain game performance.

- **Realism vs. Fun**: Balancing realism with gameplay fun is crucial. AI should provide a challenge without becoming frustratingly difficult.

- **Testing and Debugging**: AI behavior can be complex and challenging to debug. Implement debugging tools, visualizations, and monitoring to diagnose issues.

- **Data Collection (Machine Learning)**: For machine learning-based AI, collecting sufficient training data and ensuring that the AI generalizes well can be challenging.

- **Player Experience**: AI behavior should enhance the player's experience and immersion. Poorly designed or overly aggressive AI can negatively impact the game.

In conclusion, AI is a fundamental component of modern video games, shaping the behaviors and interactions of NPCs and entities. Implementing AI involves defining goals, selecting appropriate algorithms, and fine-tuning behaviors. Whether using scripted AI, rule-based AI, machine learning, or navigation AI, thoughtful AI design contributes to engaging and enjoyable gameplay experiences.

14.2 Basics of Machine Learning in Game Development

Machine learning (ML) has gained prominence in the field of game development for its ability to create adaptive and intelligent game systems. In this section, we will explore the basics of machine learning in the context of game development, including its applications, algorithms, and considerations.

Machine Learning Applications in Games

Machine learning finds applications in various aspects of game development, enhancing both single-player and multiplayer experiences. Here are some common applications of ML in games:

1. **NPC Behavior**: ML can be used to train NPCs to adapt to player strategies, making them more challenging opponents. NPCs can learn from player interactions and improve their decision-making over time.
2. **Procedural Content Generation**: ML algorithms can generate game content such as levels, maps, quests, and even art assets. This enables the creation of procedurally generated games with infinite replayability.
3. **Player Modeling**: ML models can analyze player behavior to create player profiles and predict their preferences. This allows for personalized gameplay experiences, including tailored challenges and content recommendations.
4. **Cheating Detection**: ML algorithms can detect cheating or suspicious behavior in multiplayer games by analyzing player actions and patterns. This helps maintain fair and competitive gameplay.
5. **Voice and Natural Language Processing**: ML-powered voice recognition and natural language processing enable more immersive interactions with NPCs through voice commands and chatbots.

Machine Learning Algorithms in Games

Game developers can leverage a variety of machine learning algorithms to achieve their goals. Here are some common ML algorithms used in game development:

1. Supervised Learning:

- Supervised learning involves training a model on labeled data, allowing it to make predictions or classifications based on new input. This is used for tasks like player behavior prediction and content recommendation.

2. Reinforcement Learning:

- Reinforcement learning (RL) is well-suited for training AI agents to make decisions in dynamic environments. RL agents learn by receiving rewards or penalties based on their actions, making it suitable for NPC behavior and game AI.

3. Neural Networks:

- Deep neural networks, including convolutional neural networks (CNNs) and recurrent neural networks (RNNs), are used for tasks such as image recognition, natural language processing, and even game character animations.

4. Genetic Algorithms:

- Genetic algorithms are used for evolving and optimizing game content, such as level design, character parameters, or AI behavior. They work by simulating the principles of natural selection.

5. Clustering and Dimensionality Reduction:

- Clustering algorithms like k-means can group players or in-game entities based on similarities. Dimensionality reduction techniques like principal component analysis (PCA) can help reduce the complexity of data.

6. Decision Trees and Random Forests:

- Decision trees and random forests are used for classification and decision-making tasks, such as predicting player preferences or game outcomes.

Data Considerations

Data is the lifeblood of machine learning, and game developers must consider several aspects related to data:

- **Data Collection**: Collecting relevant data is crucial for training ML models. Data can include player interactions, game events, and performance metrics.

- **Data Preprocessing**: Data often requires cleaning, normalization, and feature engineering before it can be used for training. This step ensures that the data is in a suitable format for ML algorithms.

- **Data Privacy and Ethics**: Handling player data responsibly and ethically is essential. Game developers must comply with privacy regulations and protect player information.

Challenges and Considerations

Implementing machine learning in games comes with its own set of challenges and considerations:

- **Performance**: ML computations can be resource-intensive. Optimization is crucial to ensure that ML algorithms do not impact game performance.

- **Training Data**: Collecting and labeling training data can be time-consuming and require careful planning.

- **Overfitting**: ML models can overfit to the training data, leading to poor generalization. Cross-validation and hyperparameter tuning help mitigate this issue.

- **Interpretability**: Some ML models, especially deep neural networks, are complex and difficult to interpret. Understanding how the model makes decisions is important for debugging and fine-tuning.

- **Iterative Process**: Implementing ML in games often involves an iterative process of data collection, model training, and testing to achieve the desired results.

In conclusion, machine learning is a powerful tool for enhancing various aspects of game development, from AI behavior to procedural content generation. By understanding the basics of ML algorithms, considering data-related challenges, and optimizing for performance, game developers can leverage machine learning to create more adaptive, engaging, and immersive gaming experiences.

14.3 Adaptive Game Difficulty

Adaptive game difficulty, powered by AI and machine learning, is a crucial aspect of modern game design. It involves tailoring the game's challenge level to individual players to provide a balanced and enjoyable gaming experience. In this section, we will explore the concept of adaptive game difficulty, its implementation, and its impact on player engagement.

The Need for Adaptive Difficulty

Traditional game difficulty settings (e.g., easy, normal, hard) are static and do not consider the player's skill level or preferences. Adaptive difficulty addresses this limitation by dynamically adjusting various aspects of the game to match the player's abilities. The goal is to keep players engaged and challenged without causing frustration or boredom.

Elements of Adaptive Difficulty

Adaptive difficulty systems analyze player behavior and game data to make real-time adjustments. Here are some elements that can be adapted:

1. **Enemy AI**: The behavior and capabilities of enemies can change based on the player's performance. For example, enemies may become more aggressive or use advanced tactics if the player is excelling.
2. **Game Mechanics**: Adaptive difficulty can modify game mechanics, such as altering the damage dealt by weapons, the availability of resources, or the time limits for

challenges.

3. **Puzzle Complexity**: Puzzle games can adjust the complexity of puzzles, making them more or less challenging based on the player's problem-solving abilities.
4. **Hints and Tutorials**: Adaptive tutorials and hints can be provided to assist players who are struggling, while experienced players may receive fewer or more advanced tips.
5. **Resource Management**: In resource-based games, the availability of resources (e.g., health packs, ammunition) can be adjusted to match the player's performance.

Implementation Techniques

Implementing adaptive difficulty requires careful planning and the use of AI and machine learning techniques. Here are common methods for implementing adaptive difficulty:

1. Player Profiling:

- Create player profiles based on their behavior, skill level, and preferences. Machine learning models can analyze this data to understand the player's style and adapt the game accordingly.

2. Dynamic AI Tuning:

- Adjust the behavior and abilities of AI-controlled entities based on the player's performance. For example, reduce enemy accuracy or aggression for less experienced players.

3. Reinforcement Learning:

- Employ reinforcement learning algorithms to optimize game challenges. The game environment provides rewards or penalties based on the player's actions, allowing the AI to adapt difficulty dynamically.

4. Analytics and Data Tracking:

- Collect gameplay data and use analytics tools to monitor player progress and behavior. This data can inform decisions about difficulty adjustments.

5. User Feedback:

- Encourage player feedback and use it to fine-tune the adaptive difficulty system. Players can provide valuable insights into their gaming experience.

6. Difficulty Modes:

- Offer different difficulty modes that players can choose from initially. Use adaptive difficulty within each mode to further customize the experience.

Player Engagement and Retention

Adaptive difficulty systems aim to enhance player engagement and retention in several ways:

- **Reduced Frustration**: Players are less likely to become frustrated when the game adjusts to their skill level, providing a more enjoyable experience.

- **Challenging Rewards**: Players are rewarded for improving their skills, making achievements and victories more satisfying.

- **Extended Playtime**: Adaptive difficulty can keep players engaged for longer periods, as they are less likely to abandon a game due to excessive difficulty.

- **Personalized Experience**: Players appreciate a personalized gaming experience that caters to their abilities and preferences.

- **Accessibility**: Adaptive difficulty can make games more accessible to a broader audience, including players with varying levels of experience.

Ethical Considerations

While adaptive difficulty can greatly enhance the gaming experience, it's essential to consider ethical implications. Ensuring fairness and transparency in difficulty adjustments is crucial to maintain player trust. Avoiding manipulative practices that encourage excessive in-game purchases or discourage fair play is important.

In conclusion, adaptive game difficulty is a powerful tool that leverages AI and machine learning to create personalized gaming experiences. By analyzing player behavior and adjusting game elements in real time, game developers can enhance player engagement, retention, and satisfaction. Ethical considerations and player feedback are vital in implementing adaptive difficulty systems that provide a fair and enjoyable gaming experience for all players.

14.4 Data-Driven Game Design

Data-driven game design is a methodology that relies on collecting and analyzing player data to inform and enhance the game development process. In this section, we will explore the concept of data-driven game design, its benefits, implementation strategies, and its impact on creating more engaging and player-centric games.

The Role of Player Data

Player data is a valuable resource that provides insights into how players interact with a game. It encompasses a wide range of information, including gameplay statistics, preferences, behavior patterns, and feedback. By leveraging this data, game developers can make informed decisions that lead to better-designed and more enjoyable games.

Benefits of Data-Driven Game Design

Implementing data-driven game design offers numerous advantages:

1. **Player-Centric Design**: Data-driven approaches prioritize the player's experience and preferences, resulting in games that resonate better with the target audience.
2. **Iterative Improvement**: Continuous data analysis allows developers to iteratively refine game mechanics, balance, and content based on player feedback and behavior.
3. **Content Personalization**: Personalized content recommendations and gameplay experiences can be delivered to individual players, enhancing engagement and retention.
4. **Monetization Optimization**: Understanding player spending patterns can lead to more effective monetization strategies, such as in-game purchases and

microtransactions.

5. **Bug Detection**: Data-driven approaches can help identify and address bugs, crashes, and issues that affect the player's experience.

Implementation Strategies

To implement data-driven game design successfully, developers can employ the following strategies:

1. Data Collection:

• Collect a wide range of player data, including gameplay statistics, session logs, player feedback, and demographic information. Game telemetry systems are commonly used for automated data collection.

2. Data Analysis Tools:

• Utilize data analysis tools and platforms that can process and visualize large volumes of player data. These tools can reveal player behavior patterns, preferences, and pain points.

3. A/B Testing:

• Conduct A/B tests to compare different game design elements and variations. This allows developers to determine which design choices are more effective based on player engagement and feedback.

4. Player Segmentation:

- Segment players based on behavior and preferences. This enables personalized content recommendations and game experiences tailored to different player groups.

5. Machine Learning and Predictive Analytics:

- Employ machine learning models to predict player behavior, such as churn prediction, player retention, and spending patterns. These models can inform design decisions and monetization strategies.

6. Player Feedback Integration:

- Actively incorporate player feedback mechanisms within the game. This includes in-game surveys, forums, and support for reporting issues. Responding to player feedback builds trust and enhances the player-developer relationship.

7. Iterative Development:

- Embrace an iterative development approach where game updates and improvements are based on ongoing data analysis and player feedback.

Ethical Considerations

While data-driven game design offers many benefits, it also raises ethical concerns related to player privacy and fairness. It's essential for developers to:

- **Respect Player Privacy**: Collect only the data necessary for improving the game experience and obtain player consent where required. Safeguard player data and adhere to privacy regulations.

- **Avoid Exploitative Practices**: Use player data responsibly and avoid manipulative practices that exploit player behaviors, such as excessive in-game purchases or addiction tactics.

- **Transparency**: Be transparent about data collection practices and inform players about how their data will be used.

Player-Centric Design

Data-driven game design is a powerful tool for achieving player-centric game development. By leveraging player data, developers can create games that are more engaging, enjoyable, and tailored to the needs and preferences of their player base. This player-focused approach fosters a strong connection between players and developers, ultimately leading to more successful and sustainable games in the highly competitive gaming industry.

14.5 AI for Non-Player Character Behavior

Artificial Intelligence (AI) plays a crucial role in shaping the behavior of non-player characters (NPCs) in video games. In this section, we will delve into how AI is employed to create realistic and engaging NPC behavior, the techniques used, and the challenges game developers face in implementing AI for NPCs.

Importance of Realistic NPC Behavior

Realistic and intelligent NPC behavior is essential for immersing players in the game world and enhancing the overall gaming experience. NPCs are often responsible for various in-game roles, including:

- **Enemy AI**: NPCs that act as opponents, providing challenges and combat scenarios for players.

- **Allies and Companions**: NPCs that assist players, offer guidance, or accompany them on their journey.

- **Quest Givers**: NPCs that provide quests, missions, or objectives to progress the game's narrative.

- **Supporting Characters**: NPCs that populate the game world, contributing to its realism and storytelling.

AI Techniques for NPC Behavior

Game developers employ a range of AI techniques to create compelling NPC behavior:

1. Finite State Machines (FSMs):

- FSMs model NPC behavior as a series of states with associated transitions. This approach is suitable for NPCs with simple, predefined behaviors, such as patrolling guards.

2. Behavior Trees:

- Behavior trees provide a more flexible way to define NPC behavior. They consist of nodes that represent specific actions or conditions, allowing for complex decision-making processes.

3. Navigation and Pathfinding:

- NPCs need to navigate the game world intelligently. Pathfinding algorithms like A* are used to calculate optimal paths, while obstacle avoidance techniques prevent NPCs from colliding with objects.

4. Decision-Making Algorithms:

- NPCs make decisions based on various factors, including player proximity, health, and available actions. Decision-making algorithms help NPCs choose the most appropriate actions.

5. Learning Algorithms:

- Some games use machine learning to train NPCs. Reinforcement learning can enable NPCs to adapt to player strategies and improve their performance over time.

6. Dialogue Systems:

- NPCs engage with players through dialogue systems that allow for branching conversations and choices.

Natural language processing (NLP) may be employed for more dynamic interactions.

Challenges in NPC AI

Developing AI for NPCs presents several challenges:

- **Performance**: NPCs must make quick decisions in real-time, requiring efficient algorithms and optimization to avoid impacting game performance.

- **Balancing Difficulty**: Ensuring that enemy NPCs offer a fair challenge without being too difficult or too easy for players can be a delicate balance.

- **Realism vs. Fun**: NPCs must behave realistically within the context of the game, but their behavior should also contribute to an enjoyable gameplay experience.

- **Complex Environments**: Navigating complex 3D environments with dynamic obstacles and terrain can be challenging for NPCs.

- **Data and Training**: Machine learning-based NPCs require substantial data and training to perform effectively, which can be resource-intensive.

- **Dynamic Game Worlds**: Games with dynamic, open worlds require NPCs that adapt to changing conditions and events.

Advancements in NPC AI

Advancements in AI and computing power continue to push the boundaries of NPC behavior in games. Some recent trends and developments include:

- **Deep Learning**: Deep neural networks are being used to improve NPC animations, natural language processing for dialogue, and even creating more human-like behavior.

- **Reinforcement Learning**: NPCs are becoming more adaptive through reinforcement learning, allowing them to respond to player actions in increasingly sophisticated ways.

- **Cloud AI Services**: Game developers can leverage cloud-based AI services for voice recognition, real-time translation, and other advanced interactions with NPCs.

- **Emotion Modeling**: NPCs can exhibit emotions and reactions based on the game's narrative and player interactions, enhancing immersion.

In conclusion, AI for NPC behavior is a fundamental aspect of modern video games, contributing to realism, immersion, and player engagement. Game developers use a variety of AI techniques to create diverse and dynamic NPC behaviors, but they also face challenges in balancing realism and fun. As AI technology continues to advance, NPCs in games will become even more sophisticated, providing players with increasingly immersive and memorable gaming experiences.

Chapter 15: Cross-Platform Development Challenges

15.1 Managing Different Screen Sizes and Resolutions

Cross-platform game development involves creating games that can run on a variety of devices with varying screen sizes and resolutions. Managing these differences is essential to ensure that your game looks and performs well on all target platforms. In this section, we will explore the challenges of handling different screen sizes and resolutions in cross-platform game development and discuss strategies and techniques to address them effectively.

Importance of Screen Size and Resolution Management

Screen size and resolution management is crucial for the following reasons:

1. **User Experience**: Players expect games to look and feel consistent across different devices. Inconsistent screen sizes and resolutions can result in a poor user experience.
2. **Accessibility**: Ensuring that your game is playable on a wide range of devices makes it more accessible to a broader audience, increasing its potential reach.
3. **Market Expansion**: Supporting multiple platforms with varying screen characteristics allows you to tap into different markets and potentially increase revenue.
4. **Rating and Reviews**: Negative reviews due to issues related to screen size and resolution can harm your game's reputation and affect its success.

Challenges in Handling Screen Size and Resolution Differences

Cross-platform development introduces several challenges related to screen size and resolution:

1. **Aspect Ratios**: Different devices may have varying aspect ratios, which can result in stretching or letterboxing if not handled properly.
2. **Pixel Density**: Devices with different pixel densities (DPI or PPI) may require different asset resolutions for optimal visual quality.
3. **User Interface (UI) Scaling**: UI elements need to scale appropriately to fit different screen sizes while maintaining usability and readability.
4. **Performance Optimization**: Rendering graphics at higher resolutions can be demanding on hardware, so optimizations are necessary to maintain performance across devices.

Strategies for Managing Screen Size and Resolution Differences

To effectively manage screen size and resolution differences in cross-platform game development, consider the following strategies:

1. Responsive Design:

- Implement a responsive design approach where UI elements and game content adapt dynamically based on the screen size and aspect ratio.

2. *Asset Scaling:*

- Create multiple versions of game assets (textures, images, sprites) at different resolutions to accommodate various screen densities.

3. *Viewport and Camera Control:*

- Use a dynamic viewport and camera system that adjusts to the screen size and aspect ratio, ensuring that the game world is correctly framed.

4. *Letterboxing and Pillarboxing:*

- When necessary, apply letterboxing (horizontal bars) or pillarboxing (vertical bars) to maintain the game's original aspect ratio on screens with different aspect ratios.

5. *Dynamic Font Scaling:*

- Implement font scaling based on screen size to ensure that text remains readable and appropriately sized.

6. *Performance Profiles:*

- Create different performance profiles with varying graphics settings to accommodate low-end and high-end devices.

7. Testing Across Devices:

- Thoroughly test your game on different devices and resolutions to identify and address issues.

Code Example: Asset Loading Based on Screen Density

Here's a simplified code example in C++ for loading assets based on screen density:

```
// Determine the device's screen density (DPI or PPI).

float screenDensity = GetScreenDensity();

// Load appropriate assets based on screen density.

if (screenDensity >= 2.0f) {

LoadHighResolutionAssets();

} else {

LoadStandardResolutionAssets();

}
```

Conclusion

Managing different screen sizes and resolutions is a critical aspect of cross-platform game development. By implementing responsive design, asset scaling, and other strategies, you can ensure that your game provides a consistent and enjoyable experience on a wide range of devices. Thorough testing and optimization are key to overcoming the challenges posed by varying screen characteristics and delivering a successful cross-platform game.

15.2 Handling Various Input Methods

Cross-platform game development not only involves accommodating different screen sizes and resolutions but also handling various input methods that players use across different devices. In this section, we will explore the challenges of managing different input methods and discuss strategies and techniques to ensure that your game is playable and enjoyable on diverse platforms.

Diversity of Input Methods

Modern gaming spans a wide range of devices, each with its unique input methods, including:

1. **Keyboard and Mouse**: Common on desktop and laptop computers, this input method provides precise control but may be absent on mobile devices.
2. **Touchscreen**: Used in smartphones and tablets, touchscreen input offers intuitive interaction but may lack physical feedback.
3. **Game Controllers**: Gamepads, joysticks, and other controllers are popular for console gaming, each with its button layout and features.
4. **Motion Controls**: Some devices incorporate gyroscopes and accelerometers for motion-based input, requiring specific handling.
5. **Voice and Gesture**: Smart devices and VR systems allow voice commands and gestures, adding another layer of interaction.

Challenges in Handling Different Input Methods

Adapting your game to various input methods presents several challenges:

1. **User Experience Consistency**: Maintaining a consistent and enjoyable user experience across diverse input methods can be challenging.
2. **Control Mapping**: Different input methods may require different control mappings, making it necessary to provide customization options.
3. **Precision and Responsiveness**: Ensuring that controls are precise and responsive regardless of the input method used is crucial for gameplay satisfaction.
4. **UI Design**: User interfaces (UI) must be adaptable to accommodate different input methods, such as touch-friendly menus and controller navigation.
5. **Feedback**: Providing appropriate feedback (visual, audio, haptic) to match the chosen input method enhances player immersion.

Strategies for Handling Different Input Methods

To address the challenges of handling various input methods in cross-platform game development, consider the following strategies:

1. Unified Input Handling:

- Develop a unified input handling system that abstracts the underlying input methods, allowing the game to interpret input consistently.

2. Customizable Controls:

- Offer control customization options, allowing players to map controls according to their preferences and the input method they are using.

3. Input Profiles:

- Implement input profiles that automatically adjust control mappings and sensitivity based on the detected input method.

4. Responsive UI:

- Design responsive user interfaces that adapt to touchscreen, controller, and keyboard/mouse input, ensuring usability and readability.

5. Feedback Variation:

- Vary feedback mechanisms (visual, audio, haptic) to match the chosen input method, enhancing player engagement.

6. Testing Across Devices:

- Thoroughly test your game on different devices with varying input methods to identify and address issues.

Code Example: Unified Input Handling

Here's a simplified code example in C# for a unified input handling system that abstracts input methods:

```
public class InputManager

{

public static bool GetFireButton()
```

```
{
// Detect the appropriate input method (e.g., keyboard, controller, touchscreen).
// Map the input to a common action (e.g., fire button).
// Return true when the action is triggered.
}
// More methods for handling other input actions.
}
```

Conclusion

Handling various input methods is a critical aspect of cross-platform game development. By implementing a unified input handling system, providing customizable controls, and designing responsive UI, you can ensure that your game is accessible and enjoyable for players using different devices and input methods. Thorough testing and consideration of player feedback are essential for delivering a seamless and immersive gaming experience across diverse platforms.

15.3 Cross-Platform Performance Optimization

Cross-platform game development often requires careful performance optimization to ensure that games run smoothly and efficiently on various devices with different hardware capabilities. In this section, we will explore the challenges of cross-platform performance optimization and discuss strategies and techniques to achieve optimal performance across multiple platforms.

Importance of Performance Optimization

Optimizing game performance is crucial for the following reasons:

1. **Player Experience**: Smooth gameplay, quick load times, and responsive controls contribute to a positive player experience.
2. **Market Reach**: Ensuring that your game runs on a wide range of devices allows you to tap into larger markets and reach a broader audience.
3. **User Retention**: Players are more likely to continue playing and engaging with your game if it performs well and doesn't drain their device's resources.
4. **Ratings and Reviews**: Poor performance can lead to negative reviews and lower ratings, affecting the game's reputation and success.

Challenges in Cross-Platform Performance Optimization

Cross-platform performance optimization presents several challenges:

1. **Hardware Variability**: Devices have varying hardware specifications, including CPU, GPU, RAM, and storage. Optimizing for this variability is challenging.
2. **Operating Systems**: Different platforms may run different operating systems, each with its own performance characteristics and limitations.
3. **Graphics Rendering**: Graphics rendering can be a bottleneck, especially on mobile devices. Optimizing rendering pipelines and shaders is essential.
4. **Memory Management**: Efficient memory usage and management are critical to prevent crashes and improve

loading times.

5. **Battery Life**: Mobile devices rely on battery power, so optimizing for lower power consumption is essential for prolonged gameplay.
6. **Network Performance**: Online multiplayer games need efficient network code to minimize latency and provide a smooth experience.

Strategies for Cross-Platform Performance Optimization

To address the challenges of cross-platform performance optimization, consider the following strategies:

1. Profiling and Benchmarking:

- Use profiling tools to identify performance bottlenecks on different platforms. Benchmark your game to measure performance improvements accurately.

2. Graphics Optimization:

- Employ techniques like level of detail (LOD) models, occlusion culling, and texture compression to optimize graphics rendering.

3. Memory Management:

- Implement efficient memory allocation and deallocation to avoid memory leaks and excessive usage.

4. Code Optimization:

- Optimize code for CPU and GPU performance, including reducing unnecessary calculations and minimizing draw calls.

5. Asset Optimization:

- Compress and optimize game assets to reduce storage space and improve loading times.

6. Battery Optimization:

- Implement power-efficient algorithms and minimize background processing to extend battery life on mobile devices.

7. Network Optimization:

- Use efficient network protocols and minimize data transfer to reduce latency in online multiplayer games.

8. Platform-Specific Tweaks:

- Tailor optimization techniques to each platform's specific hardware and operating system characteristics.

Code Example: Graphics Optimization with LOD

Here's a simplified code example in Unity C# for implementing Level of Detail (LOD) models for graphics optimization:

// Attach this script to a game object with multiple LODs.

```
public class LODController : MonoBehaviour
{
private LODGroup lodGroup;
private void Start()
{
lodGroup = GetComponent<LODGroup>();
}
public void SetLOD(int level)
{
// Set the LOD level based on the player's distance from the object.
lodGroup.ForceLOD(level);
}
}
```

Conclusion

Cross-platform performance optimization is essential to ensure that your game reaches a wide audience and provides an enjoyable gaming experience on various devices. By profiling your game, optimizing graphics, managing memory, and implementing platform-specific tweaks, you can achieve optimal performance across multiple platforms. Thorough testing and ongoing optimization efforts are key to delivering a high-quality, cross-platform gaming experience.

15.4 Testing Across Multiple Platforms

Testing plays a crucial role in cross-platform game development, ensuring that your game functions correctly and performs well on various devices and operating systems. In this section, we will explore the importance of testing across multiple platforms and discuss strategies and best practices for comprehensive cross-platform testing.

The Significance of Cross-Platform Testing

Cross-platform testing is essential for the following reasons:

1. **Diverse Hardware and Software**: Different devices and platforms have varying hardware specifications, operating systems, and input methods. Testing helps ensure compatibility.
2. **User Experience**: A seamless and consistent user experience is vital for player satisfaction, and testing uncovers issues that could disrupt this experience.
3. **Market Reach**: By testing on multiple platforms, you can tap into larger markets and expand your game's potential audience.
4. **Quality Assurance**: Comprehensive testing reduces the likelihood of crashes, bugs, and performance issues, improving the overall quality of your game.

Challenges in Cross-Platform Testing

Cross-platform testing presents unique challenges:

1. **Device Fragmentation**: The sheer number of devices and OS versions makes it challenging to cover all combinations thoroughly.

2. **Resource Limitations**: Acquiring and maintaining a diverse set of physical devices for testing can be costly and impractical.
3. **Compatibility Issues**: Differences in hardware and software may lead to compatibility problems that need to be addressed.
4. **Testing Tools**: Finding and using effective cross-platform testing tools and frameworks can be time-consuming.

Strategies for Cross-Platform Testing

To address the challenges of cross-platform testing, consider the following strategies:

1. Device Emulators and Simulators:

• Use device emulators and simulators to test on a wide range of platforms without the need for physical devices. However, be aware that they may not replicate real-world performance accurately.

2. Cloud-Based Testing Services:

• Leverage cloud-based testing services that provide access to a variety of real devices and platforms. These services can save time and resources.

3. Automated Testing:

• Implement automated testing scripts that can be executed on different platforms, reducing the manual testing workload.

4. Beta Testing and User Feedback:

- Engage in beta testing with a diverse group of players to gather feedback and uncover platform-specific issues.

5. Testing Documentation:

- Maintain comprehensive testing documentation to keep track of tested platforms, issues, and resolutions.

6. Platform-Specific Testing:

- Prioritize testing on platforms with larger user bases and adjust your testing efforts based on your target audience.

Code Example: Automated Cross-Platform Testing

Here's a simplified example of using Python and Appium for automated cross-platform testing of a mobile game:

```
from appium import webdriver

desired_caps = {

'platformName': 'iOS',

'platformVersion': '15.0',

'deviceName': 'iPhone 13',

'app': '/path/to/your/appium/app',

}

# Initialize the Appium driver for iOS.
```

```
driver = webdriver.Remote('http://localhost:4723/wd/hub', desired_caps)

# Write test scripts for gameplay and functionality.

# Repeat the process for Android or other platforms as needed.

# Perform assertions and gather test results.

# Close the driver and report test results.

driver.quit()
```

Conclusion

Cross-platform testing is a critical phase in game development that ensures your game runs smoothly and reliably on various devices and platforms. By using emulators, cloud-based testing services, and automated testing scripts, you can efficiently cover multiple platforms. Engaging with beta testers and maintaining thorough documentation further enhances your ability to deliver a high-quality, cross-platform gaming experience.

15.5 Dealing with Platform-Specific Limitations

Cross-platform game development often involves navigating platform-specific limitations and constraints that can impact gameplay and functionality. In this section, we will explore the challenges of dealing with platform-specific limitations and discuss strategies to overcome them effectively.

Understanding Platform-Specific Limitations

Each platform has its unique set of limitations and constraints, including:

1. **Hardware Restrictions**: Different devices have varying levels of CPU, GPU, and memory capabilities, affecting what your game can achieve in terms of graphics and performance.
2. **Operating System Differences**: Various platforms run different operating systems, each with its own quirks, APIs, and restrictions that impact game development.
3. **Input Methods**: Handling various input methods, such as touchscreens, controllers, and keyboard/mouse, requires adapting gameplay and controls to match the platform.
4. **Performance Variances**: Games must be optimized differently for devices with varying hardware and performance capabilities.
5. **Certification Requirements**: Platforms often have strict certification and submission guidelines that your game must adhere to for distribution.

Challenges in Dealing with Platform-Specific Limitations

Dealing with platform-specific limitations presents several challenges:

1. **Resource Management**: Efficiently managing resources such as memory, storage, and CPU usage while accommodating platform variations can be complex.
2. **Feature Parity**: Ensuring that your game maintains feature parity across platforms while accounting for limitations can be challenging.

3. **Testing Complexity**: Testing across multiple platforms with different limitations requires comprehensive testing strategies.
4. **Performance Optimization**: Optimizing for both high-end and low-end devices while meeting platform-specific requirements is a balancing act.

Strategies for Dealing with Platform-Specific Limitations

To address platform-specific limitations effectively, consider the following strategies:

1. Platform Detection:

• Implement a platform detection system that identifies the user's device and adjusts gameplay, graphics settings, and controls accordingly.

2. Conditional Logic:

• Use conditional logic in your codebase to enable or disable platform-specific features and functionality as needed.

3. Asset Management:

• Optimize asset loading and management to account for varying device capabilities and storage constraints.

4. User Interface (UI) Adaptation:

- Design adaptable user interfaces that work seamlessly on different screens and input methods.

5. Performance Profiles:

- Create performance profiles that automatically adjust game settings based on the detected hardware capabilities.

6. Platform-Specific Code:

- When necessary, implement platform-specific code sections to address unique challenges or leverage platform-specific features.

Code Example: Platform-Specific Input Handling

Here's a simplified code example in Unity C# for handling platform-specific input methods:

```
void Update()

{

if (Application.platform == RuntimePlatform.Android)

{

// Handle touchscreen input for Android.

}

else if (Application.platform == RuntimePlatform.WindowsPlayer)

{
```

```
// Handle keyboard and mouse input for Windows.

}

else if (Application.platform == RuntimePlatform.IPhonePlayer)

{

// Handle touchscreen input for iOS.

}

}
```

Conclusion

Dealing with platform-specific limitations is an inherent part of cross-platform game development. By understanding the unique constraints of each platform, implementing platform detection and adaptation, and optimizing for various hardware capabilities, you can navigate these limitations effectively and deliver a consistent and enjoyable gaming experience across multiple platforms. Thorough testing and player feedback are essential for identifying and addressing platform-specific issues in your game.

Chapter 16: Extending Cocos2d-x with Plugins

16.1 Using Existing Plugins

In this section, we'll explore how to leverage existing plugins to enhance your Cocos2d-x game development workflow. Plugins can save you time and effort by providing pre-built functionality and integrations with third-party services. Whether you need to add analytics, social media sharing, or other features to your game, using existing plugins can streamline the process.

Why Use Existing Plugins?

Before we dive into the practical aspects of using existing plugins, let's discuss why they are valuable in Cocos2d-x game development:

1. **Time Efficiency:** Developing certain features from scratch can be time-consuming. Existing plugins offer ready-made solutions that can be quickly integrated into your project.
2. **Reliability:** Established plugins are often well-maintained and thoroughly tested, reducing the risk of bugs or compatibility issues.
3. **Feature Richness:** Plugins often come with a range of features and configurations, allowing you to choose the ones that best suit your game.
4. **Community Support:** Many plugins have active communities around them, providing documentation, forums, and resources to help you get the most out of them.

Now, let's explore how to find, install, and use existing plugins in your Cocos2d-x project.

Finding Existing Plugins

1. **Cocos2d-x Forums:** The official Cocos2d-x forums are a good place to start. You can find announcements and discussions about various plugins there.
2. **GitHub:** Many Cocos2d-x plugins are hosted on GitHub. You can search for repositories related to Cocos2d-x and browse through available plugins.
3. **Package Managers:** Some plugins may be available through package managers like Cocos Package Manager (CPM) or Conan. Check if the plugin you need is listed there.

Installing and Using Plugins

Let's assume you've found a plugin that fits your needs. Here are the general steps to install and use it:

1. **Download the Plugin:** If the plugin is available as a downloadable package, download it to your computer.
2. **Integration:** Depending on the plugin, integration can vary. Some plugins might require you to add specific lines to your CMakeLists.txt file to include them in your project.
3. **Initialization:** In your game's code, initialize and configure the plugin. This typically involves providing API keys or configuring settings.
4. **Usage:** Start using the plugin's functionality in your game. This may involve making API calls, handling callbacks, or using the provided functions and classes.

Here's a simple example of integrating a hypothetical "Social Sharing" plugin:

```
// Include the plugin header

#include "SocialSharingPlugin.h"

// Initialize the plugin

SocialSharingPlugin::initialize("your_api_key");

// Trigger social sharing when a user completes a level

void onLevelComplete() {

SocialSharingPlugin::share("I just completed level 10 in my awesome game!");

}
```

Remember to refer to the plugin's documentation for specific integration and usage instructions.

Plugin Compatibility and Updates

It's important to keep in mind that plugin compatibility can be an issue when updating Cocos2d-x or your game engine. Before updating, check if your plugins have updates or if they are compatible with the new version. Plugin maintainers often release updates to ensure compatibility with the latest engine releases.

In conclusion, leveraging existing plugins can greatly enhance your Cocos2d-x game development process. It allows you to add functionality efficiently and tap into the expertise of the Cocos2d-x community. Just be mindful of compatibility and updates to ensure a smooth development experience.

16.2 Developing Custom Plugins

In this section, we'll delve into the process of creating custom plugins for your Cocos2d-x game. While existing plugins can be valuable, there may be cases where you need unique functionality that isn't readily available. Developing custom plugins allows you to tailor solutions to your specific game requirements.

Plugin Development Prerequisites

Before we begin, ensure you have the following prerequisites in place:

1. **Cocos2d-x Environment:** Set up your Cocos2d-x development environment, including the necessary libraries and tools.
2. **C++ Proficiency:** Familiarity with C++ programming is essential since Cocos2d-x primarily uses C++ for game development.
3. **IDE:** Choose an Integrated Development Environment (IDE) that suits your workflow, such as Visual Studio, Xcode, or Cocos Creator.
4. **Plugin Idea:** Clearly define the purpose and functionality of your custom plugin. What problem does it solve, and how will it integrate into your game?

Steps to Create a Custom Plugin

Let's outline the steps to create a custom Cocos2d-x plugin:

1. Project Setup

Start by creating a new project or opening an existing one. Your custom plugin will be part of your game project, so ensure it's set up correctly.

2. Create a Plugin Directory

Organize your project by creating a directory specifically for your custom plugin. This helps keep your code modular and maintainable.

3. Write Plugin Code

Begin writing the code for your plugin. Here's a simplified example of a custom "PlayerStats" plugin that tracks player statistics:

```
// PlayerStatsPlugin.h

#pragma once

#include "cocos2d.h"

class PlayerStatsPlugin {

public:

static void initialize();

static void trackScore(int score);

static int getHighScore();

};

// PlayerStatsPlugin.cpp
```

```
#include "PlayerStatsPlugin.h"

int highScore = 0;

void PlayerStatsPlugin::initialize() {

// Initialize any necessary data or configurations.

}

void PlayerStatsPlugin::trackScore(int score) {

// Track player scores and update highScore if needed.

if (score > highScore) {

highScore = score;

}

}

int PlayerStatsPlugin::getHighScore() {

return highScore;

}
```

4. Build the Plugin

Ensure your custom plugin builds successfully within your Cocos2d-x project. Update your project's CMakeLists.txt or equivalent configuration files to include your plugin files.

5. Test the Plugin

Create test scenarios within your game to verify that the plugin functions as expected. Test different aspects of your custom functionality, and make adjustments as needed.

6. Documentation

Write clear and comprehensive documentation for your custom plugin. Explain how other developers can integrate and use it in their projects.

7. Version Control

Use version control systems like Git to track changes in your custom plugin's code. This makes collaboration and maintenance more manageable.

8. Distribution

If you plan to share your custom plugin with the Cocos2d-x community or use it in multiple projects, consider packaging and distributing it as a reusable library.

9. Community Contribution

Contributing your plugin to the Cocos2d-x community can be beneficial for others and help improve your plugin through feedback and collaboration.

10. Maintenance

Regularly update and maintain your custom plugin to ensure compatibility with new Cocos2d-x versions and address any issues that arise.

Remember that developing custom plugins offers flexibility and customization options for your Cocos2d-x games. By following these steps and best practices, you can create tailored solutions to enhance your game development process.

16.3 Integrating Third-Party SDKs

Integrating third-party Software Development Kits (SDKs) is a common practice in game development, and Cocos2d-x provides a flexible framework for incorporating these SDKs into your projects. These SDKs can enhance your game with various functionalities, such as analytics, advertising, in-app purchases, and more. In this section, we'll explore how to integrate third-party SDKs effectively.

Choose the Right SDKs

Before you start integrating SDKs into your Cocos2d-x project, it's crucial to select the appropriate SDKs for your game's requirements. Consider the following factors:

1. **Functionality:** Identify the specific features or services your game needs. For example, if you want to monetize your game, you might need an advertising or in-app purchases SDK.
2. **Compatibility:** Ensure that the selected SDKs are compatible with your target platforms and Cocos2d-x version.

3. **Documentation:** Check if the SDKs have clear and well-maintained documentation. Proper documentation makes integration smoother.
4. **Community Support:** SDKs with an active community can provide valuable resources and help troubleshoot issues.

Adding SDKs to Your Project

Integrating third-party SDKs typically involves the following steps:

1. Obtain SDKs

Visit the official website or repository of the SDK provider to download the necessary SDK files or libraries. These files are usually provided in a compressed format.

2. Include SDK Files

Unzip the downloaded SDK files and place them in your Cocos2d-x project directory. Depending on the SDK, you may need to include header files, libraries, and configuration files.

3. Configure Build Files

To ensure that the SDK is included in your project build, you may need to make adjustments to your project's build system (e.g., CMake or Xcode). This often involves modifying CMakeLists.txt files or project settings.

4. Initialize the SDK

In your game's code, you'll need to initialize the SDK by calling its initialization function. This is typically done in the game's startup sequence. For example, initializing an analytics SDK might look like this:

```
// Include the analytics SDK header
#include "AnalyticsSDK.h"
// Initialize the analytics SDK
AnalyticsSDK::initialize("your_api_key");
```

5. Use SDK Features

Once the SDK is initialized, you can start using its features. For instance, if you integrated an advertising SDK, you can display ads at specific points in your game. Refer to the SDK's documentation for details on using its functions and features.

Handling SDK Dependencies

Some SDKs may have dependencies on other libraries or SDKs. Ensure that you satisfy these dependencies by including the required files and configurations in your project.

Testing and Debugging

Thoroughly test the integration of third-party SDKs in your game. Pay attention to how they interact with your game's code and ensure that they function as expected. Debug any issues that arise during testing.

Version Compatibility

Keep an eye on updates and new versions of the SDKs you've integrated. SDK providers often release updates to address issues and improve compatibility. Make sure to update your SDKs when necessary, but also test the new versions thoroughly to avoid unexpected problems.

Managing Multiple SDKs

In some cases, you may need to integrate multiple SDKs into your game. Be mindful of potential conflicts or compatibility issues between these SDKs. It's essential to ensure that they can coexist peacefully within your project.

Error Handling and Logging

Implement robust error handling and logging mechanisms for the integrated SDKs. This will help you identify and address issues as they arise and provide valuable information for debugging.

In summary, integrating third-party SDKs can add valuable functionalities to your Cocos2d-x game projects. However, it's essential to choose the right SDKs, follow proper integration procedures, and thoroughly test and maintain the integrations to ensure a smooth gaming experience for your players.

16.4 Plugin Maintenance and Updates

Once you've integrated custom or third-party plugins into your Cocos2d-x game, the journey doesn't end there. Maintaining and updating these plugins is crucial to ensure that your game continues to run smoothly and remains compatible with new versions of

Cocos2d-x or other dependencies. In this section, we'll explore the best practices for plugin maintenance and updates.

Version Compatibility

One of the primary reasons for plugin maintenance is ensuring compatibility with different versions of Cocos2d-x. As Cocos2d-x evolves, changes in APIs and libraries can affect the functionality of your plugins. Here's how to manage version compatibility:

- **Regularly Check for Updates:** Keep an eye on official announcements and updates for Cocos2d-x. Check if your plugins have new versions or updates that address compatibility issues.

- **Testing:** Before updating Cocos2d-x or your game engine, thoroughly test your plugins with the new version to identify any compatibility problems. This includes testing both your custom plugins and third-party ones.

- **Adjust Plugin Code:** If you encounter issues, you may need to adjust your plugin code to adapt to changes in Cocos2d-x. This could involve modifying function calls or updating dependencies.

- **Maintain Multiple Versions:** If you have multiple projects using different versions of Cocos2d-x, consider maintaining different branches or versions of your plugins to ensure compatibility with each project.

Dependency Management

Plugins often rely on external libraries, frameworks, or SDKs. These dependencies can also evolve and require updates. Here's how to manage them:

- **Check Dependency Updates:** Regularly check for updates and new versions of the dependencies your plugins rely on. SDKs, libraries, and third-party tools may release updates that improve performance, security, or compatibility.

- **Update Dependencies Carefully:** When updating dependencies, be cautious and test the changes thoroughly. An update might introduce new issues, so it's essential to verify that the updated version works well with your game.

- **Documentation:** Keep clear documentation of the dependencies used by your plugins, including version information. This helps in case you need to roll back to a previous version or troubleshoot compatibility issues.

Bug Fixes and Enhancements

Plugin maintenance also involves addressing bugs and making enhancements. Here are some practices to follow:

- **Bug Tracking:** Establish a bug tracking system to keep tabs on reported issues. Users or fellow developers may encounter problems with your plugins, and having a systematic way to track and prioritize bug fixes is essential.

- **Release Notes:** Maintain release notes for your plugins to document changes, bug fixes, and enhancements in each version. This helps users understand what has been improved or fixed in a particular release.

- **Feedback and Collaboration:** Be open to feedback from the community or users of your plugins. Collaboration can lead to valuable contributions, bug reports, and ideas for enhancements.

Security Updates

Security is a critical aspect of plugin maintenance. Outdated or vulnerable plugins can expose your game to security risks. Here's how to address security concerns:

- **Stay Informed:** Keep up-to-date with security news and vulnerabilities related to the technologies and libraries your plugins use. Be aware of any security advisories for your dependencies.

- **Promptly Apply Security Patches:** If a security vulnerability is identified in a dependency or your plugin code, take immediate action to apply patches or updates to mitigate the risk.

- **Inform Users:** If a security issue affects your plugin, communicate the issue and the solution to your users. Transparency is essential in maintaining trust.

Version Control and Backups

Maintain version control for your plugin code. Use a version control system like Git to track changes, manage branches, and facilitate collaboration. Additionally, regularly back up your plugin code and documentation to prevent data loss in case of unforeseen issues or accidents.

Communication

Keep channels of communication open with users of your plugins. If you plan to discontinue support or development for a particular plugin, inform users in advance to allow them to make alternative arrangements.

In conclusion, plugin maintenance and updates are integral parts of managing Cocos2d-x game projects. By staying vigilant about version compatibility, dependency management, bug fixes, security updates, and effective communication, you can ensure that your plugins continue to enhance your games without causing unexpected issues.

16.5 Community Contributions and Sharing

One of the strengths of the Cocos2d-x community is its collaborative spirit. Developers from around the world contribute their knowledge and expertise to create a vibrant ecosystem of plugins and extensions. In this section, we'll explore the importance of community contributions and how you can share your own plugins with the community.

Benefits of Community Contributions

Community contributions play a significant role in the growth and sustainability of the Cocos2d-x ecosystem. Here are some benefits:

- **Expanded Functionality:** Contributions can extend the capabilities of Cocos2d-x by providing new features and functionalities through plugins.

- **Faster Development:** Developers can leverage existing community-contributed plugins to speed up their game development process, reducing the need to reinvent the wheel.

- **Quality Assurance:** Plugins developed and maintained by the community are often well-tested, improving their reliability and performance.

- **Knowledge Sharing:** Community contributions are valuable learning resources for developers looking to understand best practices, coding standards, and advanced techniques.

Sharing Your Plugins

If you've developed a custom plugin that you believe could benefit other Cocos2d-x developers, consider sharing it with the community. Here's how you can do that:

1. Documentation

Before sharing your plugin, ensure it is well-documented. Create clear and comprehensive documentation that explains how to integrate and use the plugin. Include code examples, usage guidelines, and any dependencies required.

2. Version Control

Host your plugin's code on a version control platform like GitHub. This allows other developers to easily access, fork, and contribute to your project. Use descriptive commit messages to maintain transparency and make it easier for others to understand your changes.

3. Open Source Licensing

Choose an open source license for your plugin. Popular choices include the MIT License, Apache License, or GNU General Public License (GPL). Clearly state the chosen license in your project's repository to specify how others can use and modify your code.

4. Publish on Package Managers

Consider publishing your plugin on package managers or registries like Cocos Package Manager (CPM) or Conan. This makes it more accessible to other Cocos2d-x developers who can easily integrate it into their projects.

5. Forums and Communities

Engage with the Cocos2d-x community by sharing your plugin on the official forums and relevant online communities. Provide information about its functionality and how it can benefit other developers.

6. Collaboration

Be open to collaboration with other developers who might want to contribute to or improve your plugin. Collaborative efforts can lead to more robust and feature-rich plugins.

7. Updates and Maintenance

Regularly update and maintain your plugin to address issues, incorporate improvements, and ensure compatibility with new versions of Cocos2d-x. A well-maintained plugin is more likely to gain adoption within the community.

8. Seek Feedback

Encourage users of your plugin to provide feedback, report issues, and suggest enhancements. Feedback from the community can help you refine your plugin and make it more useful.

Etiquette and Best Practices

When sharing your plugins with the Cocos2d-x community, it's essential to follow certain etiquette and best practices:

- **Respect Licensing:** If you use third-party libraries or code in your plugin, ensure that you respect their licenses and give proper attribution.
- **Provide Support:** Be responsive to questions and issues raised by users of your plugin. Providing support can enhance your plugin's reputation.

- **Acknowledge Contributors:** If other developers contribute to your plugin, acknowledge their contributions and give them credit.

- **Keep Documentation Updated:** Maintain up-to-date documentation to reflect changes and improvements in your plugin.

- **Be Patient:** Not all plugins gain instant popularity. Building a community around your plugin may take time.

By sharing your knowledge and creations with the Cocos2d-x community, you contribute to the growth and strength of the platform, fostering collaboration and innovation among developers. Additionally, you can benefit from the contributions of others, creating a win-win situation for the entire community.

Chapter 17: Localization and Internationalization

17.1 Basics of Game Localization

Game localization and internationalization are essential processes for making your game accessible and appealing to a global audience. Localization involves adapting your game to different languages and cultures, while internationalization focuses on designing your game from the start to be easily localized. In this section, we'll delve into the basics of game localization and why it's crucial for reaching a diverse player base.

Understanding Game Localization

Localization is the process of adapting your game to different regions, languages, and cultures to ensure that players from various backgrounds can enjoy it. This involves more than just translating text; it encompasses every aspect of your game, including text, graphics, audio, and cultural nuances.

Key Elements of Game Localization:

1. **Text Translation:** Translate all in-game text, including dialogues, menus, tutorials, and subtitles, into the target languages. Pay attention to character limits, text expansion, and readability.
2. **Audio Localization:** Provide voiceovers or subtitles in the target languages. Ensure that the audio matches the lip-syncing or timing of the original content.
3. **Graphics and Symbols:** Adapt images, icons, and symbols to be culturally relevant and sensitive. What's acceptable in

one culture may not be in another.

4. **Cultural References:** Modify or replace cultural references, jokes, and humor to resonate with the target audience. Avoid content that could be offensive or misunderstood.
5. **Date and Time Formats:** Adjust date and time formats, currency symbols, and measurement units to match regional conventions.
6. **Legal and Compliance:** Ensure that your game complies with regional laws, age ratings, and content restrictions.

The Importance of Localization

Localization is not just about making your game accessible to a wider audience; it's also about creating a more immersive and enjoyable experience for players. Here are some reasons why localization is crucial:

1. Market Expansion:

Localization opens up new markets and revenue opportunities. It allows you to tap into player bases in different countries and regions, potentially increasing your game's sales and popularity.

2. Player Engagement:

Players are more likely to engage with a game that speaks their language and reflects their culture. A localized game enhances player immersion and emotional connection.

3. Competitive Advantage:

In a global gaming market, offering a localized experience gives your game a competitive edge. Players are more likely to choose a game that caters to their language and preferences.

4. Brand Reputation:

A commitment to localization demonstrates your dedication to providing a high-quality gaming experience. It can enhance your brand's reputation and foster player loyalty.

Internationalization (i18n) and Localization (L10n)

To effectively localize a game, it's essential to consider internationalization (often abbreviated as i18n) during the game's development. Internationalization is the process of designing and developing your game to be adaptable for future localization. Here's how to approach internationalization:

1. Text Handling:

Use a text management system that supports multiple languages and character sets from the beginning. Avoid hardcoding text and ensure that the user interface (UI) is designed to accommodate text expansion.

2. Separate Content from Code:

Keep in-game text and content separate from the game's code. Use external files or databases to store text, making it easier to replace and update for different languages.

3. Unicode Support:

Use Unicode encoding for text to ensure compatibility with a wide range of languages and characters.

4. Flexible UI:

Design a flexible UI that can adjust to different text lengths. Consider dynamic UI elements that can expand or contract based on the language.

5. Cultural Sensitivity:

Avoid cultural bias in your game's design and content. Be aware of potential cultural differences and consult with native speakers or experts during development.

6. Test Early:

Test the internationalization aspects of your game during development, even if you're not planning immediate localization. Identifying and addressing issues early can save time and effort later.

In summary, game localization is a vital process for expanding your game's reach and creating a more inclusive gaming experience. Understanding the basics of localization and incorporating internationalization practices into your game development workflow are key steps toward successfully reaching a global audience.

17.2 Cultural Considerations in Localization

When localizing a game, it's not just about translating text; it's also about understanding and respecting the cultural differences of the target audience. Cultural considerations play a crucial role in creating a successful localized game that resonates with players from different regions. In this section, we'll explore some of the key cultural factors to keep in mind during the localization process.

Language Variations

Languages can have various dialects, regional variations, and script differences. For example, English is spoken in many countries, but British English differs from American English in spelling, vocabulary, and pronunciation. When localizing, consider whether you need to adapt your translations to suit specific regional variations of the target language.

Cultural References

Games often include cultural references, jokes, and humor that may not be universally understood. When localizing, it's essential to replace or adapt these references to be relevant and relatable to the target audience. What's funny in one culture may not have the same impact in another, and references to specific events or celebrities may need to be changed.

Sensitivity to Symbols and Imagery

Symbols and imagery can have different meanings and connotations in various cultures. For example, colors may symbolize different emotions or concepts, and certain symbols may carry religious or cultural significance. Ensure that the visual elements of your game are culturally sensitive and do not inadvertently offend or misinterpret cultural symbols.

Holidays and Traditions

Consider local holidays and traditions when localizing your game. You may want to incorporate holiday-themed content or events that align with the target culture's celebrations. However, be cautious not to stereotype or misrepresent these traditions, and consult with cultural experts or native speakers if needed.

Social and Ethical Norms

Different cultures have varying social norms and ethical standards. Content that is acceptable in one culture may be considered offensive or inappropriate in another. Pay attention to cultural sensibilities and avoid content that could potentially offend or alienate players.

Localization Testing

Localization testing is a critical phase of the process. Test the localized version of your game with native speakers or players familiar with the target culture. They can provide valuable feedback on the accuracy of translations, cultural appropriateness, and any issues related to cultural references.

Inclusivity and Representation

Consider inclusivity and representation in your localized game. Ensure that characters, storylines, and visuals are diverse and inclusive to reflect the cultural and ethnic backgrounds of your players. Avoid stereotypes and strive for authentic and respectful representation.

Regional Regulations and Laws

Be aware of regional regulations and laws that may affect your game's content. Some countries have strict regulations regarding certain themes, content, or age ratings. Ensure that your localized game complies with these regulations to avoid legal issues.

User Feedback and Iteration

After releasing the localized version of your game, pay attention to user feedback from the target audience. Players may provide insights into cultural aspects that need further refinement. Be open to making iterative improvements to enhance the localization based on user input.

In summary, cultural considerations are integral to successful game localization. Understanding and respecting the cultural differences of your target audience can lead to a more immersive and enjoyable gaming experience for players from diverse regions. Collaborating with cultural experts and native speakers can be invaluable in ensuring that your localized game is culturally sensitive and appealing.

17.3 Multi-Language Support Implementation

Implementing multi-language support in your game involves more than just translating text. It requires careful planning and coding to ensure that your game can seamlessly switch between languages and provide an excellent experience for players of various linguistic backgrounds. In this section, we'll explore the steps to implement multi-language support in your Cocos2d-x game.

Step 1: Design for Localization from the Beginning

The best approach to multi-language support is to design your game with localization in mind from the start. Follow these principles:

- **Separate Text from Code:** Avoid hardcoding text into your game's code. Instead, store all text in external files or a localization database.

- **Dynamic UI:** Design user interface elements to be flexible and accommodate text of varying lengths. Ensure that UI components can expand or contract as needed.

- **Unicode Encoding:** Use Unicode encoding for all text in your game to support a wide range of languages and characters.

Step 2: Prepare Text for Translation

Before sending text for translation, prepare it appropriately:

- **String IDs:** Assign unique string IDs to all text elements in your game. This makes it easier to manage translations and ensures consistency.

- **Context Information:** Provide context information for translators. Explain where and how each text string is used within the game to help translators understand its context.

Step 3: Translate Text

Hire professional translators or use reputable translation services to translate your game's text into the target languages. Ensure that translators are familiar with gaming terminology and context to provide accurate translations.

Step 4: Implement Localization

Now comes the technical part of implementing localization in your game:

- **Localization Files:** Create separate localization files or databases for each supported language. These files should map string IDs to their translated counterparts.

- **Language Selection:** Implement a language selection screen where players can choose their preferred language. Store the selected language as a preference or setting.

- **Load Localization Data:** Load the appropriate localization file or database based on the selected language when the game starts.

- **Text Replacement:** Replace in-game text with the corresponding translated text based on the loaded localization data.

Step 5: Handle Text Expansion and Contraction

Different languages may have text that expands or contracts compared to the source language. Handle these variations by:

- **Dynamic Text Boxes:** Use dynamic text boxes that can adjust their size to accommodate longer or shorter text.

- **Text Alignment:** Ensure that text alignment is appropriate for the target language, as some languages read from right to left.

- **Testing:** Thoroughly test all supported languages to verify that text fits correctly within UI elements and does not overlap or get cut off.

Step 6: Cultural Considerations

Consider cultural differences when implementing multi-language support:

- **Date and Time Formats:** Adjust date and time formats to match regional conventions.

- **Currency Symbols:** Use the appropriate currency symbols and formats for each language.

- **Cultural Sensitivity:** Ensure that graphics, symbols, and content are culturally sensitive and do not inadvertently offend or misinterpret cultural norms.

Step 7: Testing and Quality Assurance

Testing is a crucial phase of multi-language support:

- **Localization Testing:** Test the game thoroughly in each supported language to identify any translation issues, text overflow, or layout problems.

- **Beta Testing:** Conduct beta testing with players who speak the target languages to gather feedback and address any remaining localization issues.

Step 8: Ongoing Maintenance

Localization is an ongoing process. Regularly update and maintain your game's translations to address issues, provide updates, and ensure compatibility with new game content.

In summary, implementing multi-language support in your Cocos2d-x game involves careful planning, coding, and consideration of cultural differences. By designing for localization from the beginning, preparing text for translation, and following best practices, you can create a game that appeals to a global audience and provides an enjoyable experience in multiple languages.

17.4 Internationalization Best Practices

Internationalization (often abbreviated as i18n) is the process of designing and developing your game to be adaptable for future localization. While localization focuses on translating and customizing your game for specific regions, internationalization sets the foundation for this process. In this section, we'll explore internationalization best practices to ensure that your game is ready for global audiences.

1. Use Unicode for Text Handling

Unicode is a standardized character encoding system that supports a vast range of characters from different languages and scripts. It's essential to use Unicode encoding for all text in your game to ensure compatibility with various languages. Avoid using legacy encodings that may limit your game's language support.

In Cocos2d-x, you can work with Unicode-encoded strings using the built-in *std::string* class, which is Unicode-friendly.

2. Externalize Text and Assets

Avoid hardcoding text directly into your game's source code and graphics. Instead, externalize text and assets by storing them in separate files or databases. This makes it easier to replace and update text during localization without modifying the codebase.

In Cocos2d-x, you can load text from external files using file I/O operations or by using localization frameworks and tools.

3. Use String IDs

Assign unique string IDs to all text elements in your game. These IDs serve as references to the actual text content. Using string IDs allows for easy management of translations and ensures consistency across the game.

For example, you can create a mapping of string IDs to text content in a JSON or XML file, which can be loaded at runtime based on the selected language.

```
{
"welcome_message": "Welcome to the game!",
"start_button": "Start",
"options_menu": "Options"
}
```

4. Support Dynamic Text Layout

Different languages may have text that expands or contracts compared to the source language. Ensure that your game's user interface (UI) elements can handle dynamic text layout. Use dynamic text boxes that can adjust their size to accommodate longer or shorter text.

Cocos2d-x provides UI components like *Label* and *Button* that can adapt to dynamic text lengths, but you may need to configure them properly for localization.

5. Consider Right-to-Left (RTL) Languages

Some languages, such as Arabic and Hebrew, are written from right to left (RTL). Ensure that your game's UI can support RTL languages if you plan to localize for regions where these languages are prevalent. This includes text alignment, layout, and rendering.

Cocos2d-x provides support for RTL languages through its text rendering capabilities and layout tools.

6. Maintain a Language Selection Mechanism

Implement a language selection screen within your game, allowing players to choose their preferred language. Store the selected language as a preference or setting, and load the appropriate localization data based on this choice.

You can use Cocos2d-x's built-in user interface components to create a language selection menu and save the chosen language in the game's settings.

7. Collaborate with Native Speakers

To ensure accurate translations and cultural sensitivity, collaborate with native speakers of the target languages. Native speakers can provide valuable insights into language nuances, cultural references, and context-specific issues.

Consider involving linguistic and cultural experts during the internationalization and localization process.

8. Test Thoroughly

Internationalization and localization testing are crucial steps. Test your game in multiple languages to identify any issues related to text layout, overflow, or cultural appropriateness. Conduct beta testing with players who speak the target languages to gather feedback and address any remaining localization issues.

By following these internationalization best practices, you can build a solid foundation for localizing your game to reach a global audience effectively. Designing with internationalization in mind from the beginning will make the localization process smoother and more efficient, ultimately leading to a better gaming experience for players worldwide.

17.5 Legal Considerations in Global Markets

Expanding your game to international markets brings not only linguistic and cultural challenges but also legal considerations. Different countries have varying regulations, laws, and requirements that you must comply with when distributing and operating your game globally. In this section, we'll explore some of the key legal considerations you should be aware of when taking your game to the global stage.

1. Age Ratings and Content Restrictions

Many countries have age rating systems for video games, and these systems can vary significantly from one region to another. For example, the ESRB rating system is commonly used in North America, while PEGI is prevalent in Europe. Be aware of the age rating requirements in the countries you target and ensure that your game complies with them. Failure to do so can result in legal consequences or restrictions on distribution.

2. Compliance with Privacy Laws

Data protection and privacy laws, such as the General Data Protection Regulation (GDPR) in the European Union, govern how user data is collected, processed, and stored. Ensure that your game complies with these laws, especially if it collects and stores user information. This may include obtaining user consent for data processing and providing clear privacy policies.

3. Intellectual Property Rights

Respect intellectual property rights when using copyrighted materials, trademarks, and other intellectual property in your game. Make sure you have the necessary licenses or permissions to use third-party content, and avoid infringing on the intellectual property of others. Different countries have varying copyright laws, so consult with legal experts when needed.

4. Consumer Protection Laws

Understand consumer protection laws and regulations in the countries where you distribute your game. These laws may cover issues such as refund policies, advertising practices, and fair competition. Ensure that your game's terms of service and refund policies are clear and comply with local regulations.

5. Taxation and VAT/GST

Taxation rules and value-added tax (VAT) or goods and services tax (GST) rates can differ significantly between countries. Determine your tax obligations in each market and be prepared to handle tax collection and reporting accordingly. Some digital distribution platforms may assist with tax compliance, but it's essential to understand your responsibilities.

6. Licensing and Publishing Agreements

If you partner with local publishers or distributors in international markets, carefully review and negotiate licensing and publishing agreements. Ensure that these agreements protect your intellectual property, define revenue sharing, and outline responsibilities and obligations for both parties. Consult with legal experts to create agreements that work in your favor.

7. Localization of Legal Documents

Translate and localize legal documents, including terms of service, privacy policies, and end-user license agreements (EULAs), into the languages of the target markets. Ensure that these documents comply with local laws and regulations. Localized legal documents help users understand their rights and responsibilities in their native languages.

8. Cultural Sensitivity

Be culturally sensitive in your game content, including visuals and narratives. Avoid content that could be considered offensive or disrespectful in specific cultures. Cultural insensitivity can lead to legal issues and harm your game's reputation.

9. Legal Consultation

Consult with legal experts who specialize in international law and the gaming industry. They can provide guidance on complying with regional regulations, protecting your intellectual property, and ensuring legal compliance in global markets.

In summary, expanding your game to global markets requires careful consideration of legal requirements and regulations. Being proactive in understanding and addressing these legal considerations is essential to ensure a successful and legally compliant international launch. Consult with legal experts as needed to navigate the complexities of global legal compliance.

Chapter 18: Mobile Game Specifics

18.1 Mobile Performance Optimization

Mobile game development presents unique challenges due to the wide range of devices with varying hardware capabilities. To create a successful mobile game, you need to optimize performance to ensure a smooth and enjoyable experience on a variety of smartphones and tablets. In this section, we'll explore mobile performance optimization techniques for Cocos2d-x game development.

1. Profile and Benchmark

Before diving into optimization, it's essential to profile your game to identify performance bottlenecks. Profiling tools help you determine which parts of your game are consuming the most resources, such as CPU usage, GPU load, and memory usage. Popular profiling tools for mobile game development include Android Profiler and Instruments (for iOS).

Once you've identified performance bottlenecks, benchmark your game on multiple devices to understand how it performs on different hardware configurations. This will help you set performance goals and prioritize optimizations.

2. Efficient Asset Loading

Mobile devices have limited storage and memory, so it's crucial to optimize asset loading. Use texture atlases to reduce the number of texture swaps and minimize memory usage. Implement asset streaming to load assets dynamically as needed, rather than loading everything upfront. This reduces the initial load time and memory footprint.

3. Resolution and Screen Sizes

Support multiple screen resolutions and aspect ratios by designing flexible UIs and using assets that scale well. Avoid using high-resolution assets on devices that don't require them, as this can lead to unnecessary memory consumption and decreased performance. Use adaptive layouts to ensure your game looks good on various screens.

4. Graphics Optimization

Optimize graphics rendering for mobile devices by reducing the number of draw calls and triangles. Use tools like Cocos2d-x's SpriteBatchNode to batch sprites together for efficient rendering. Implement level-of-detail (LOD) techniques for 3D models to reduce polygon counts on lower-end devices.

5. Memory Management

Mobile devices have limited memory, so effective memory management is crucial. Use object pooling to recycle objects rather than creating and destroying them frequently. Unload assets that are no longer in use to free up memory. Monitor and manage memory allocations to avoid memory leaks.

6. Threading and Parallelism

Leverage multi-threading to distribute CPU-intensive tasks across multiple cores. Cocos2d-x provides tools for background loading and parallelism, allowing you to offload tasks like asset loading and data processing to separate threads, improving overall performance.

7. Battery Usage

Optimize battery usage by minimizing background processes and reducing unnecessary CPU and GPU load when the game is in the background. Implement a power-efficient rendering strategy, such as frame rate capping, to conserve battery life.

8. Touch Input and Gestures

Mobile devices rely heavily on touch input and gestures. Optimize touch handling code to respond quickly to user interactions. Implement touch event pooling to reduce the overhead of creating and destroying touch objects.

9. Mobile-specific Features

Utilize mobile-specific features to enhance the user experience. This may include integrating with device sensors (e.g., accelerometer and gyroscope), utilizing haptic feedback, and implementing push notifications for engagement and retention.

10. Cross-Platform Development

Consider cross-platform development frameworks like Cocos2d-x to streamline the development process and reduce the effort required to optimize for multiple mobile platforms (iOS and Android). Cocos2d-x provides tools and libraries that abstract platform-specific details.

11. Testing and Performance Profiling

Regularly test your game on a range of devices with different specifications and operating systems. Use profiling tools to identify and address performance bottlenecks as they arise. Continuous testing and optimization are essential to ensure a consistently smooth gaming experience on all target devices.

By following these mobile performance optimization techniques, you can create mobile games that run efficiently and provide an enjoyable experience across a wide range of devices. Mobile game development requires a balance between delivering high-quality visuals and ensuring smooth performance, making optimization a critical aspect of your development process.

18.2 Handling Touch Input and Gestures

Touch input is fundamental in mobile game development, as it's the primary way players interact with your game. Handling touch input and gestures effectively is essential to provide a responsive and enjoyable gaming experience. In this section, we'll explore how to handle touch input and gestures in your Cocos2d-x mobile game.

1. Basic Touch Handling

Cocos2d-x provides straightforward ways to handle basic touch input. You can enable touch events for specific layers or nodes in your scene. Here's a basic example of how to handle touch events in Cocos2d-x:

```
bool YourGameScene::init() {

if (!Layer::init()) {

return false;

}

// Enable touch events for this layer

setTouchEnabled(true);
```

```
// Register touch event listener

auto listener = EventListenerTouchOneByOne::create();

listener->onTouchBegan =
CC_CALLBACK_2(YourGameScene::onTouchBegan, this);

listener->onTouchMoved =
CC_CALLBACK_2(YourGameScene::onTouchMoved, this);

listener->onTouchEnded =
CC_CALLBACK_2(YourGameScene::onTouchEnded, this);

_eventDispatcher->addEventListenerWithSceneGraphPriority(listener,
this);

return true;

}

bool YourGameScene::onTouchBegan(Touch* touch, Event* event)
{

// Handle touch begin

return true; // Return true to indicate that the touch event is consumed

}

void YourGameScene::onTouchMoved(Touch* touch, Event* event)
{

// Handle touch move

}

void YourGameScene::onTouchEnded(Touch* touch, Event* event)
{
```

```
// Handle touch end

}
```

In this example, we enable touch events for the layer and register touch event listeners for handling touch begin, move, and end events.

2. Multi-Touch Support

Mobile devices often support multi-touch input, allowing players to interact with the game using multiple fingers simultaneously. Cocos2d-x provides support for handling multiple touch points. You can modify the example above to handle multi-touch input by iterating through all active touches:

```
bool YourGameScene::onTouchBegan(Touch* touch, Event* event)
{

// Handle touch begin

// Iterate through all active touches

for (auto& touch : touches) {

int touchID = touch->getID();

Vec2 touchLocation = touch->getLocation();

// Handle each touch individually

}

return true;

}
```

3. Gesture Recognition

In addition to basic touch handling, you may want to recognize common gestures such as swipes, pinches, and taps. Cocos2d-x provides gesture recognition through extensions and third-party libraries. One popular library is Cocos2d-x's own *ui::Layout* class, which includes gesture recognition for swipes and pinch gestures.

```
auto listener = EventListenerTouchOneByOne::create();

listener->onTouchBegan = [](Touch* touch, Event* event) {

return true;

};

listener->onTouchMoved = [](Touch* touch, Event* event) {

// Detect swipe gestures

Vec2 delta = touch->getDelta();

if (delta.x > 50) {

// Right swipe

} else if (delta.x < -50) {

// Left swipe

}

if (delta.y > 50) {

// Up swipe

} else if (delta.y < -50) {

// Down swipe
```

```
}

};

_eventDispatcher->addEventListenerWithSceneGraphPriority(listener,
this);
```

This code demonstrates how to detect swipe gestures by tracking touch movement. You can adapt this approach to recognize other gestures based on your game's requirements.

4. Virtual Joysticks and Buttons

For games that require virtual joysticks, buttons, or on-screen controls, you can implement these elements using Cocos2d-x's UI components. The *ui::Button* class allows you to create interactive buttons that respond to touch events. Similarly, you can create joystick-like controls by tracking touch movement and converting it into character movement.

```
auto leftButton = ui::Button::create("left_button.png",
"left_button_selected.png");

leftButton->setPosition(Vec2(100, 100));

leftButton->addTouchEventListener([&](Ref* sender,
ui::Widget::TouchEventType type) {

if (type == ui::Widget::TouchEventType::BEGAN) {

// Handle button press

} else if (type == ui::Widget::TouchEventType::ENDED) {

// Handle button release

}
```

```
});

addChild(leftButton);
```

In this example, we create a simple left button that responds to touch events. You can create similar buttons for other directions or actions.

By effectively handling touch input and gestures, you can create intuitive and responsive controls for your mobile game, enhancing the overall player experience. Customize touch input to suit your game's mechanics and provide a smooth and enjoyable gaming experience on mobile devices.

18.3 Mobile Networking Considerations

In today's mobile gaming landscape, many games rely on network connectivity to provide multiplayer features, social interactions, cloud-based features, and more. Handling mobile networking effectively is crucial for providing a seamless online experience for your players. In this section, we'll explore important considerations and best practices for mobile networking in Cocos2d-x game development.

1. Network Libraries and APIs

Cocos2d-x provides support for networking through its network libraries and APIs. You can use these tools to create and manage network connections, send and receive data, and implement online features in your game. Familiarize yourself with Cocos2d-x's networking capabilities and APIs to leverage them effectively.

2. Cross-Platform Compatibility

When implementing networking features, consider cross-platform compatibility. Ensure that your networking code works seamlessly on both iOS and Android devices. Cocos2d-x's networking libraries are designed to be cross-platform, making it easier to develop networking features that work consistently on various mobile devices.

3. Security and Encryption

Security is a critical aspect of mobile networking. Protect sensitive user data and prevent unauthorized access to your game's servers. Use secure communication protocols such as HTTPS and implement data encryption to safeguard user information. Cocos2d-x provides support for secure socket layer (SSL) encryption, which can be used for secure network communication.

4. Latency and Performance

Mobile networks can introduce latency and fluctuations in network performance. Design your game's networking features to handle network delays gracefully. Implement techniques such as prediction and interpolation to provide a smooth experience for players, especially in real-time multiplayer games.

5. Bandwidth Usage

Mobile data plans often have limited bandwidth, so optimize your game's networking to minimize data usage. Compress data when transmitting it over the network and reduce unnecessary data transfers. Consider implementing client-side prediction and server reconciliation to minimize the amount of data that needs to be exchanged.

6. Offline Mode

Ensure that your game has an offline mode or fallback mechanisms in case of network disruptions. Players should still be able to enjoy the game's core features and content even when they have limited or no network connectivity. Implementing offline features can enhance player retention and user satisfaction.

7. Error Handling and Recovery

Network errors are inevitable in mobile gaming. Implement robust error handling and recovery mechanisms to gracefully handle network failures, timeouts, and unexpected errors. Provide clear error messages and options for players to retry or take appropriate actions.

8. Cross-Platform Multiplayer

If your game offers multiplayer functionality, consider implementing cross-platform multiplayer support. This allows players on different mobile platforms to play together. Ensure that matchmaking, game state synchronization, and communication protocols are compatible across platforms.

9. Backend Services

Consider using backend-as-a-service (BaaS) providers or cloud platforms to simplify server management and scalability. Services like Firebase, AWS, or Google Cloud can handle server infrastructure, user authentication, and real-time database synchronization, freeing you to focus on game development.

10. Data Synchronization

If your game involves data synchronization, implement conflict resolution strategies to handle situations where multiple players update the same data simultaneously. Ensure that player progress and game data are synchronized accurately across devices and platforms.

11. Testing and Optimization

Regularly test your game's networking features on various mobile devices and network conditions. Optimize network requests, minimize latency, and reduce data usage through profiling and testing. Consider using simulated network conditions during development to replicate real-world network scenarios.

By addressing these mobile networking considerations, you can create a robust and reliable online experience for your players. Effective mobile networking implementation is crucial for multiplayer games, social features, leaderboards, and other online interactions that enhance player engagement and retention.

18.4 Battery Usage and Optimization

Battery life is a precious resource on mobile devices, and players expect games to be power-efficient to avoid rapid battery drain. Optimizing your mobile game for minimal battery usage is essential for providing a positive player experience and improving device longevity. In this section, we'll explore strategies and best practices for optimizing battery usage in your Cocos2d-x mobile game.

1. Frame Rate Control

One of the most effective ways to conserve battery life is by controlling the frame rate of your game. Running your game at a high frame rate when it's not necessary can consume unnecessary power. Implement a frame rate capping mechanism that adjusts the frame rate based on the device's capabilities and the game's requirements. For example, you can limit the frame rate to 30 or 60 frames per second (FPS) when the game is in the foreground and reduce it further when in the background.

```
Director::getInstance()->setAnimationInterval(1.0f / targetFPS);
```

2. Efficient Rendering

Optimize rendering to reduce GPU load and minimize battery consumption. Use techniques such as sprite batching, texture atlases, and occlusion culling to reduce the number of draw calls and render only what's visible on the screen. Minimize the use of complex shaders and effects that require significant GPU processing.

3. Background Processing

When your game is in the background, reduce background processing to a minimum. Suspend or pause background tasks that are not critical to the player experience. For example, if your game uses background threads for non-essential tasks like data synchronization, consider suspending those threads when the game is not in the foreground.

4. Audio Optimization

Audio can also impact battery life. Implement audio streaming and loading strategies to minimize memory and CPU usage. Use compressed audio formats and adjust the audio quality settings to strike a balance between audio fidelity and resource consumption.

5. Network Activity

Minimize network activity when the game is not actively using network features. Frequent polling for updates or maintaining constant connections can drain the battery. Implement smart network management that reduces network activity during periods of inactivity.

6. Location Services

If your game uses location services, request location updates at reasonable intervals. Constantly polling for location data can significantly impact battery life. Use location updates only when necessary, and provide options for players to disable location services if they choose.

7. Power-Conserving Animations

Optimize animations and transitions to be power-efficient. Avoid excessive use of animations that continuously run in the background, as they can consume CPU and GPU resources. Implement animations that pause or scale down when not in focus.

8. Background Music and Sound Effects

Allow players to control audio settings, including background music and sound effects volume. Some players may prefer to conserve battery by turning off audio when playing on the go. Implement options for players to mute or adjust audio settings.

9. Battery Monitoring

Monitor device battery levels and adapt your game's behavior accordingly. When the battery level is low, consider implementing power-saving modes that further reduce resource consumption, such as lower graphics settings or reduced frame rates.

10. Testing on Different Devices

Test your game on a variety of mobile devices with different hardware capabilities and battery capacities. Ensure that your battery optimization strategies work effectively across a range of devices and operating systems.

11. Player Education

Educate players about battery-saving options within your game. Provide tips and information on how to optimize their device settings for extended gameplay without excessive battery drain.

By implementing these battery optimization strategies, you can create a mobile game that conserves battery life while delivering an engaging and enjoyable player experience. Prioritizing battery efficiency is not only player-friendly but also contributes to positive user reviews and increased player retention.

18.5 Integrating with Mobile-Specific Features

Mobile devices offer a wealth of unique features and capabilities that can enhance the gameplay experience and set your game apart. Integrating mobile-specific features into your Cocos2d-x game can improve user engagement and make your game more appealing to a broader audience. In this section, we'll explore some key mobile-specific features and how to integrate them effectively.

1. Accelerometer and Gyroscope

Mobile devices are equipped with built-in sensors like accelerometers and gyroscopes. These sensors detect motion and rotation, allowing you to create games that respond to the physical movement of the device. For example, you can implement tilt-based controls for racing games or use gyroscopes for aiming in shooting games. To integrate these features, you can use Cocos2d-x's built-in classes like *Device::getRotation()* and *Device::getAcceleration()*.

```
// Enable accelerometer and gyroscope

Device::setAccelerometerEnabled(true);

Device::setGyroscopeEnabled(true);

// Register event listeners

auto accelerometerListener = EventListenerAcceleration::create([](Acceleration* acceleration, Event* event) {

// Handle accelerometer data

});

auto gyroscopeListener = EventListenerGyroscope::create([](Gyroscope* gyroscope, Event* event) {

// Handle gyroscope data

});

_eventDispatcher->addEventListenerWithSceneGraphPriority(accelerom
this);
```

```
_eventDispatcher->addEventListenerWithSceneGraphPriority(gyroscop
this);
```

2. Haptic Feedback

Many modern mobile devices offer haptic feedback, also known as vibration feedback. You can use haptic feedback to enhance the tactile experience of your game. Implement haptic feedback for actions like button presses, explosions, or collisions to provide tactile confirmation to players. Cocos2d-x provides APIs for triggering haptic feedback on supported devices.

```
// Check if haptic feedback is supported
if (Device::hasHapticFeedback()) {
// Trigger haptic feedback
Device::vibrate(0.5f); // Vibrate for 0.5 seconds
}
```

3. Touch ID and Face ID

For security and convenience, some mobile devices offer biometric authentication features like Touch ID and Face ID. You can use these features to secure in-game transactions or access restricted content. Integrate biometric authentication into your game's login or payment systems to provide a seamless and secure experience for players.

4. Push Notifications

Push notifications are a powerful tool for engaging players and keeping them informed about in-game events, updates, and promotions. Implement push notifications to notify players of new content, achievements, or time-limited offers. You can use platform-specific APIs or third-party services like Firebase Cloud Messaging (FCM) for push notifications.

5. Augmented Reality (AR)

Augmented reality features can provide immersive and interactive experiences. You can integrate AR capabilities to enable players to interact with virtual objects in the real world. Platforms like ARKit (iOS) and ARCore (Android) offer AR development tools that can be used in conjunction with Cocos2d-x to create AR-enhanced games.

6. Social Media Integration

Leverage social media integration to allow players to share their achievements, high scores, or in-game experiences with their friends and followers. Implement features that enable players to connect their social media accounts, post updates, and invite friends to play the game.

7. In-App Purchases

Mobile devices are known for in-app purchases (IAPs), and integrating them effectively can be a monetization strategy for your game. Implement IAPs for virtual goods, power-ups, or premium content. Cocos2d-x provides APIs for managing in-app purchases on both iOS and Android platforms.

8. Camera and Photo Integration

Allow players to use their device's camera to capture photos or videos within the game. You can use this feature for player avatars, creating custom in-game content, or for sharing moments with other players.

Implement camera integration using platform-specific APIs or third-party libraries.

9. Location-Based Features

Leverage the device's GPS capabilities to create location-based gameplay elements. You can implement features like geocaching, location-based quests, or real-world exploration mechanics. Platforms like GPS Kit (iOS) and Google Location Services (Android) provide location data that can be integrated into your game.

10. Device-Specific APIs

Both iOS and Android offer a range of device-specific APIs and services that can enhance your game. Examples include Apple's Game Center for iOS and Google Play Games Services for Android. These platforms provide leaderboards, achievements, multiplayer matchmaking, and other features that can enhance player engagement.

By integrating mobile-specific features into your Cocos2d-x game, you can create a more immersive and engaging player experience. Consider the unique capabilities of each platform and target audience preferences when deciding which features to implement. Effective integration of these features can help your game stand out in the competitive mobile gaming market.

Chapter 19: Advanced Topics in Game Design

19.1 Narrative and Storytelling Techniques

Game design goes beyond mechanics and visuals; it encompasses the art of storytelling and creating immersive narratives that captivate players. In this section, we'll explore advanced narrative and storytelling techniques that can elevate your Cocos2d-x game to new heights.

1. World Building

Effective storytelling often begins with world-building. Create a rich and immersive game world with its history, cultures, and lore. Develop detailed backstories for characters, locations, and factions within your game. This depth adds layers to your narrative and provides players with a sense of immersion.

2. Character Development

Compelling characters are at the heart of any great story. Design characters with distinct personalities, motivations, and arcs. Allow their actions and decisions to impact the game world and storyline. Make characters relatable and provide opportunities for players to form emotional connections with them.

3. Branching Narratives

Consider implementing branching narratives that allow players to make choices that influence the story's direction. These choices can lead to multiple endings or divergent storylines, enhancing replayability and player agency. Use conditional statements and decision trees to manage branching narratives efficiently.

```
if (playerChoice == "HelpNPC") {

// Storyline where the player helps an NPC

} else if (playerChoice == "IgnoreNPC") {

// Storyline where the player ignores the NPC

}
```

4. Non-linear Storytelling

Non-linear storytelling breaks away from traditional linear narratives and lets players explore the story at their own pace. Incorporate open-world elements or nonlinear levels where players can choose their objectives and the order in which they tackle them.

5. Environmental Storytelling

Use environmental storytelling to convey narrative elements through the game world itself. Details like abandoned buildings, graffiti, or item placements can hint at a story without explicit exposition. This allows players to piece together the narrative through exploration.

6. Subtext and Themes

Incorporate subtext and themes that add depth to your narrative. Address complex topics or moral dilemmas that encourage players to think critically and engage with the story on a deeper level. Subtext can be conveyed through character dialogues, symbolism, or subtle storytelling cues.

7. Foreshadowing

Foreshadowing is a powerful storytelling tool. Plant hints or clues about future events early in the game to create anticipation and intrigue. This can be achieved through dialogues, item descriptions, or visual cues that players might not fully grasp until later in the game.

8. Player-Driven Stories

Empower players to create their narratives within the game world. Implement sandbox or emergent gameplay elements that enable players to craft their unique stories through their choices, actions, and interactions with the game's systems.

9. Audio and Sound Design

Sound design plays a significant role in storytelling. Use music, sound effects, and voice acting to evoke emotions and set the tone for different story moments. Consider how audio can enhance the narrative's impact.

10. Dynamic Events

Incorporate dynamic events that occur based on player actions or triggers within the game. These events can create memorable story moments and make the world feel alive and responsive to the player's presence and decisions.

11. Pacing and Rhythm

Carefully manage the pacing and rhythm of your narrative. Balance moments of tension and excitement with periods of reflection and exploration. Pacing can influence how players perceive the story's progression and emotional impact.

12. Ethical Considerations

Be mindful of ethical considerations when crafting your narrative. Avoid harmful stereotypes or insensitive content. Aim to create stories that resonate with diverse audiences and promote inclusivity and empathy.

13. Playtesting and Iteration

Iterate on your narrative through playtesting and player feedback. Observe how players engage with the story, identify pacing issues, and refine character development based on player reactions. Playtesting is essential for fine-tuning the storytelling experience.

14. Storytelling Tools

Consider using specialized storytelling tools and engines that offer features for branching narratives, dialogue trees, and interactive storytelling. These tools can streamline the process of implementing complex narratives.

By incorporating these advanced narrative and storytelling techniques into your Cocos2d-x game, you can create a memorable and emotionally engaging experience for players. A well-crafted narrative can elevate your game beyond its mechanics, leaving a lasting impression on players and fostering a deeper connection with your game world.

19.2 Creating Immersive Game Worlds

Creating an immersive game world is a fundamental aspect of game design that directly influences player engagement and enjoyment. Immersive worlds captivate players, making them feel like they've stepped into another reality. In this section, we'll delve into techniques for crafting immersive game worlds using Cocos2d-x.

1. Detailed Environments

Begin by designing detailed and visually captivating environments. Pay attention to small details like foliage, architecture, and terrain. These elements contribute to the world's believability. Use tools in Cocos2d-x to efficiently create and render complex scenes, such as the TileMap feature for 2D environments or 3D model integration for 3D worlds.

```
// Creating a simple TileMap in Cocos2d-x

auto tilemap = TMXTiledMap::create("maps/level1.tmx");

addChild(tilemap);
```

2. Consistent Art Style

Maintain a consistent art style throughout your game world. Visual coherence is essential for immersion. Whether your game features pixel art, realistic 3D graphics, or a stylized cartoon style, ensure that all assets, characters, and environments adhere to the chosen style.

3. Dynamic Lighting and Shadows

Implement dynamic lighting and shadows to add depth and realism to your game world. Use techniques like shadow mapping and shader effects to create convincing lighting effects that react to in-game events, time of day, or player actions.

```
// Adding dynamic lighting to a Cocos2d-x scene

auto light = Light::create();
```

```
light->setPosition3D(Vec3(0, 10, 0));

light->setLightType(LightType::DIRECTIONAL);

addChild(light);
```

4. Soundscapes

Sound design plays a crucial role in immersion. Use ambient soundscapes, background music, and spatial audio to create a sense of place within your game world. Consider how sound can convey information about the environment, such as the rustling of leaves in a forest or the distant echoes in a cavern.

5. Interactive Elements

Include interactive elements in your game world that respond to player actions. This could involve destructible objects, moving platforms, or NPCs with dynamic behaviors. Interactivity reinforces the sense that the game world is alive and reactive.

6. Lore and Backstory

Develop a rich lore and backstory for your game world, even if it's not explicitly conveyed in the main storyline. Create historical events, legends, and myths that provide depth and context to the world. You can scatter hints and lore-related items throughout the game for players to discover.

7. Day-Night Cycle and Weather

Implement a day-night cycle and dynamic weather systems to make the world feel dynamic and ever-changing. These elements can influence gameplay, affecting visibility, NPC behavior, and the overall mood of the game.

```
// Creating a day-night cycle in Cocos2d-x

auto dayNightLayer = DayNightLayer::create();

addChild(dayNightLayer);
```

8. Environmental Storytelling

Use environmental storytelling to convey narrative elements through the game world itself. Details like abandoned campsites, cryptic symbols, or ruined structures can hint at past events or hidden secrets, encouraging players to explore and piece together the story.

9. World Map and Navigation

Consider implementing a world map or navigation system that allows players to explore a larger game world seamlessly. Provide landmarks, waypoints, and fast travel options to enhance player orientation and reduce frustration.

10. Player Agency

Give players agency in shaping the game world. Allow their decisions and actions to have meaningful consequences that impact the world's state. This can lead to multiple endings or divergent storylines, enhancing replayability and player investment.

11. Cultural Diversity

Create diverse cultures and societies within your game world, each with its traditions, languages, and customs. Diversity adds richness and authenticity to the world, making it feel more expansive and believable.

12. Hidden Secrets and Easter Eggs

Include hidden secrets, Easter eggs, and rewards for exploration. These surprises can delight players and motivate them to thoroughly explore every corner of your game world.

13. Environmental Challenges

Design environmental challenges that require players to interact with the world creatively. This could involve solving puzzles, navigating treacherous terrain, or using the environment itself as a weapon or tool.

14. Playtesting and Iteration

Iterate on your game world design through playtesting and player feedback. Observe how players engage with the world, identify areas that may break immersion, and refine the design based on player experiences.

An immersive game world can transport players to fantastical realms, historical settings, or futuristic landscapes. By carefully crafting your game world using these techniques, you can create a captivating and memorable experience that keeps players eagerly exploring and engaging with your game.

19.3 Player Psychology and Engagement

Understanding player psychology is essential for designing games that captivate and retain players' attention. By leveraging psychological principles, game designers can create experiences that are not only entertaining but also highly engaging. In this section, we'll explore key aspects of player psychology and how they can be applied to game design using Cocos2d-x.

1. Reward Systems

Reward systems are a fundamental aspect of player engagement. Implementing well-designed reward structures can motivate players to progress and invest more time in your game. Consider using a variety of rewards, including achievements, in-game currency, cosmetics, and power-ups. Use Cocos2d-x's achievements system and data storage capabilities to track and reward player progress.

```
// Unlocking an achievement in Cocos2d-x

AchievementManager::unlockAchievement("First_Milestone");
```

2. Progression Mechanics

Players enjoy a sense of progression and achievement. Implement progression mechanics such as leveling up, skill trees, or unlocking new content over time. Show players how far they've come and what they can achieve next to keep them engaged.

3. Flow State

Create a flow state where players are fully immersed in the game, losing track of time and distractions. Maintain an optimal balance of challenge and skill to keep players in this state. Avoid overly frustrating or trivial gameplay segments.

4. Social Interaction

Leverage social interaction by implementing multiplayer modes, leaderboards, and social media integration. Social competition and cooperation can significantly enhance player engagement. Use Cocos2d-x's networking capabilities for multiplayer features.

```
// Setting up multiplayer functionality in Cocos2d-x
```

```
MultiplayerManager::createGameRoom();

MultiplayerManager::joinGameRoom("RoomID");
```

5. FOMO (Fear of Missing Out)

Create events, limited-time offers, and special promotions to trigger players' fear of missing out. Time-limited content or discounts can motivate players to log in regularly and participate in the game.

6. Autonomy and Choice

Give players a sense of autonomy and choice. Allow them to make meaningful decisions that impact the game's outcome. Choices can include character customization, story branching, or strategic decisions.

7. Immersion and Escapism

Design your game to provide a sense of immersion and escapism. Engage players in a captivating narrative, detailed game world, or compelling characters that transport them to another reality.

8. Challenge and Mastery

Humans crave challenges and the feeling of mastery. Gradually increase the difficulty of your game to match players' growing skills. Provide opportunities for players to learn and improve, fostering a sense of accomplishment.

9. Surprise and Delight

Incorporate elements of surprise and delight, such as unexpected events, humorous interactions, or hidden secrets. These moments can create memorable experiences and keep players engaged.

10. Feedback and Progress Tracking

Offer clear feedback to players about their progress and performance. Use UI elements, animations, and notifications to inform players of their achievements, goals, and milestones.

```
// Displaying progress feedback in Cocos2d-x
HUD::showAchievementNotification("Level Up!");
```

11. Emotion and Storytelling

Emotional storytelling can deeply engage players. Craft narratives that evoke a range of emotions, from excitement and joy to empathy and sadness. Players who form emotional connections with the game are more likely to stay engaged.

12. Player Empowerment

Empower players by making them feel capable and influential within the game world. Provide tools, abilities, and resources that enable players to overcome challenges and make an impact on the game's universe.

13. Anticipation and Teasers

Generate anticipation and excitement by teasing upcoming content, updates, or events. Release teasers, trailers, or sneak peeks to keep players eager to see what's next.

14. Playtesting and Feedback

Regularly conduct playtesting and gather player feedback to understand how players are engaging with your game. Use this feedback to refine and improve engagement strategies.

By integrating these psychological principles into your Cocos2d-x game design, you can create experiences that resonate with players on a deep level. Engaged players are more likely to continue playing your game, recommend it to others, and become loyal members of your gaming community.

19.4 Ethical Game Design

Ethical game design is a critical consideration for game developers. As creators of interactive experiences, designers have a responsibility to craft games that are not only enjoyable but also respectful of players' well-being and societal values. In this section, we'll explore the importance of ethical game design and principles to guide your decision-making when developing games with Cocos2d-x.

1. Player Well-Being

Prioritize player well-being by ensuring that your game does not promote addictive or harmful behaviors. Avoid excessive use of gamification techniques that can lead to compulsive gameplay. Implement features that encourage healthy breaks, such as reminders to rest or take a walk.

```
// Implementing periodic rest reminders

Scheduler::schedule([](float dt) {

// Display a reminder to take a break

}, 1800); // Schedule a reminder every 30 minutes
```

2. Fair Monetization

If your game includes monetization strategies, ensure that they are fair and transparent. Avoid predatory practices like pay-to-win mechanics, loot boxes with random rewards, or overly aggressive advertising. Clearly communicate pricing and in-app purchase options to players.

3. Inclusivity and Representation

Strive for inclusivity and representation in your game. Create characters and narratives that reflect diverse backgrounds, cultures, genders, and identities. Avoid harmful stereotypes and offensive content that can perpetuate bias or discrimination.

4. Age-Appropriate Content

Label your game with age-appropriate content ratings and provide parental controls. If your game is intended for mature audiences, clearly indicate this to prevent exposure to inappropriate content by younger players.

```
// Implementing parental controls in Cocos2d-x

UserSettings::setAgeRestriction(true);
```

5. Privacy and Data Security

Respect player privacy and adhere to data protection regulations. Clearly communicate how player data is collected, used, and stored. Implement robust data security measures to protect player information from breaches or unauthorized access.

6. Accessibility

Design your game with accessibility in mind. Ensure that it can be enjoyed by players with disabilities by providing options for customizable controls, text-to-speech features, and visual aids.

Conduct accessibility testing to identify and address potential barriers.

7. Social Responsibility

Consider the broader societal impact of your game. Avoid promoting violence, hate speech, or harmful ideologies. Use your platform as a game developer to contribute positively to social issues or raise awareness about important topics.

8. Transparency

Be transparent with your players about game updates, changes, and community guidelines. Maintain open communication channels to address player concerns and feedback. Transparency builds trust with your player base.

```
// Displaying changelogs and update notes in Cocos2d-x
UI::showChangelog("Version 1.2.0", "Bug fixes, balance adjustments, and new content added.");
```

9. Ethical Testing

Conduct ethical testing by seeking player consent and providing clear explanations when conducting playtests or experiments within your game. Avoid manipulating player behavior without their informed consent.

10. Community Moderation

Implement robust community moderation tools to prevent harassment, toxic behavior, and inappropriate content in player-generated spaces like forums or chat rooms. Enforce strict rules of conduct to maintain a positive and inclusive community.

11. Accountability

Take accountability for any mistakes or missteps in game development. Acknowledge and rectify issues promptly, and demonstrate a commitment to ethical game design principles.

12. Ethical Leadership

Promote ethical game design principles within your development team and the wider gaming industry. Encourage discussions about ethics and responsible game development practices among peers and collaborators.

Ethical game design is not only a moral imperative but also a strategic choice. Games that prioritize player well-being and ethical principles tend to foster healthier player communities, enjoy longer-term success, and create a positive reputation for developers. By following these ethical guidelines, you can contribute to a more responsible and inclusive gaming industry.

19.5 Innovations in Game Mechanics

In the constantly evolving landscape of game development, innovative game mechanics can set your Cocos2d-x game apart and create unique player experiences. In this section, we'll explore various innovative game mechanics and how you can incorporate them into your game design.

1. Procedural Generation

Procedural generation is a technique that generates game content dynamically, such as levels, maps, or quests. It can result in endless variations of gameplay and exploration. Implement procedural generation algorithms to create randomized or semi-randomized game elements.

```
// Procedural level generation in Cocos2d-x

auto generatedLevel = ProceduralLevelGenerator::generateLevel();
```

2. Time Manipulation

Incorporate time manipulation mechanics that allow players to control time within the game world. This can involve time travel, time loops, or the ability to pause, rewind, or fast forward in specific scenarios. Time manipulation adds depth to puzzles and challenges.

```
// Implementing time manipulation in Cocos2d-x

TimeController::pauseTime();
```

3. Non-Linear Narratives

Move away from linear storytelling and embrace non-linear narratives. Implement branching storylines, player choices that affect the plot, and multiple endings based on player decisions. Non-linearity increases replayability and player agency.

4. Emergent Gameplay

Create emergent gameplay experiences where interactions between game elements produce unexpected and unique outcomes. Emergent gameplay encourages player experimentation and creativity.

```
// Enabling emergent gameplay in Cocos2d-x

EmergentGameplay::enable();
```

5. Permadeath and Rogue-like Elements

Incorporate permadeath mechanics or rogue-like elements into your game. When players die, they must start over, but they retain some progression or knowledge from previous attempts. Permadeath adds tension and rewards skillful play.

6. Dynamic Ecosystems

Design dynamic ecosystems within your game world. Create ecosystems with interconnected flora and fauna that evolve over time. Player actions can influence the balance of these ecosystems, affecting gameplay and the environment.

7. Physics-Based Interactions

Leverage physics-based interactions to make the game world feel more tactile and responsive. Incorporate realistic physics simulations for objects, characters, and environmental elements. Players can use physics to their advantage in puzzles and challenges.

```
// Adding physics-based interactions in Cocos2d-x

PhysicsController::enablePhysics();
```

8. Player-Generated Content

Allow players to generate and share their content within the game. Implement level editors, character customization tools, or community-driven content creation platforms. Player-generated content enhances replayability and community engagement.

9. Augmented Reality (AR) Integration

Explore AR integration to blend digital experiences with the real world. AR can enable location-based gameplay, interactive storytelling in physical spaces, and unique gaming experiences tied to the player's environment.

```
// Integrating AR features in Cocos2d-x

ARController::enableAR();
```

10. Multiverse and Cross-Platform Play

Consider creating a multiverse where players can access their characters and progress across different games or platforms. Cross-platform play allows players on various devices to interact and collaborate within the same game world.

11. Emotional AI

Implement emotional AI systems that enable non-player characters (NPCs) to react dynamically to player actions and emotions. NPCs can display empathy, fear, or other emotional responses, enhancing immersion and player engagement.

```
// Adding emotional AI to NPCs in Cocos2d-x

NPC::enableEmotionalAI();
```

12. Player-Driven Economy

Create a player-driven in-game economy where players can buy, sell, and trade virtual goods and resources. The player-driven economy can impact gameplay and strategy.

```
// Implementing a player-driven economy in Cocos2d-x

EconomyManager::enablePlayerTrading();
```

13. Voice and Gesture Control

Explore voice and gesture control mechanics for player input. Allow players to interact with the game world using voice commands or gestures, adding a new layer of immersion and interactivity.

```
// Implementing voice and gesture control in Cocos2d-x

InputController::enableVoiceInput();
```

14. Dynamic Soundscapes

Create dynamic soundscapes that react to gameplay events and player actions. Soundscapes can adjust based on the player's choices, creating a more immersive audio experience.

Incorporating innovative game mechanics into your Cocos2d-x game can lead to novel and memorable player experiences. However, it's essential to balance innovation with usability and player guidance to ensure that these mechanics enhance, rather than detract from, the overall gaming experience.

20. The Future of Cocos2d-x and Game Development

20.1 Emerging Trends in Game Development

The world of game development is in a constant state of evolution, with new technologies and trends shaping the industry's future. As a Cocos2d-x developer, it's essential to stay informed about these emerging trends to create cutting-edge games. In this section, we'll explore some of the prominent trends that are likely to shape the future of game development.

1. Metaverse and Virtual Worlds

The concept of the metaverse, a virtual universe where players can interact, socialize, and create, has gained significant attention. Game developers are exploring ways to build immersive virtual worlds that connect players from around the globe. This trend goes beyond traditional gaming, encompassing virtual reality, augmented reality, and persistent online spaces.

2. Blockchain and NFT Integration

Blockchain technology and non-fungible tokens (NFTs) have made their way into the gaming industry. These technologies enable true ownership of in-game assets and provide players with opportunities to trade and sell their items outside of the game. Game developers are exploring blockchain integration for digital asset ownership and secure transactions.

3. Cloud Gaming

Cloud gaming services are becoming more prevalent, allowing players to stream games on a variety of devices without the need for high-end hardware. This trend offers accessibility and convenience, and game developers need to consider optimizing their titles for cloud gaming platforms.

```
// Cloud gaming optimization in Cocos2d-x

CloudGaming::optimizeForStreaming();
```

4. Artificial Intelligence (AI) and Machine Learning

AI and machine learning are influencing game development in various ways. AI-driven NPCs can provide more realistic and dynamic interactions, while machine learning can be used for procedural content generation and player behavior prediction.

```
// Implementing AI and machine learning in Cocos2d-x

AIController::integrateMachineLearning();
```

5. Cross-Platform and Cross-Reality Play

The gaming landscape is becoming increasingly cross-platform and cross-reality. Players expect to access their games on various devices, from mobile to PC to VR headsets. Developers need to embrace cross-platform development and ensure seamless experiences across different realities.

6. Sustainability and Eco-Friendly Gaming

Sustainability is gaining traction in the gaming industry. Game developers are incorporating eco-friendly practices into their development processes, including energy-efficient design, reduced carbon footprints, and awareness campaigns within games.

7. Accessibility and Inclusivity

Ensuring that games are accessible to players of all abilities is a growing concern. Developers are implementing features such as customizable controls, text-to-speech, and colorblind-friendly options to make their games inclusive.

```
// Enhancing accessibility in Cocos2d-x games

AccessibilityManager::enableInclusiveFeatures();
```

8. Dynamic Narrative Experiences

Games with dynamic narratives that adapt to player choices are becoming more popular. This trend offers replayability and a personalized gaming experience. Developers are using advanced branching dialogue systems and player-driven storytelling tools.

```
// Implementing dynamic narrative systems in Cocos2d-x

NarrativeManager::createDynamicStoryEngine();
```

9. Cybersecurity and Player Data Protection

With the increasing importance of online and multiplayer features, cybersecurity and player data protection are critical. Game developers are investing in robust security measures and complying with data protection regulations to safeguard player information.

10. Emerging Platforms and Technologies

New platforms and technologies, such as extended reality (XR), haptic feedback devices, and brain-computer interfaces, continue to emerge. Game developers are exploring these technologies to create innovative and immersive experiences.

11. Community-Driven Development

Community-driven development involves closer collaboration between developers and players. Developers are engaging their communities for feedback, ideas, and even content creation, fostering a sense of ownership and involvement among players.

```
// Implementing community-driven development in Cocos2d-x

CommunityManager::collaborateWithPlayers();
```

12. Live Services and Continuous Updates

Live services model involves providing ongoing content updates and events to keep players engaged. Developers are adopting this approach to maintain player interest and extend the lifecycle of their games.

```
// Implementing live services in Cocos2d-x games

LiveServiceManager::deliverRegularContentUpdates();
```

As a Cocos2d-x developer, staying informed about these emerging trends and technologies is essential for remaining competitive in the game development industry. Embracing innovation and adaptability will enable you to create games that resonate with players and meet the evolving demands of the gaming community. The future of Cocos2d-x and game development holds exciting possibilities, and by staying ahead of the curve, you can be a part of shaping that future.

20.2 Cocos2d-x in the Evolving Tech

Landscape

Cocos2d-x has been a stalwart in the game development industry, offering a robust and flexible framework for creating 2D and 2.5D games across various platforms. However, as technology continues to advance and the gaming landscape evolves, it's essential to consider how Cocos2d-x fits into this changing tech landscape.

1. Cross-Platform Development

Cocos2d-x's strength has always been its ability to facilitate cross-platform development. This remains a crucial aspect of modern game development as players expect to access games on a variety of devices, including smartphones, tablets, PCs, consoles, and emerging platforms like virtual reality (VR) and augmented reality (AR). Cocos2d-x's cross-platform capabilities continue to make it a valuable tool for developers aiming to reach a wide audience.

```
// Cross-platform development with Cocos2d-x

PlatformManager::enableCross-PlatformCompatibility();
```

2. Integration with Emerging Technologies

One of the challenges and opportunities in the evolving tech landscape is the integration of emerging technologies. Game developers are increasingly exploring technologies like VR, AR, mixed reality (MR), and haptic feedback devices to create more immersive gaming experiences. Cocos2d-x's adaptability allows developers to incorporate these technologies into their games seamlessly.

```
// Integrating AR features in Cocos2d-x

ARController::enableARIntegration();
```

3. Optimizing for Cloud Gaming

Cloud gaming services are becoming a significant part of the gaming ecosystem. Cocos2d-x developers need to optimize their games for cloud gaming platforms to ensure smooth streaming experiences for players. This involves considerations for network latency, scalability, and data management.

```
// Optimizing Cocos2d-x games for cloud gaming

CloudGaming::optimizeForStreaming();
```

4. Enhanced Graphics and Performance

As hardware capabilities continue to advance, players expect increasingly sophisticated graphics and smoother performance. Cocos2d-x remains adaptable in this regard, allowing developers to leverage advanced graphics rendering techniques and optimize performance for a wide range of devices.

```
// Implementing advanced graphics in Cocos2d-x

GraphicsManager::enableAdvancedRendering();
```

5. Community and Open Source Contributions

Cocos2d-x's vibrant community and open-source nature have been key to its success. In the evolving tech landscape, community-driven development becomes even more valuable. Developers can collaborate, share knowledge, and contribute to the framework's growth, ensuring its relevance in a changing industry.

```
// Contributing to the Cocos2d-x open-source project

CommunityManager::joinOpenSourceInitiatives();
```

6. Data-Driven Design

Data-driven design, driven by analytics and player feedback, is becoming increasingly important. Cocos2d-x developers can integrate analytics tools and data-driven decision-making processes into their development pipelines to create games that resonate with players.

```
// Implementing data-driven design in Cocos2d-x

AnalyticsManager::integratePlayerFeedback();
```

7. Security and Player Data Protection

With the growing importance of online and multiplayer features, ensuring cybersecurity and player data protection is paramount. Cocos2d-x developers must stay updated on security best practices and compliance with data protection regulations to safeguard player information.

```
// Strengthening security measures in Cocos2d-x games

SecurityManager::enhanceDataProtection();
```

8. Innovation and Adaptability

To thrive in the evolving tech landscape, Cocos2d-x developers should prioritize innovation and adaptability. Embrace emerging trends and technologies, experiment with new gameplay mechanics, and be open to trying novel approaches to game design.

```
// Fostering innovation and adaptability in Cocos2d-x development

InnovationManager::encourageCreativeExploration();
```

Cocos2d-x has a rich history and a strong foundation in game development, making it well-positioned to evolve alongside the industry. Developers who continue to leverage its strengths while embracing emerging technologies and trends can create games that captivate players in the ever-changing landscape of interactive entertainment.

20.3 Augmented and Virtual Reality in Cocos2d-x

Augmented Reality (AR) and Virtual Reality (VR) are transformative technologies that have gained significant traction in the gaming industry. As players seek more immersive experiences, game developers are exploring ways to incorporate AR and VR into their titles. In this section, we'll delve into how Cocos2d-x can adapt to and harness the potential of AR and VR.

1. Augmented Reality (AR)

AR overlays digital elements onto the real world, enhancing the player's environment. To integrate AR into Cocos2d-x games, developers can utilize AR development kits and libraries compatible with the framework. This allows for creating AR experiences that blend the digital and physical worlds.

```
// Incorporating AR features in Cocos2d-x using ARKit or ARCore

ARController::enableARIntegration();
```

2. Virtual Reality (VR)

VR immerses players in a completely digital environment. Cocos2d-x can adapt to VR by leveraging VR SDKs and platforms. Developers can create VR experiences that transport players to fantastical worlds or simulate real-world scenarios, all within the VR headset.

// Enabling VR support in Cocos2d-x using Oculus or SteamVR

VRController::enableVRIntegration();

3. Cross-Reality Experiences

The integration of both AR and VR in a single experience is known as Mixed Reality (MR) or cross-reality. Cocos2d-x developers can explore the creation of cross-reality games where AR elements interact with the VR environment, providing a truly unique gaming experience.

// Developing cross-reality games in Cocos2d-x

CrossReality::enableARVRInteraction();

4. Immersive Storytelling

AR and VR offer new avenues for storytelling. Developers can use these technologies to immerse players in narratives where they become active participants. Interactive storytelling in Cocos2d-x can be enriched through AR markers or VR environments that respond to player choices.

// Implementing interactive storytelling in AR and VR with Cocos2d-x

Storytelling::createImmersiveNarratives();

5. Spatial Audio

Audio plays a crucial role in AR and VR experiences, providing spatial cues that enhance immersion. Cocos2d-x supports spatial audio, allowing developers to create audio environments that adapt to the player's position and orientation in the virtual or augmented world.

```
// Implementing spatial audio in Cocos2d-x

AudioManager::enableSpatialSound();
```

6. Gesture and Voice Controls

AR and VR often involve gesture and voice controls for interaction. Cocos2d-x developers can integrate these input methods into their games, enabling players to interact with the virtual or augmented environment naturally.

```
// Implementing gesture and voice controls in Cocos2d-x for AR and VR

InputManager::enableGestureAndVoiceInput();
```

7. Training and Simulation

Beyond gaming, AR and VR are valuable for training simulations and educational experiences. Cocos2d-x's adaptability makes it a suitable choice for creating training modules and simulations that leverage AR and VR for real-world applications.

```
// Developing training simulations in Cocos2d-x with AR and VR components

TrainingSimulations::simulateRealWorldScenarios();
```

8. Performance Optimization

AR and VR demand high-performance hardware and software. Cocos2d-x developers must optimize their games to ensure smooth experiences, minimal latency, and high frame rates, especially on mobile VR platforms.

```
// Optimizing performance for AR and VR in Cocos2d-x
PerformanceManager::optimizeForVR();
```

9. User Experience and Comfort

Comfort and user experience are critical in AR and VR. Developers should consider factors like motion sickness, user interface design, and ergonomics when creating AR and VR games in Cocos2d-x.

```
// Designing comfortable user experiences for AR and VR in Cocos2d-x
UXDesign::prioritizeComfortAndImmersion();
```

As AR and VR technologies continue to evolve, Cocos2d-x remains a versatile framework for game developers looking to explore these immersive realms. Whether it's creating games, training simulations, or interactive storytelling experiences, Cocos2d-x's adaptability allows developers to harness the potential of AR and VR to captivate and engage players in new and exciting ways.

20.4 The Role of AI in Future Game Development

Artificial Intelligence (AI) is poised to play a central role in the future of game development. AI technologies offer new possibilities for creating dynamic, immersive, and engaging gaming experiences. In this section, we'll explore how AI is shaping the future of game development and how Cocos2d-x can embrace these advancements.

1. AI-Driven Gameplay

AI-driven gameplay is a future trend where AI algorithms control non-player characters (NPCs) and adversaries in more dynamic and realistic ways. Game developers can leverage AI techniques such as reinforcement learning and neural networks to create NPCs that adapt to player strategies and provide more challenging and unpredictable gameplay.

```
// Implementing AI-driven gameplay in Cocos2d-x using neural networks

AIGameplay::integrateNeuralNetworks();
```

2. Personalized Player Experiences

AI can analyze player behavior and preferences to deliver personalized gaming experiences. Cocos2d-x developers can use AI-powered recommendation systems to suggest in-game content, difficulty levels, and challenges tailored to individual players.

```
// Implementing personalized gaming experiences with AI in Cocos2d-x

Personalization::utilizeAIRecommendations();
```

3. Dynamic Content Generation

AI algorithms can generate game content dynamically, including levels, maps, quests, and even narrative elements. This approach allows for endless variations in gameplay and can keep players engaged over the long term.

```
// Implementing dynamic content generation with AI in Cocos2d-x

ContentGeneration::leverageAIAlgorithms();
```

4. Natural Language Processing (NLP)

NLP is becoming more relevant in game development, enabling players to interact with games using natural language. Cocos2d-x developers can integrate NLP-based chatbots or voice assistants to enhance player engagement and provide assistance within the game.

```
// Integrating natural language processing into Cocos2d-x games

NLPIntegration::addChatbotAssistant();
```

5. Emotional AI

Emotional AI is a growing field where AI models can recognize and respond to human emotions. Cocos2d-x can incorporate emotional AI to create NPCs and characters that display empathy, adapt their behavior based on player emotions, and provide more immersive interactions.

```
// Adding emotional AI to NPCs in Cocos2d-x

EmotionalAI::createEmpatheticCharacters();
```

6. AI for Content Moderation

Content moderation is essential for online and multiplayer games. AI-powered content moderation tools can help identify and filter inappropriate content, ensuring a safe and enjoyable gaming environment.

```
// Implementing AI-based content moderation in Cocos2d-x

ContentModeration::enhanceCommunitySafety();
```

7. AI-Enhanced Graphics and Animation

AI can enhance graphics and animation in games. Cocos2d-x developers can leverage AI algorithms for upscaling, real-time image enhancement, and even generating realistic animations and visual effects.

// Enhancing graphics and animation with AI in Cocos2d-x

AIEnhancedGraphics::applyImageUpscaling();

8. Data-Driven Game Design

AI can analyze player data to inform game design decisions. Cocos2d-x developers can use AI to identify player preferences, pain points, and areas for improvement, leading to data-driven game design and optimization.

// Implementing data-driven game design with AI in Cocos2d-x

DataDrivenDesign::leveragePlayerAnalytics();

9. AI-Powered Quality Assurance

AI can assist in quality assurance (QA) processes by automating testing, identifying bugs, and providing performance analysis. Integrating AI into the QA pipeline can lead to more reliable and polished games.

// Implementing AI-powered quality assurance in Cocos2d-x development

AIQA::automateTestingAndBugsIdentification();

10. Ethical Considerations

As AI becomes more prevalent in gaming, ethical considerations become essential. Cocos2d-x developers should ensure that AI applications in games adhere to ethical standards, including fairness, transparency, and responsible data usage.

```
// Adhering to ethical AI practices in Cocos2d-x game development

EthicalAI::prioritizeFairnessAndTransparency();
```

The role of AI in future game development is expansive and promises to push the boundaries of what's possible in interactive entertainment. Cocos2d-x's adaptability and open-source nature position it well to embrace these AI-driven innovations, enabling developers to create games that are more immersive, personalized, and engaging than ever before.

20.5 Preparing for the Next Generation of Gaming

The gaming industry is in a constant state of evolution, with new technologies and trends shaping the future of interactive entertainment. As a Cocos2d-x developer, it's essential to anticipate and prepare for the next generation of gaming experiences. In this section, we'll explore key considerations to help developers stay ahead in the ever-changing landscape of game development.

1. Advanced Hardware Capabilities

Next-gen gaming platforms will undoubtedly feature advanced hardware, enabling more realistic graphics, faster processing, and improved AI capabilities. Cocos2d-x developers should familiarize themselves with the latest hardware specifications to leverage these capabilities effectively.

```
// Harnessing advanced hardware capabilities in Cocos2d-x

HardwareIntegration::optimizeForNextGenPlatforms();
```

2. Ray Tracing and Realistic Lighting

Real-time ray tracing and advanced lighting techniques are becoming standard in the gaming industry. Cocos2d-x developers can explore implementing ray tracing for more realistic shadows, reflections, and lighting effects in their games.

```
// Implementing ray tracing in Cocos2d-x for realistic lighting

RayTracing::enableRealisticLighting();
```

3. 5G and Low Latency Networking

5G networks offer low-latency connectivity, enabling seamless online multiplayer experiences and streaming. Developers should optimize their games for low latency and consider innovative online features made possible by 5G.

```
// Optimizing Cocos2d-x games for low-latency 5G networking

Networking::leverage5GSpeeds();
```

4. Immersive Audio Experiences

Next-gen gaming will emphasize immersive audio experiences, including spatial sound and 3D audio. Cocos2d-x developers should integrate these audio technologies to enhance immersion and player engagement.

```
// Implementing spatial sound and 3D audio in Cocos2d-x games
```

Audio::createImmersiveAudioEnvironments();

5. Cross-Platform and Cross-Reality Gaming

Cross-platform and cross-reality gaming will continue to expand, requiring developers to ensure seamless experiences across various devices and realities, including VR, AR, and traditional gaming platforms.

// Ensuring cross-platform and cross-reality compatibility in Cocos2d-x

CrossPlatform::enableMulti-RealitySupport();

6. Sustainability and Green Game Development

Sustainability in game development is gaining importance. Cocos2d-x developers can adopt eco-friendly practices, reduce carbon footprints, and raise awareness of environmental issues within their games.

// Incorporating sustainability practices in Cocos2d-x game development

EcoFriendlyGaming::promoteGreenGameDesign();

7. Player Data Privacy and Security

Player data privacy and security remain paramount. Developers must stay updated on data protection regulations and implement robust security measures to safeguard player information.

// Strengthening player data privacy and security in Cocos2d-x games

DataSecurity::protectPlayerData();

8. Accessibility and Inclusivity

Ensuring games are accessible to players of all abilities is an ongoing concern. Cocos2d-x developers should continue to improve accessibility features, including customizable controls, text-to-speech, and colorblind-friendly options.

```
// Advancing accessibility features in Cocos2d-x games

Accessibility::prioritizeInclusivity();
```

9. Ethical Game Design

Ethical game design practices, including fair monetization models and responsible player engagement, will be increasingly important. Developers should prioritize ethical considerations in their game design and monetization strategies.

```
// Adhering to ethical game design principles in Cocos2d-x development

EthicalDesign::createFairMonetizationModels();
```

10. Community Building and Engagement

Building and engaging with the gaming community is crucial for long-term success. Developers can foster a sense of ownership and involvement among players, encouraging community-driven content creation and feedback.

```
// Building and engaging with the gaming community in Cocos2d-x

CommunityEngagement::cultivatePlayerInvolvement();
```

The future of game development holds exciting possibilities, but it also presents new challenges. Cocos2d-x's adaptability and open-source nature make it a valuable tool for developers looking to embrace these advancements and create games that resonate with players in the next generation of gaming. By staying informed, experimenting with new technologies, and prioritizing player experience and ethics, Cocos2d-x developers can be at the forefront of the evolving gaming landscape.

www.ingramcontent.com/pod-product-compliance
Lightning Source LLC
LaVergne TN
LVHW090258210926
848480LV00001B/59